Jon Trades

An anecdotal memoir

By Robert Jon Anderson

Introduction: Hello, My Name Is _____

I am a Minister without portfolio, a Professor without a podium. I am a regular guy, who has done and achieved many irregular things.

I am a High School drop-out (although I went back years later to complete the requirements for my diploma). I have continued my education throughout my life, often in a library. I have used libraries to teach myself some of the principals of physics, philosophy, psychology, astronomy and history. I have also taken college courses in Literature, Film, Mechanical Engineering, Emergency Medical Technician Basic Training, and various other trade programs including Advanced Digital Imaging and OSHA's 40-hour Safety course. I am a sponge drinking the nectar of the universe's knowledge.

I titled this work "Jon of all trades" for two reasons: My middle name is "Jon", a fairly uncommon spelling of a common name, and obviously as a play on "Jack" of all trades. That description fairly suits me and my life. I studied computers and the Internet, when that field began to burst into the public consciousness in the early 1990s; I then moved on to Graphic Design and digital Imaging and various forms of printing; when I tired of that, I did a complete turn-about and entered the construction industry, purely to keep myself amused and interested in the act of going to work.

I get bored and complacent easily, so I constantly challenge myself, not by reading about new and exciting adventures, but by going out and living new and exciting adventures.

I have been employed as, at one time or another: a dishwasher, a Marine navigator, a sandwich-maker, a grill cook, a janitor, a Copy Shop apprentice, a Copy Shop manager, a stock clerk, a cashier, a Graphic Artist, a Pre-press specialist, a machinist, a taxi driver, a carpenter, a construction foreman, a Geotechnical Driller's apprentice, a Geotechnical Driller, a construction project manager, a concrete finisher, a cost estimator, a hospital housekeeping supervisor and an EMS dispatcher. My one rule of thumb, when I undertake any new field of employ, is to give myself the goal of being the best person at that job as quickly as possible. I am only in competition with myself. At one point, I also taught Bible School – and I am an unrepentant and avowed agnostic / spiritual wanderer.

I am a former member of MENSA (I allowed my dues to lapse), a fairly smart fellow who is seemingly (according to my own perceptions, as well as those of my friends, whom I asked for their input) assembled from the parts of Don Quixote, Hunter S. Thompson, Donald Duck, John Belushi, Robin Williams, David Foster Wallace, Steve Jobs, Iron Man, David Fincher, Bobby Shaftoe, Carl Sagan, Hugh Hefner, Howard Hughes, Martin Heidegger and Andy Warhol. Not to mention 10,234 anonymous Joe-Schmoes – we were not all someone famous in a past life.

These pages to follow will also show that I wish to add a few more fields to my paid endeavors: That of a writer and an artist. (I have several unpaid "hobbies" that I feel are my true strengths: I write, I paint, and I play bass guitar and write songs. I am also a parent. I do not understand the concept of "free time").

I know that many people enjoy biographies, autobiographies, memoirs, journals and other, assorted tales of recollection that purport to tell someone's story in a non-fiction format.

In general, I do not. I think back to school, when I was forced to read a biography of William Penn (a religious goober for whom the state of Pennsylvania was inexplicably named; although, in and of itself, having a state named after ones' self is not necessarily a glorious honor – the state of Virginia is merely an homage to a virgin queen), which I hated. I have enjoyed some biographical reading, but, I am here to tell you, this collection of anecdotes and essays is a different kind of exercise.

I will try to entertain you. I hate being bored, when listening to a story, and I won't force it on you. I can assure you that if you are looking for names, dates and numbers in a journal or memoir, you may be disappointed. I purposefully have arranged these tales in a manner that makes sense to me, not to Father Time. If you like to laugh, and enjoy crisp writing and loquacious rambling, with the occasional recounting of the bizarre, then have I got the book for you. In fact, you are holding it in your hands.

Always, I believe in love, and treating my fellow man with respect and empathy. Truly we are all inhabitants of one world.

If a horseshoe crab can find true love, so can a man who keeps his hair brushed.

I hope will become more and more apparent to you, my honored reader, I can write a fairly good stick. Why, you may be asking yourself, have I never heard of this guy? He is 42 (*edit - 49 years old, as of this revision in 2018) years old, what has he been doing? Well, as you will see in the following pages, I have been living life.

I began writing when I was 12 years old – but, I have been drawing since I was 5 years old. Which field of Artistic endeavor should I choose? When I was 16, I took up the guitar (and then the bass guitar when it became apparent that my friend and lifelong co-conspirator, Chris, was much better at the six-string than I was), and we formed a garage band and pursued a musical career for a while. Complications truly began to set in – do I concentrate on writing, on painting, on songwriting and music? When I was 19, and working full time (and attending classes in martial arts, as well as keeping up my alcohol-drinking proficiency), I attended film school at night. I got married at the age of 21 (and I am still wed to that amazing woman). It became necessary to apply myself at work, when, during the summer of 1990, shortly after I had married, and while I was writing and painting during my free time (and rehearsing with the band in the evenings), we discovered that Clarissa was pregnant. Something had to give. During her pregnancy, I also joined a local theater group, and spent several evenings a week rehearsing for a play. I could not concentrate on becoming a world-famous author, painter, musician and film director (and actor) while working a full-time job – and trying damned hard to be good at that job – while also being a husband and father. As it turns out, my children (I have two, a boy and a girl) are quite worth the delay of my own personal artistic pursuits. One child is now grown, the other is firmly entrenched in his teenage years, and the words have called to me, once again.

So, here I am. A confluence of events, hastened by a crushing recession and the loss of any Yuppie chits I had accumulated, has left me in a state where I have nothing else to lose, except my dreams. Those I will not surrender meekly. Instead, I have been encouraged by my good friend and voracious reader, Betsy, who has spurred me to hone my craft, and to tell my story. Courtesy holsters many weapons. If you're rude, get ready to duck.

This is no cautionary tale – this is a convoluted triumph of achievement. Follow me, if you will.

Be the art.

For mom, for dad, for Clarissa, Mad and Elias.

This is a work of recollections and personal histories – where applicable, all names have been changed, except wherein the author has received specific permission.

Part One: Origin Sin

A. Life, backward

A criticism of this book I received was that "only James Joyce could get away with stream-of-consciousness when telling his story," which I reject out of hand. Joyce was obscure, to be sure, but he was not the first -- nor will he be the last -- writer to employ every available technique to tell a story. I do not utilize techniques to advertise my own literary cleverness, I use different methodologies to establish a cadence of prose, part of which is essential to the storytelling itself. For drama, I may write breathlessly; for introspection, I may muse in a seemingly circular pattern. You may rest assured that my writing is deliberate and intentional, and I have edited this tome to within an inch of its life. I wrote what I meant to write. If it does not curry your favor, I take the blame, but don't think that I stumbled upon this book at the bequest of a Genie and slapped my name on it. I do what I mean to do.

Traveling backward through life from now, until the end (beginning). This is an exercise I did, in which I categorize my life into sound-bites. I started from the moment I sat at the computer that night, and then went backward, through my move to Texas, my business failing, meeting my wife, my first sexual experience, childhood and so forth. It is merely a different   way   to   look   at   one   man's story._____

Tired. Remember to stay focused. Have to do Christmas shopping. Wake up early enough to give Birthday presents and cake. What to eat. Friends ill, deaths in families, busy season. Lonely. Quiet. Talking to myself.Tired. Maybe a good idea?Fuzzy, not so tired. Finish column. Hair pisses me off. What clothes.A good idea for stories. Good idea for activities. The breadth and scope are daunting, but I will have help.I don't deserve such good friends. How much love and hospitality can I receive in this life? Driving forever through the scape of my mind and the Earth.Good to see friends. Desert abundance of nothingness. Redheads can be irksome, it is a stereotype for a reason.Ah, a social network again. Perhaps I can make many, many friends of women and find out what makes them so different from me.Texas, since I have nowhere else to go. Sparse and beautiful and frighteningly lost in time.

Everything I gain, I lose, except my family and friends. Money is transitory, property is relative. The Earth will survive us, at least I have my brain and hands.Finally working for myself. Building things at a good price for good quality. I feel like I can control my own destiny.I see. Mastering the body can help to master the mind. Fear is unfamiliarity with the unknown; to know yourself is to conquer fear.As a good friend once told me, New York kicked my ass. Drugs and rampant hedonism and I am lucky my family persevered and stayed.This woman appeals to me. She is perfect on the surface, but with so many flaws buried beneath, she might be able to tolerate my own myriad discrepancies.So this is sex. I like this. I wish to find more women with which to do this.The ocean has been next to me and ignored for so long I feel like a monk who has seen the face of his God. Sailing is pure and clean and execution and silence. Never have I struggled so hard as I am with this physical activity, but I feel like a re-born person. Everything about me feels different, and the strength surges through my veins like an electric charge. I really want to talk to girls but I can't figure out how to put a sentence together.This boy, then, understands me. He is so different from myself, yet seems unperturbed by my unusual behavior or manner of speaking. I can be next to him.I understand everything the teacher says, but the other kids don't understand me. I don't like this feeling. I will talk to the teachers--at least they talk back.This boy I knew was killed walking down the same sidewalk I travel every week, to Church. What is a drunk driver? I don't think I will do that.Warm weather. Shorts. I hate shoes even though I keep getting stitches. Outside there are many other kids. One has a tape player and we can listen to an Elvis movie. A bike is fun to get around. Swim.The house is like a castle. I shouldn't do bad things. I feel good here, even though I don't feel good sometimes.

Some things make me happy, some things make me unhappy.

Do not tell mother and father anything that makes mother and father unhappy.

Do what mother and father says, mother and father happy.

mother happy mother smile. father happy father smile. mother unhappy mother frown. father unhappy father frown.

mother happy mother smile. father happy father smile.

warm. mother. good smell. food. movement. father. hands. noises. feet. colors. funny.

warm. mother. good smell. food. movement. father. hands. noises. feet. colors.

warm. mother. good smell. food. movement. father. hands. noises.

warm. mother. good smell. food. movement. father.

warm. mother. good smell. food. movement.

warm. mother. good smell. food.

warm. mother. good smell.

cold. bright. loud. hell.

dark. warm. safe. heaven.

B. Some childhood vignettes.

I have stories to tell, and the means to tell them. I have actually kept myself from dozing, here at 2:50 a.m., by constructing recollections into a semi-coherent piece, so I have arisen from the appeal of slumber to write them down.1. When I was around 7 or 8 years old, my family lived in a trailer park in Mayport, Florida, for about three years, during a time period where my father was saving every penny he earned to purchase a house. I later learned that trailer parks were the Home Base for "white trash"; at the time, I was happy to have a lot of other children to play with. It was there that I learned to ride a bicycle, where I learned to appreciate the joys of climbing trees (directly behind the trailer park's property was a vast, undeveloped section of woods), and where I learned of the dangers of 1970s-era playgrounds.

The playground, centrally located within the trailer park, appeared to have received no maintenance, or indeed attention, since it had been built (as a guess, probably 10 years prior to my residence, which was 1975-1978. The grass was overgrown, the see-saw had no seat, only exposed steel, only one of the four swings was functional--you get the picture. Adjacent to the dilapidated playground was an area that had formerly been a swimming pool; by the time we moved in, it was a giant concrete pit filled with refuse.The grassy field surrounding the trailer park's "recreation area" was also untended, averaging growth of about two feet. The residents of the park warned the children against playing in this third-world garbage dump, and naturally, we did anyway.

I received at least three injuries in this area, two of them serious enough to warrant medical attention (and the third one should have, except for my failure to inform my mother about it) during my three years living nearby.

The first was sustained running throughout the overgrown grassy field--during one such running chase (and I must interject here that I never, ever wore shoes except to school and church), I opened up a gash on the sole of my left foot by tramping on a broken glass bottle. Off to the Naval Dispensary we went, where I received 7 stitches. The following year, in the same field, I stepped on a ragged and turn beer can (on the same left foot), and returned to the Navy Base to frustrate a different corpsman who had to use the largest needle he could find to penetrate the "shoe-leather-like callouses" (his words), this time with 9 stitches. The scars are superimposed on my foot. The third event was when a friend and I were horsing around near the see-saw, and my playmate jumped on one end, causing the end I was near to rapidly rise and strike me in the jaw, momentarily causing me to black out.I loved that trailer park.2. My father's mother was a crusty New England Yankee who was harsh in language, disapproving of children, and generally scared the shit out of my sisters and I. We had only met her twice before in our lives when she visited Florida in the late 1970s--my guess is 1979--and we agreed, silently but in unison, to try to stay out of her way. She had the particular approach, indigenous to rotten relatives, of arriving with a multitude of gifts for us children, although it was July and nowhere near Christmas time. I remember my younger sister received an inflatable beach ball, among other things (there were several dime-store gifts for each of the three of us), and one summer afternoon, we were playing in the backyard as the adults sat at the outdoor lounge, smoking and being grown-up and disapproving. A brief description of the backyard, for you imaginists: the back of the house was L-shaped, with a concrete patio filling in the contours of the "L" to create a square; lining the side wall, between the house and the patio, were a couple of trees, including a lime tree. Lime trees, for those who don't know, have thorns around the trunk.

My sister and I were bouncing the ball around, mostly playing out back because the adults were there, and on one pass I threw, the ball got away and hit the lime tree. It stuck there, instead of rebounding, and when I retrieved it, I saw why: it had stuck to one of the thorns. The thorn left a pinprick in the ball, and, thinking about it carefully, I extracted the ball and placed my index finger carefully over the hole, and approached the adult table. I asked them if we had any scotch tape. The adults asked me why, and I explained that the ball had suffered a minor puncture, and a small piece of scotch tape would be more than big enough to seal the leak. My grandmother gestured for me to hand her the ball, and I did so, carefully holding my finger over the leak, into her hands. She saw the small hole, and then pushed against it, which immediately pressed the vinyl inwards, and what a second before had been a pinprick shredded the ball in half. She looked up from the destroyed husk of vinyl in her hands and glared at me with such a visage of reprimand that I immediately blushed and tried to stammer out an apology. I had made a minor, careless mistake, and she scowled as if she were inclined to sentence me to execution the next morning.

Many years later, my grandfather died, and a few years after that, my grandmother contracted emphysema. As she neared her most fragile, final years, I was then a young parent living in New York City. I had been loath to remain in contact with most of my relatives (which is still true today), but my grandmother contacted my father, her son, and got my phone number in NYC. What she never said, but I inferred, was that she wished to reconnect with my father's only son, and her first great-granddaughter, and began to call on a semi-regular purpose, asking for pictures of my daughter, and any and all family pictures of my young family (we have since added a son). I would chat with her, for a few minutes at a time, and though I never denied her request, I never gave it much thought, and thus didn't send her any photos. In the mid-1990s, she died of her emphysema, having never seen a picture of her granddaughter.

C. Wrestling

I just did a status update on my Facebook page that had this cryptic bit of nonsense:

By All Means, DRILK!

There is one other human being in the world who knows what that means, so in the interest of disclosure, I am going to de-mystify some "secret language" shite.

During some down times (i.e., unemployed, beggar days), Chris and I would play with a tape recorder (do you remember those? They recorded sounds, via a machine no bigger than a lunchbox, onto loops of magnetic tape, using electricity), and we would say whatever came into our minds (a truly frightening thought), and also play music, read stories, and just generally fuck around with sonic experimentation. From one of these sessions came "By all means DRILK", courtesy of Chris. I find that I have to digress again. (Merely explaining a little phrase is complicated, within my wee little life; is it any wonder that our planet is full of Babel - diversified misunderstandings?)

In high school, Chris and I were on the wrestling team. We had, as a coach, the most thoroughly unqualified and congenitally idiotic human being it has ever been my misfortune to be instructed by (fuck the dangling participle, I'm rolling). Coach Sullivan was his name, a squat, pudgy, chinless yet bearded specimen of a man, a born loser with sweatpants and whistle. Always the whistle. This semi-human turd learned the art of Greco-Roman wrestling by attending "Dollar Jell-O Shot Night" at "Mabel's Mud Wrestling and Goat-Roping Emporium", I assume; his knowledge of wrestling tactics, not to mention physical fitness, was far exceeded by my own--and I learned at the knee of "Rowdy" Roddy Piper and "Nature Boy" Rick Flair (not to mention Andre the Giant, Kendu Nagasaki and other bizarre caricatures) on Saturday Morning's "Pro" wrestling programs. To summarize, he was a muddled, constantly baffled buffoon who spent his days "teaching" American History and attempting to date student cheerleaders (it was rumored), and his afternoons spouting contradictory and unhelpful motivational aphorisms to sweating teenage boys.

As we grunted and sweated on the mat, he would prowl about, with his ubiquitous whistle (I do believe it was the whistle that drew him to coaching; whenever he would wheeze some bizarre instruction to the team, his words would squeak as he exhaled through the whistle's chamber, which made wrestling practice a constant chore, as we wrestlers tried to stifle laughter at everything he said and did). He rattled off the cliches--"no, pain, no gain" and "give 110% effort". He would scream like a nerdling sci-fi fan who had been cheated of an opportunity to touch Chewbacca's fur at a convention. He would exhort us to work harder, to drink milk, to be a winner. As we performed timed drills, he would stomp about and signal a new drill with a TWEET on his whistle; if any wrestler dared to jump the gun, he would scream, "NEVER ANTICIPATE THE WHISTLE!!" (The whistle was a magic wand, you see).

TWEET GIVE 110% TWEET THERE IS NO "I" IN "TEAM" TWEET FASTER TWEET NO NO NEVER ANTICIPATE THE WHISTLE.

Despite all of that, I loved wrestling. I was not very good at it, but it was the first time in my life that I pushed myself harder than I thought I could go. It was unbelievable exertion, but it helped me to learn how to compete, how to exercise and train for strength, and how adults were kinda full of shit. During one practice, we heard this exhortation, and Sullivan (whom Chris and I unflatteringly nicknamed "Bunnywick") lost any credibility that he might have had left with his team:

TWEET GIVE 120% TWEET FASTER TWEET NO ALWAYS ANTICIPATE THE WHISTLE!!!!!!!!!!!!

Always. anticipate . The. Whistle.

Don't you mean never, Coach?

Fuck that dude. Anyway, back to Chris and I and a tape recorder---

We were screaming Bunnywick aphorisms back and forth, and toggling the "pause" button (on those old recorders, you would click "record" and "play" at the same time, and when you wished, you would pause the recording, and start again by releasing "pause"), making funny conglomerations of sounds, and Chris growled in a James Earl Jones-esque voice, "By all means, Drink Milk!", only I had toggled the pause button and it seamlessly recorded as "By all means Drilk" which struck us as funny and we've used it ever since to denote a bit of pompous silliness or to confuse the shit out of someone we've just met or just to denote a Wednesday so now you know.

Size doesn't matter. It's not the size of the boat, it's the motion of the ocean -- you just know some Angry Incher came up with that quote. Somewhere, a meerkat female is getting hot and bothered at the thought of an Angry Inch. I have no idea why I am pursuing this line -- I myself am adequately provided for, South of the Navel, so I have no frame of reference. I have never had any women request a foot long dildo, however, so I am thinking that the average wanger is sufficient to slog through the soggy cave in search of cervix. Most willing participants are able to please each other, so -- try harder. Keep it up.

That reminds me of a humiliating incident from High School, and it was only humiliating because of the comments and sniggering. I used to have an OCD-like preference (it started when I was very young, maybe 4 years old) of pulling my penis up, to "store" it, as it were, in the waistband of my underwear (I cannot for the life of me remember why, except that it was more physically comfortable, then). So, my wiener was always pointed up. Not a big deal for a toddler, but once I reached puberty, the Dong-Fairy arrived, and some inches were added to my length.

After one particular wrestling match (which I won, in fact), in the locker room afterward, one of the Seniors on the team was laughing and joking with other team-mates when I entered to change from tights back into street clothes. They were suddenly silent, when I opened my locker, and the instigator, an Italian douchebag named Mark Manicotti (or something equally slanderous; not his real name) turned to me and asked, laughing, "Hey Anderson, you wear a steel-belted jockstrap, or what?"

I had no idea to what he was referring; I was in good spirits, having just won my match (my first victory as a wrestler), and I shrugged.

"A little excited out there about winning?" The other wrestlers behind me giggled, enjoying the "witty" put-downs he was laying on me. A few more barbs and comments later, I realized that he thought I was sporting a boner, out on the mat, because of the way my penis was tucked into my jockstrap. My first thought was -- How small do you think an erection is? I am one of those guys whose flaccid length is little indication of the finished product -- I quadruple in size (different men are different, as you may expect; for some men, the erection and flaccid state are similar in length, if not girth). I demurred, assuring him that I found little erotic about pushing my body to its physical limits (wrestling is physically exhausting*), and I even demonstrated (while clothed) that I just kept mine tucked "up" -- which is apparently unusual (and the habit has left me, probably because of this incident).

The next few weeks of school (of course the jack-ass was a loudmouth gossip, worse than skinned-knee schoolgirls in the play-yard), I endured jokes and snarky comments: Everybody in the school thought that I had gotten an erection during a wrestling match. What. The. Fuck. I was half-tempted to demonstrate both states for an objective panel of judges; if I knew then what I know now (as regards penis size; I had no idea what the average size was then), I would have gladly whipped it and embarrassed his small cock (we showered together, the team, as well as stripping down to the buff for "weigh-in," so everyone's dong was on display at some time or other), and put the matter to rest. Actually, now I would just black both of his eyes and call the issue good. Perhaps break some fingers (the easiest attack to make on a human -- the fingers are like little pretzel sticks, waiting to be shattered).

Our coach was nicknamed by the upperclassmen "Poosh" (Chris and I called him "Bunnywick", a tag Chris lay on him). Each senior was allowed a little blurb or quote beneath his / her yearbook picture, as way of speaking their mind. As final fuck-you from Mark Gastronomy, beneath HIS yearbook picture (which all of my classmates gleefully and cruelly pointed out to me) he left me this message, immortalized for all time: "Rob, keep it up and don't give Poosh a hard time out there on the mats". For his final Senior message, he chose to fuck with a Sophomore (who had done nothing to him personally). Stay classy, Mark. I hope your wife (if you managed to find one) died of leukemia and you spend your days trying to get the dog drunk so you can fuck it.

D. Little things teach big lessons

Some of us grew up in the 1970s, when we would walk to school 5 miles in the snow, uphill BOTH ways, wearing tie-dyed T-shorts and coke spoons.We also were treated to some Saturday cartoon shorts that were not attempting to force children to wheedle our parents to make purchases; a little education was chunked in there in a watchable and fondly remembered fashion. The SchoolHouse Rock shorts.

To each their own. Marijuana + SchoolHouse Rock = A Good Thing. On my iPod shuffle, I have the Preamble on my playlist. It's true. I learned the preamble to the Constitution of the United States of America from a song that aired as part of a Saturday Morning Cartoon.

Today's Lesson: Learn From Everything."Some people can read War and Peace and come away thinking it's a simple adventure story. Others can read the ingredients on a chewing gum wrapper and unlock the secrets of the Universe."--Lex Luthor, Superman, 1978

E. Sailing.

Right about the time I turned 16 years of age, my parents divorced. My mother moved to New York, to enter a seminary, and my father bought a little 22-foot sailboat. It was the kind that could be towed on a trailer, with a retractable keel (a keel, on a sailboat, is critical, as it is the part that descends down into the water to create a counter-drag to the effect of wind pushing against the sails; without a keel, in a stiff wind, the boat could tip over and capsize, which is considered bad).Every weekend, I would hang out late with my friend Chris on a Friday night, generally to a very late hour, drinking and smoking pot and drinking codeine cough syrup and swallowing tabs of LSD and generally not-give-a-fucking about my education, or indeed my life, as I was reacting to the divorce in a very predictable fashion: self-destructive behavior.Then, my father and I would wake up early on a Saturday, usually around 5 or 6 a.m. (early for one who was binging until 1 or 2 a.m.), hook the boat to his truck, and then we'd go to breakfast at the Red Diner (I always called it that, I have no idea what its name was), which also led me to my life-long appreciation of coffee. Those early Saturday mornings started me on the road of caffeine addiction. We would eat, then truck down to the big river, and drop the boat in, and then sail all day, and return at dusk.Eventually, this became a bit of a hassle, so my father began renting a berth in a marina, which leads me to the rest of the story.When I was 16, I spent a summer on a sailboat.I have so many memories from that summer, it has become one of my most important formative years.Since the owner and captain of the boat was an elderly lady (who berthed in the same yard as my dad's boat, which is how we met), it was as if I spent the summer alone. I had no friends of my own age (aside from brief overlaps where her-- Betty was her name--grandson spent a few weeks aboard the boat, and Chris was along for a week or two), so I spent the summer learning and observing.It began as sailing lessons, for me, at a price that my father asked and to which I agreed: I would return to school (I had dropped out the previous year), if he paid for sailing lessons. Then, I ended up crewing on Betty's boat.

I learned boating and navigation from the ground up. I learned how to recognize maritime signal laws and buoys (Red Right Returning is the mnemonic for one, meaning when one is returning to port, to keep the Red buoy on your right to mark the channel), I learned the signal flags (Alpha, Bravo, etc, each have a flag with a different pattern).I learned how to be responsible and to perform duties. I learned how to steer a craft, under sail, and tack into the wind. I learned how to dock a boat on the drift, before I learned how to drive. I learned how to trim sheets, tie down lanyards, how to tie knots, and to secure a winch.

I learned how to take compass readings, to measure the wind, how to adjust for swells and waves when steering.

I learned how to recognize weather (and its meanings), I learned how to tie into a pontoon caravan (when several boats are anchored in a bay, they tie together for socialization purposes), I learned how to grill on a deck barbecue. I learned how to duck to avoid a swinging mainsail boom. I learned to anticipate lulls and luffing, I learned how to enjoy the dolphins surfing on the bow waves. I learned that Port (four letters, ending in "T", just like left) meant left, and Starboard meant right. I came to understand Leeward and windward. I enjoyed rinsing the boat off, in port, because the freshwater hose would attract manatees, who would surface for a drink of fresh water (uncorrupted by fish shit and bilge and diesel).I enjoyed fishing for catfish and crabs, and watching seagulls pace the boat.I learned the methods of freeing a boat that had run aground.I met seamen from all over the world.

In the Bahamas, I learned the joys of crystalline, transparent water, and observed images of fish, coral reefs and undersea vegetation that looked like pictures from an art gallery.

Most of all, I learned how to be alone with my own thoughts, as my body undertook an important, but unthinking task, such as steering the boat as it scooted along, for dozens and dozens of miles. With one eye on the compass, I could enjoy conversations with myself, and not feel as if "I should be doing something", because I was doing something. With no one to talk to, I made friends with myself.

F. Wine Grenades

Long before perceived time was measured by the number of Presidents that have governed during my life span (now 8, and counting), I was Younger and Stupider. It is inexorable that time flows in one direction, from youth towards senility, but wisdom is an optimistic addition. I like to think that I have gathered some wisdom in my Forty-plus years of inhaling oxygen.

Chris and I, lifelong troublemakers-in-arms, fellow artists and minstrels, moved to New York City during the late 1980s, where we immediately began to understand poverty. Released from the shelter of parental funding, we soon spent large portions of our days combing the (literal) streets of New York for two things: returnable cans, to gather money so that we could eat; and, discarded cigarette butts for the tobacco content. If we found 40 cans in a day, at five cents a can that was $2.00. Macaroni and Cheese was 5 boxes for a dollar, and cheap hot dogs were $1.00 for a pack of 8. That would feed us for a day. Cigarette butts, if you collected enough of them, you could shred the small remaining amounts of tobacco left in each one into a pile, and then re-roll them with rolling papers. That made for some eclectic-tasting cigarettes, I assure you.In the late summer of 1988, our fortunes shifted as we found employment at a printing company in Manhattan's SoHo district. With gainful employment under our belts, life became less about survival and more about amusing ourselves and finding women with whom to have deep, meaningful conversations and deep, meaningful penetration. We were 20 years old.

After working at the print shop for a span of several months, we had begun to meet and interact with customers, our favorites of which were of course the young Tomatoes. SoHo is a district filled with art galleries, and galleries invariably hire young, attractive, recently graduated women to act as interns, grievously underpaid versions of "gofers" or "administrative assistants" or "slaves". We, being the retail salesmen, and they, being the designated peons, interacted on a regular basis. We were like sharks swimming in a chum-filled school of deliciously curvy mackerel.

From a neighborhood business, a Wine and Food magazine, came a couple of comely lasses that apparently had taken a like-minded interest in us two strapping lads. It came to pass that we were invited to a Wine-tasting event (such things were held regularly at their loft, on the 5th floor of a building across the street from our shop). The interns were given the opportunity to have their own party, to compensate for the lack of money or benefits, I suppose, and so the loft on this night was filled with twenty-somethings filled with self-importance and hormones.It may be relevant to note that Chris and I, genius-level intellects though we may be, were somewhat rough around the edges and flirting dangerously close to barbarism as a creed. We were only a year or so removed from an incident involving the stabbing of a crackhead and our own rampant marijuana, cocaine, alcohol and LSD usage. It could be said that Couth we were Un. But we were pretty, and funny. I suppose we were the "bad boys" that parents hate and young girls crave. I think they crave. I was very bad at reading women, then, and a woman had to throw herself at me for me to notice. I've gotten better, in some senses, but I still can't figure women and their motivations out. Go figure that one—I don't think I am unique among men for that particular knowledge gap.I don't recall if we went to the party directly from work—knowing how our behavior was at the time, we probably did. I don't remember arriving. The loft was an immense one, in the New York City style, ceilings 15 feet high, and an open expanse perhaps 40 or 50 feet square on a side. There were several tables set up on the side opposite the door, filled with bottles of wine.Since this part is clear, I will pause here to describe the Mother lode.

I have always enjoyed the taste of the grape; I still enjoy wine, to this day. I still get a feeling of childish glee when I discover a moderately-priced wine that has a beautiful finish and a smooth drinkability. At this party, there must have been provided ten or fifteen cases of wine. There were bottles of wine everywhere. Feeling somewhat like hobos invited to the White House, we were greeted at the door by whichever Cupcakes had invited us—I remember one named Kim, it was probably her that invited both of us. There were a goodly number of young women, and pseudo-hip young men in attendance. Kim led us to the wine and from that point on, the memories become less clear.For some godforsaken reason there was a skateboard available in the loft; when Chris and I had exhausted our limited, primitive social skills, we naturally began to explore avenues of disruption and mayhem. Chris had attempted to chat up a young woman on multiple occasions; he asked for her name and was given the answer, "Rose". After another visit to the wine table, he met her again and asked for her name. Somewhat less enthralled at this point, the terse reply was again, "Rose". It must have registered somewhere with Chris that he had committed a faux pas; however, in his cups he was undauntable. He made use of the skateboard, in the loft, circling the room to the growing consternation of the somewhat more conservative attendees. Whenever he circled, he made a point of saying "Hi, Rose" to the young woman in whose bed he would NOT be spending the night. My part this early in the tale is minimal. I do believe I engaged in conversations and bemusedly watched Chris circle the room. Soon enough, however, we had both reached critical mass in our levels of intoxication, and it was time for the barbarians to emerge.I do remember being somewhat offended at the ostentatious abundance of fermented grapes that had been provided; perhaps that was the triggering factor in our decision to begin hurling it out of the fifth-floor windows at unoffending passers-by. Whatever the reason, Chris and I decided that it would be jolly fun to see who could come the closest to a pedestrian with a wine grenade, but fail to hit them. Shards and splashes did not count as a "hit"—we were agreed upon that. A growing rumble of alarm began to circulate the "straights" at the party; having come from good schools in Connecticut and New Jersey, having majored in Art History in college, none of these were preparation for co-existing with borderline-insane drunks who lived by no rules, who asked for and gave no quarter. It was liberating to be admired and feared, simultaneously, as it became apparent to those who tried to curtail our activity that nothing short of a Taser rifle would stop us from doing whatever the Hell we wanted to.Many bottles of wine later, perhaps twenty or so, when the young women, nearly in tears, prevailed upon our less-savage instincts, muttering vaguely about "their jobs" and "police", finally convinced us to seek further entertainment at some other activity.It was the first and last event to which we were invited at that loft.

After such a joyous and intoxicating beginning to the evening, Chris and I tasked ourselves with finding new and more destructive outlets for our youthful aggression. In New York City, the small open kiosks that are used as some bus stops are made of a layer of plexiglass. It appeared, when the idea presented itself to us, that to our drunken eyes, it was fragile enough to be broken with a sharp and determined blow. We brutally assaulted the plexiglass, first one of us, then the other, with no visible effect upon the bus shelter. Far too drunk to ponder such failure, we made our way down the streets, like mad Don Quixotes, tilting at bus shelters. We punched them, we kicked them, we hurled shoulders against them, and we were completely unsuccessful, all the way back home.The next morning I woke up with agonizing pains in my hands and forearms that registers to this day, 21 years later.This story has no moral, other than testosterone + alcohol + intelligence = mayhem.Stay in school, and don't do drugs.

G. Oh, Henry

During my era of poverty in New York City, Chris and I did occasional stints of helping for my mother's church, for the "Meals on Wheels" program. The pay was lousy, and it was quite warm, that early summer of 1988. Everywhere you traveled, on the streets of Manhattan during that summer, you would hear some car's radio playing "It Takes Two", the hypnotic jam performed by Rob Base and DJ EZ-Rock.There was a driver, who is so irrelevant to my personal history that I recall nothing about him, and Chris and I, and we would jump in a van for an afternoon, and do the actual deliveries into the buildings around the Upper West Side. Each block might have 3 or 4 different shut-in or elderly people to whom we were delivering, so Chris would grab meals, and I would grab some, we'd go off, and meet back at the van, to move on to a different block.Some blocks only had a single building, and we would enter together, each of us carrying meals, and thus laugh and joke and be our normal selves while helping out the nearly-dead. During one such delivery, Chris went up to the designated apartment, and I went back to the van to get more another meal for the last delivery in that building. We were not far from home, and this was the final delivery, so the driver and I exchanged good-byes, and I went up via the elevator. The door was answered by a young black man, and a gravelly voice called out from another room, "Who's that, Gregory?" (Gregory may or may not be the man's name, but Chris and I agreed that it might be). Chris was standing in the other room, with a beer in his hand. When told it was Meals on Wheels, an elderly man rolled towards the door in a wheelchair. He was square of face, and his voice was gravelly from years of booze and cigarettes. I handed him the meal, and he asked me if I wanted a beer.Since we had been dropped off, we had no particular urgency, and we were both 19 year-olds with a yen for chilled beer, I agreed, and another can was popped open. The man introduced himself as Henry, and we told him our names. We were having a beer! So, we were at least temporary buddies. We chatted, amiably enough, about what Chris and I were during in New York (which was pretty much fuck-all; we would, later that summer, find a job placement program, which led us to money and wives, but at this point, we were still smoking recycled cigarettes and drinking beers donated by old geezers who reeked of urine and decay), and finished our beverages, at which point, Henry--having been informed by Gregory that the beer supply had been emptied, asked Gregory and--oddly enough--Chris to go the corner store and buy a couple more six-packs of Schlitz. Chris was reluctant to go, and he asked if I would go with him. I was sipping my beer, not really in a hurry to re-emerge into the summer humidity, and shrugged, declaring that I would just as soon stay and finish my drink.As an older and wiser man, I am chuckling as I read this, because it is the innocence of youth that puts one into such situations. I would remain behind, and finish my beer while Henry reminisced--presumably of times when his pants were not scented with Eau De Piss. As soon as the door closed behind them, Henry began to speak quickly, and I can recall his words, verbatim, 22 years later, so I let Henry speak from (hopefully) beyond the grave:Henry: You know I live all alone, Robert. I get very lonely. Would you have sex with me? Would you let me suck your dick?Rob: No, I'm not into that. Sorry, but I like girls. (For some reason, I felt bad for the dude. I felt as if I was letting him down).When Chris returned with Gregory, several minutes later, Chris gave me a knowing look as he entered. *The bastard*. He was trying to be subtle, I realized, being reluctant to leave for the store, knowing that I was about to be propositioned by a crusty old cripple. He knew, because Henry had gone after him first, while I was bringing up the meals. I felt so cheap, and somewhat jealous. I had been chosen second.

H. Carol in New York

This series of paragraphs will tell the tale of two under-employed, semi-homeless, borderline-savage 19 year-olds attempting to woo and seduce a schoolteacher.I suppose a modicum of background information is in order; I have no illusions that you are all voices in my head (well, yes I do, but I suppress those with razor slices to my legs), and thus, you need at least some information before I try to be humorous. Otherwise the story would be, "and then I went home and soon after got a job, religion and a place to live". Not a very interesting story.

Chris and I were staying, with my older sister, in a two-bedroom apartment on 110th street, in Manhattan, at the Northwest corner of Central Park (our bedroom windows overlooked the Park itself). We were considered to be living right at the Southern edge of Harlem. A few doors down from us, westerly, was a Burger King restaurant. We spent a lot of time in that summer of 1988 trying to find ways to fill our time, as we were employed only part-time with Meals on Wheels. We collected bottles and cans; we cadged cigarettes, we begged from my mom--we were broke, irresponsible, useless teenagers, but we were living in the City, and life was never dull. My sister spent her days working as a receptionist for a podiatrist.In the apartment (which we were subletting from a man who went to the seminary in the same class as my mother; after I got fired from my hospice job in March of 1988, he no longer collected rent from us--not by his choice, but because we had no money) was an upright piano; out of tune and old, it was, nevertheless, a musical instrument, and Chris and I would use it to create all manner of audiological, experimental sonic creations (random noise that was sometimes musical). We also played with a tape recorder, reading excerpts from newspapers in silly voices, screaming into it, any and creating every strange noise we could make, playing with sound. Once a week or so (I believe it was on Thursdays), the church that sponsored the Meals on Wheels program, which was an Episcopal church on 84th street, would host a cookout for the elderly and (I suppose) the poor, in a small, lovely little fenced-in garden adjacent to the church. We were not the only group to use the mini-botanical garden, and we began to see a group come in, as our allotted time in the garden ran out, a group led by a young and pretty blond woman.I think our first interactions were playfully pleasant, some gentle ribbing on her part that we had overextended our time, providing the cookout, and of course I (and especially Chris), would immediately lob a sass-grenade in return. We were natural wise-asses, as a defense mechanism, I suppose, and also, she was very cute and the extent of our thinking was "I wonder how she looks unclothed". Neither of us were virgins, but just barely. I had been with one woman in bed, I think Chris had doubled my experience at that time with two partners.

Her name was Carol, we soon discovered, as she was very amiable, and as a couple of weeks went by, it became obvious that she was bringing her group in earlier and earlier, and thus she naturally overlapped our group by longer time periods every week. She had a tic that I remember: when she was talking to me, she would look directly at me, and close her eyelids as she spoke. Frowning or smiling, she would have normal expressions with closed eyelids. It was mildly disconcerting to me, and memorable. She was about 5'3", with a slim, athletic build and petite breasts. Her hair was straight and blond and shoulder-length, perhaps a little longer.One hot July day, she asked if I could stay, after my group left, and talk for a little while. Having absolutely no activity on my agenda until the next day (if that), I agreed, and we sat at a little picnic table and chatted. We exchanged the basic background stories, the where-are-you-from kind of information, and she asked if I could meet her back at the park that evening, after her group was done, with a cold six-pack of beer. I, of course, agreed to do so. I returned that evening, bearing a cold pack of Heineken (I think I had begged my sister for a few bucks), and my timing was correct--she was alone. We sat and drank and shared our stories. Now, I fill in some of the bits that prompt this story to be told, 22 years later.I always thought that Chris was the more interesting of the two of us, plus he was taller; we weren't exactly competing for the same woman's attentions, but, in a way we were. I asked her, How is it that you asked me to come back tonight, and not Chris? . Carol replied that Chris' teeth had bothered her; he was funny, and all that, but she wasn't looking for personality.By this time, I am pretty sure I am going to spend a night having sex. I am trying to restrain my mouth from talking too much, and I nodded and smiled a lot.After the beers were finished, we walked uptown, chatting and buzzing pleasantly. By the time we reached my apartment (which was south of hers, she living in Harlem proper), she needed to pee, so we stopped at my place. Had I mentioned we were poor? Soon, she called out from the bathroom that there was no toilet paper. Sheepish, I put a handful of Burger King napkins in her hand, which was probing out from behind the door. She still invited me to follow her uptown to her apartment, however, so I slipped into my bedroom and grabbed a couple of condoms--free samples from the AIDS hospice I had been fired from (wrongly; they accused me of having sex with a resident, which was absurd for two reasons: 1) HE HAD AIDS and 2) HE WAS A HE), and thus loaded with prophylactics, we walked the ten or so blocks to her digs.She had a nice little place, it was furnished (which mine wasn't) and had a television and stereo (which mine hadn't). She sat me down, and mixed me a vodka tonic, and pulled out a little pipe with a nice pile of marijuana in it. The evening had been rolling along nicely, and I just figured this was even better. As I lit the pipe, I took a puff, and then awaited her return (she had gone to change). After ten minutes or so, I put some jazz on the stereo, and when she finally returned, I gave her the pipe and tried to get her to dance a little.Now that she was back in her home element, she acted in a completely different manner. No longer playful and flirtatious, she behaved like a cousin that had invited me over for a beer. She chided me for not smoking more--I had learned to puff and pass; apparently, in her circle of stoners, one smoked the bowl, then re-filled and passed. Pot etiquette was different.Then she went off to sort laundry.I think my slightly-drunk, mildly stoned brain registered an unexpected progression at this point. After being left in the living room for about fifteen minutes, I went in to ask her what the hell she had invited me over for. She discussed the fact that she had a fiancé, in upstate New York, and that she "wasn't going to sleep with me". She smiled as said it. She agreed that it was late, however, and I could sleep in the spare room (She had an extra bedroom, in Manhattan, how cool). Being buzzed and disappointed and frustrated, I went to lay down, taking off only my shirt (I was wearing sweatpants, I remember, she was wearing a lycra jogging or bike-riding outfit, very form-fitting, and not helping my condition at all). I had been laying down for a while, when I felt the bed sink down as she climbed into it with me. In the dark, her lips touched mine, and as I was very inexperienced in the kissing department at this time, I let her lead me where I needed to be. A very pleasant, arousing petting session ensued; at some point, my sweatpants came off (I had no underwear on underneath) and my extremely turgid maleness poked at the sheet covering me like a Sequoia spontaneously sprouting. Then, wistfully, she patted my cheek and went to her own room. My feelings at that point are somewhat difficult to describe. I was disappointed.I lay down and dozed for an interminable amount of time, then rose, nude, and walked into her room and set my head against her arm as I sat on the floor. She mumbled drowsily, go back to bed, and I did so.The next morning, we chatted--neither of us were comfortable with the previous evening's events, or the order or resolution thereof; I saw her a few more times in the garden, and never since.This is one of the few incidents in my life that I have never re-visited, except superficially, to try to establish motivation. I really don't want to know "why" or "what did I do" or "what did I say"... I know that the physical reality, the actual event, turned into a nightmare of failed expectations and horrible enticements unfulfilled. I love and adore women, and always have, which is why I don't think about it. I don't blame "women" for Carol's bizarre schizophrenic behavior, I blame her. I don't even like the term men often call such a female, nor will I repeat it here. Mostly women say "yes", so I figure she's an anomaly, and say to Chris: You were the lucky one. The problems with the teeth saved you, at the time. And now they--like Carol--are historical.

I.   Calm before the storm

A state of confusion is an absence of focus.I would focus on bread.I crave and hate advice. I hate making a point and having it misunderstood. I cannot abide chastisement for imagined errors.The act of creation is an annoying process.

When my mood is good, I can spin yarns, to keep a horde happy, around a virtual campfire. I can tell a tale to keep another human from boredom, or to enthrall, excite, enlighten or seduce. When my mood is more blurry (can one have a blurry mood? I can), I have no interest in creating anything. I wish to walk away from that which I know and keep my humor to myself. I need a re-boot, but I don't know how to do it.I can keep going, because I will, of course, level out and become merry once more. The difference between me now, and me as a 22 year-old, is that now I know that this is a transient state, a peak or valley of a wave.These things pass.Death, murder, mayhem, rape, divorce: All of these things matter only to those being killed or ravaged or those watching their worldly possessions being swept out to sea by a hurricane--it doesn't affect the rest of us so severely. We pass a hat, we cluck our tongues, and we buy more life insurance.I am at a cusp of originality, I feel, which has the effect on me of changing everything. I question every decision of my life, from cognizance up until the word "until" that I just typed, and often I rearrange furniture in my head.I ask for forgiveness in advance, for those whom I piss off. I am not doing it to you. My head is cluttered, and I need to survive.Perhaps a week on the Congo. Perhaps an illicit affair with a steamy cauldron of sexual stories. An escape--the problem with such daydreams, however, is simple: From where, and to where, is the escape? If you open a door to a new room, it is still just a room. We don't have doors that lead to the future, only the past.I've been to the past, and it is not as great as you may remember. They had taxes and mosquitoes there, also.Since I have said little, I encourage you to take away something:By no stretch of anyone's imagination do I write as fast as I can. I type really well, almost faster than I can think. I could be pouring out five or ten times as much as I do into words, every day. The words are what piss me off--I already know the story, why should I write it down? I'd much rather be skydiving with a team of Swedish bikini models.Better yet -- brunettes. A team of really smart, short, small breasted brunettes. We have to go with my personal dating history / list of ideal women on that one.

J. Hamburgers and memory games.

Sometimes, a memory is concocted out of whole cloth by your brain. Presumably because your brain is bored (actually, your brain is like a determined librarian; if it can't find what you're looking for, it will grab a different book off of a nearby shelf and hand it to you, secure in the knowledge that you won't know the difference; why? because the instrument that would allow you to tell the difference is the *very same instrument that is lying to you in the first place*), a memory that you frequently gaze upon and fondle like a cherished collectible might be a work of autonomic fiction.I recall many things clearly; some I recall through a gauzy-haze as if the memories were Zsa Zsa Gabor on television post-1975. A fact that I remember is merely there, as if I am surrounded by road signs (Kindergarten teacher, Miss Kathy; number of stitches in the sole of left foot during second-grade school year: nine; learned the name of the capital of Belgium, Antwerp, from a PBS science-fiction movie named: The Lathe of Heaven), others I have to resort to associative identification, as if I had laid a trail of bread crumbs in my subconscious. I don't know if I can do that on cue, but I will try. Let me think, first, of something that I can't remember (which is harder than it sounds, *because I can't remember it*, by definition.) Then, I will try to rebuild the link, and dictate the steps my brain took to get there. Hang on.The trouble is, my memory is pretty sharp. My address when I was 6 years old? 612 Mayport Road. My phone number when I was 10? 249-0721. The name of the girl whose lip I accidentally cut when I threw a board over a tree limb and it dropped and hit her in the face? Wendy (why she was standing directly beneath the spot where I had just told everybody I was about to lob a hunk of wood, I couldn't say, even now).Finding the holes where few exist is difficult.I did remember when I went and paced and smoked a cigarette, just now, attempting to find a hole, a curious exercise my friend Chris and I used to do. We used to have (hell, we still do) long, meandering and conspicuously random conversations about whatever streams hit our consciousness, for extended blocks of time, and then we would attempt to re-create the entire thread of conversation, in reverse, with the goal of discovering where it had begun. Does that translate, or does it sound elementary?Come try it in my presence--it isn't easy. I don't mean we would begin on the subject of football, and end up talking about hockey, and backtrack that; I mean, we would start by discussing the very hot girl who lived diagonally from him (Ms. Monjo), which we would lead to debating the merits of certain brands of vodka, and end up, twenty minutes later, discussing something completely unrelated, like how many times Chewbacca raped Ewoks in Return of the Jedi, just offscreen (four). Then, we would go backwards, point by point, until we ended up returning to our admiration of Ms. Monjo's bikini top (pleasantly full) and the cut of the bikini bottom (also pleasantly full; this was the 1980s, and tushes were permitted on hot girls, and a healthy hint of bush pressing against the frontal "V" of a bikini was acceptable). It is a great memory exercise, I realize now; then, it was a method of staving off boredom and the inevitable search for fireworks to launch at police cars which were, unfortunately, occupied with police officers (true event, never caught, I deny everything).Aha. I just had one.Okay, for a brief time period, Chris and I both worked at a Wendy's restaurant in Jacksonville Beach; we were on different shifts, but due to overlap, we met and worked with many of the same folks. I had a flash of a pair of brothers that worked there, a Laurel and Hardy-looking pair; the heavyset one worked the dawn patrol, with me, and the skinny, hypertensive and hyperactive one worked with Chris later in the day. I tried to remember their names, and set the memory ladder to work.Some background:

Out in back of Wendy's restaurants (I assume this still happens, but I will be damned if I ever look to confirm it) was a large, oblong steel tank that looked like a fuel tank, thousands of gallons of capacity in size; its function, as those of us who worked on the grill soon discovered, was for the disposal of grease that is the inevitable by-product of applying heat to thousands of pounds of fatty meat. A bucket, hung from the front of the grill, captured the excess run-off from the cooking of hamburger; periodically, it was a (dreaded) necessity to empty this bucket into the holding tank out back. We less-than-fondly called the tank of horrors The Greasepit. This was in Florida, during the summer. Florida's climate runs from warm to hot. Have you ever smelled rancid meat, or rancid fat? It isn't pleasant. Now multiply that smell times *thousands of pounds of it that have been fermenting--cooking--in 105-degree Florida heat for weeks* (the tank was emptied perhaps once a month), and you still have no idea the pure gag reflex that was a body's defense when the lid of the tank was opened to dump the (comparatively fresh) hot, wet burger spooge inside. **Shit was rank**, I am saying. It was akin to punishment to be instructed by the supervisor that the "bucket needed dumping". Oh yeah--for $3.50 an hour.Chris' supervisor was a pudgy bastard who performed his management duties as if he were Richard Simmons dosed on Acid; when confronted with an unwiped table, or a pile of browned lettuce awaiting disposal, the supervisor would point to the offending disorder and shriek: "Hideous! Gross! Disgusting! Blah!!!' His was a simplistic mantra, from a simpler time, when you could be a wimpish prick of a boss and not get a 9mm round between your eyes for your troubles from a disgruntled ex-employee (or even a current employee--that dude sounded annoying, and I was glad I had a different supervisor).

Also at this restaurant was a Lifer Wendy's employee named Debbie. She was, shall we charitably say, not attractive. Some people are, some aren't. She was freckled like a smallpox victim, and had a gruff demeanor, and we were teenagers and therefore had disproportionate ideals of feminine beauty. She probably is not as ugly as my memory tells me she was, but at the time, she was Chris and I's ideal of the Least Desired Fuck Buddy that we knew.So, as time passed (and, we were complete and total assholes) a common insult that Chris and I began to hurl at one another was that "You just wanna go fuck Debbie in the Grease Pit", being the combination of two things that we would rather shoot nails from a nailgun through our scrotums rather than endure.My point, finally: When I attempted to recall the brothers' names, my mind told me "Fuck Debbie in the grease pit. Hideous! Gross! Disgusting! Blah! SteveandDave". and so, I had my answer. Steve and Dave.Also: They had a cool dog who was totally *not* the killer that Dave claimed (he had been asserting, for weeks, that the beast was as likely to bite my dick off as look at me; the first time I entered their apartment, the dog flopped on its back, legs in the air, awaiting a tummy scratching), and they introduced me to the joys of listening to the group "Alabama" while stoned out of my gourd. You take the good with the bad.

K. Is there a truth?

Have you ever told the truth?

It is a valid question, not meant to initiate feelings of indignation or shocked surprise. We must go past the primary response of "Of course, I always tell the truth"; if such a statement is your response, then this column is just for you.

I plan to circle from falsehood to the meaning of sincerity over to the Boston Red Sox and back to prevarications. If you have any interest in any of those subjects, you are in the wrong place. The World Wide Web is that-a-way. This is a blog of my commentary and opinions; any facts or information that manage to leak into my posts are incidental or secondary.

I was asked the question: "Why do people lie for no reason?". To answer glibly takes but a moment; to answer sincerely takes a few minutes' ponderance; to answer in the correct way takes enormous amounts of hubris and insight. I am stocked up on both, fortunately for us.

The short answer: To avoid trouble, to avoid confrontation, to gain an advantage, to gain a desired effect/goal/reward. These answers might suit the average query, for certain. Who am I to rule in a court of opinion? Well, if not me, then who? Is it an elected post? I do believe that to be a self-appointed pontificator is the duty of every weblogger.

The sincere answer: We cannot understand why people lie unless we know their motivation; it is only in the subjective view that a canard is told "with no reason". Everyone does everything for a reason, even if that reason is to perform as many random acts as possible (see Sid Vicious, the New York Knicks, G.W. Bush). We may feel that we are lied to arbitrarily, perhaps even dismissively, but we must put on our empathic shoes to feel the purpose behind any verbal evasion. A man may tell a woman that "He had a great time last night, but I just don't think I am right for you", which probably means the exact opposite: He doesn't feel that SHE is right for HIM. So, the woman may ask, "Why doesn't he just tell me the truth? I can handle it. Be an adult!" I think those sorts of answerless questions are borne of a fantasy approach -- most people prefer to avoid a confrontation, and will say whatever they (correctly or not) feel will bring closure to a situation with as little Hurling of China as possible (no man likes to find his clothes piled at the curb, soaked in gasoline, either; breaking up with a woman is an endeavor best achieved by perishing in a car crash: At least she will remember your corpse fondly).

The correct answer: No one thinks they are wrong. If you believe you are being lied to, you are probably correct. If the other person believes that they are telling you what is expedient for them, they are correct, as well.

An example, to confuse you further: Albert has a car. Bart steals his car. Albert protests, and calls the police, and Bart is arrested.

Albert: Why did you steal my car, you couthless thug, you enjoyer of Big Macs!

Bart: I didn't steal no car.

Police: We stopped you as you were driving the car, swigging a 40 oz. of Colt .45.

Bart: I don't drink.

At first glance, it seems to most of us that Bart is a bald-faced liar, a no-good criminal eager to take as he pleases, and damn the consequences. But, if we delve further into Bart's story, we discover some interesting exculpations:

Bart ran rapidly from the pack of marauding senior citizens. They had come at him as he was helping a pack of crippled orphans to cross the street. Hopped up on tolterodine and ranitidine, the Geezer Wolfpack was hell-bent on draining blood from younger men to use as an aphrodisiac. They carried disease-filled urine in glass bottles, to use as Molotov cocktails on those that stood in their path. Bart had had run-ins with the Geezerpack before, and had barely escaped with his life. As he ran from their chomping, toothless snarls, he saw that ahead, directly in the path of the ferocious gang of diapered lunatics, was a Church Choir preparing to board a bus, in preparation for giving a free concert to homeless, Veteran Polio victims. Bart knew he had little time to act. He waved his arms, to draw the attention of the Elderslayers, and as they fired bottles of death-filled beer bottles at him, he shouted to the Choir to make good their escape. At the last moment, juggling several bottles of biological death, Bart dove into an un-locked car and made his getaway. As he drove away, planning to ditch the car a few blocks away, where it would be safe from the Geezerpack, Bart made the Ultimate sacrifice, and drank down the foul contents of the bottles, to prevent the diseases from spreading to others. As he was nearly finished in saving the city, a police officer pulled him over, and completely misunderstood the entire situation.

Bart was not lying.

Albert was not lying.

The police were not lying.

Sometimes, your point of view is wrong.

So, I tell my friend this, and I hope she gets the point. This is the same friend that I asked if she would get Vajazzled, so that I could see it firsthand. I have no idea why I get tagged as a perverse man, since I know me so well. After people know me for a while, they realize I am not a pervert, I am quite sincere as to my simple tastes and desires. I have no qualms about asking a woman to see her vagina (more accurately, vulva, since the vagina is the little hole that is only fun to see when you are putting yourself inside of it). I am not a jerk, usually, so I will not talk about a naked brunette dancing around Fenway Park, home of the Boston Red Sox; I will definitely NOT mention brown and curly pubic hairs, glistening in the gloaming, sparkling with the moisture of the aroused woman, dancing freely, freely, for the first time in her life.

Not going to mention it.

Sincere: From the Latin *sin cere*, meaning "without wax". A sculptor, in the olden times before Photoshop, would create his sculpture from marble, laboring for hours and weeks and months to create perfection. Lesser works would have flaws in them, flaws that would be patched by the sculptor with wax. A masterpiece, on the other hand, would be *sin cere*, without wax, meaning the sculptor knocked that shit out of the park with no flaws. Bangin'. I love that word origin.

I would say here, "Would I lie to you?", but we already have established that I would. But, I would do it with a smile, and a reason. The road to naked women is paved with intentions -- good, bad, and indifferent. I am not sure life has much greater meaning than a man desiring to love a naked woman; procreation is creation, on a Lego-sized scale (God must have a monster Penis).

L. Memories that embarrass

Do you let me in to your mind, when you read?Do you skim the line, gleaning tidbits of humor and angst, or doyou think of us, sitting on a bench in a busy train station, talking,gesticulating, occasionally shouting over the sounds of passing express trains?It was noted, in an epistle I received early this morning,that "I, of all people, should know that my words are powerful,"an assertion that knocked me on my ass.No--I did not realize that. I know my words are honest,I try not to dance around, except to rhyme in some poetic scheme;but, that I actually reached out, and people remember what I have said,and feel it, had not occurred to me.It is disconcerting.If I look back, at an example of the stupidest thing I ever said, (and thereare many candidates), the one that makes me cringe, still (and nearly suicidal),was an attempt at suave and friendly and witty that makes me want to puke.To prove my fearless nature, (and I hate doing this, for two reasons; One, it actually does make my chest clench with anxiety, almost 30 years later, and Two, I doubt that it will translate to the present time as the absolutely humiliating moment that it seemed to be, at the time). a recap:Chris and I were swimming at a hotel pool, by the beach (several of the beachfronthotels had pools, which were for guests only, but we freely used them as our community pool), and on this particular day, there also happened to be swimming two teen aged girls (who were of the complete opposite gender from our own). Being boys, we naturally wished to engage these gorgeous creatures in some manner (I actually have no memory of how attractive they were), but, being boys, we (I) had no concept of how to execute this desire.Chris and I, of course, began to splash and attempt to drown each other, to demonstrate the massive amounts of testosterone that was coursing through our bloodstreams. We splashed and cavorted our way across the pool to a position that was in conversational talking distance from the lasses.At this point, one of the girls dove under the water (ignoring us completely), and swam to the bottom,holding her breath, and generally taking advantage of the flush of youthful health.Being the eager idiot I was, I turned to the other girl on the surface, and casually queried,

"Did the Other one drown?" Chris climbed out of the pool, then, I think. Not suave.Imagine: You are a teen boy. Your body is betraying you, every day. Hair is sprouting in the most embarrassing of places. Your body is a malfunctioning bundle of awkwardness. Your blood burns to know the flesh of a woman, but you are only a couple of years removed from playing with action figures. You want to talk to girls (who are, after all, just people like yourself, except they have the added burden of bleeding on a monthly basis from THEIR embarrassing places), but you want to say something that sounds casual, not desperate, something friendly, but not creepy, and something that will make her laugh, so that she might relax enough to part her thighs so that you can rut like a wild boar. All of these thoughts and pressures at once, and you spout some inane gibberish like a toddler who has just learned to speak, and instead of James Bond-smooth, you get Pee Wee Herman, jerking off in a porn theater creepy.

It was not my finest moment. I blame nothing but my misunderstanding of social interaction, a dilemma that plagues me still. Sometimes I forget that I am not a Godwho has dreamed you all. I would keep apologizing, but fuck you, too, you have toaccept that I am just not like other men. That's not a pick-up line, it is true.I am not like other men.And you--YOU--are not like other men, or women. I am learning, too.Every day.

M. Love, again

I have done bits on love, but perhaps it needs to be re-addressed, because we humans are complete and total buffoons about it. I have been stupid about "love" and its meanings, definitions, boundaries and complications, since the beginning of time. For I, like all of us, am my own universe, and the meaning of love must begin and end with me. If you want empathy, walk a mile in my shoes.

Love? Love. This is my way of thinking as I write. There is little-to-no preparation for this column, it is merely done as a request for a bored 27 year-old woman (a quite attractive, Portuguese woman, no less; the Spanish Spice, the fiery brunette, everything points to sex except for our Geography, and the facts that 1. I am quite married and 2. See number 1.) I love to trade words for goods, like baseball cards of sexual tension. Does that metaphor even make sense? I mean I like to gaze upon the nude female form. If I know the possessor of the form, so much the better.

I know, somewhere in the recesses of some people's sexuality, there is a spot that is intrigued, excited and stimulated by the thought of a semi-stranger gaining sexual arousal from one's existence. I know of several women who got thoroughly turned-on by the knowledge that a man gazed upon their naked flesh and became liquid in his fullness (more muddled semi-demi-hemi-metaphors; some women get off if a man masturbates at the sight of them).

Anyway, I promised to speak of love, not sex.

Let me begin in the middle: Love is not syrupy sentiments spouted in yearning. I love to write poetry myself, mostly because it is the command of cadence, the mastery of the English language, the ability to take a phrase and make it sing as if a stanza of music that appeals to me. Some people swoon, when hearing even a commonplace thought assembled into rhyming meter; good for them. But, looking upon the face of your infatuation, and claiming:

"Your eyes have never been closed to me, nor ever will;

Yours and mine have no distinction, we are the same,

for the life within carries our dialogue in a letter n the sill, our perpetual unity that is split only by a mirror's glaze;

the image of you only reminds me that within my eyes are

your eyes, and within my heart is the eternity of your gaze."

That may be poetic, or sweet, or complimentary, but it is basically saying "I want to fuck you, and I will say anything that it takes to convince you to open your legs for me." (If it is a man writing it). I cannot speak for women, in that sense, but I know that chicks often dig the florid speech. That is not love, that is the first bloom of attraction -- lust, passion, desire, call it by any name that suits your purposes, attraction is not love. Attraction is what causes a lover to want to meet a lover (coming through the rye), but what makes those lovers stick together? A deeper bond, one hopes, or the relationship is doomed.

Love is more than affection, more than sexual desire, more than a "quickening of the heartbeat" when one sees the object of attention; love is constantly-changing set of rules for engagement. To love, one has to surrender themselves to the possibility of damage. If you cannot bear the thought of being hurt or pissed on, you will find it difficult to embrace love. Love is a donation of trust, with no indication that the trust is deserved. Only when you bare your throat to the blade, and emerge unscathed, can you truly love and trust and meld with another.

Love is not difficult to find. It can be made -- if you are unselfish enough to make it. Be a good communicator, ask for what you want, and give your partner everything. When burned, reach once more for the stove. Burn yourself again.

I have had a few loves in my life, and not all of them women. When you love a member of the opposite sex, however (if that is the direction your sexual proclivities run, that is; if you are gay, just switch the genders, I don't care), it is great fun to also enjoy the flesh, as well as burning yourself on the stove of their companionship.

There are many, many, many good parts: Knowing that someone cares if you live or die. Knowing that if you empty yourself of emotion, the other person will receive it (some with more aplomb than others, but we can't all be poets).

Knowing that someone accepts our existence, as banal or unfulfilled or mundane as it may be.

I could go on, but I am beginning to get hungry for linguine with clam sauce.

N. Drilling

Some of my stories have morals or subtexts; some have a point. This one is just going to be reminiscing about working on a Geotechnical Drill Platform.

Geotechnical Drilling is the act of drilling to pre-arranged depths to take core samples so that environmental Engineers know the composition of terrain in a specific area, usually for construction purposes. If an area that is currently a wooded lot is getting eyeballed with the intention of building 2 or 3-storey houses, the bore depths will be, on average, 25 - 50 feet deep, depending on what composes the strata; if the underground material is sand or rock, 20 feet is sufficient to know that the structure will be adequately supported. If it is clay (such as most of Washington, D.C.--marshy, swampy muck; I cannot BELIEVE what is underground in our nation's capital), additional depths may be requested by the Engineers. That's the gist of why we were drilling. Every 5 feet or so, we would lower a hollow sample tube inside of the augers, with steel pipes added to the needed lengths, and beat the tube into the ground with a hydraulic- (or human-) powered "hammer". Then we'd winch the tube out, split it open, catalog the soil, and keep drilling until that boring was completed.

How were we drilling? Generally, on truck or ATV-mounted platforms, with 100-200 feet of augers carried with us, a few dozen glass sample jars, lubricating spray, a good set of wrenches (including big-ass pipe wrenches), some pairs of gloves and a shovel or two. The shovel may have been the second-most frequently used tool, after the drill rig itself. Do you know what is underground, 99% of the time? Water. Water+soil=mud. As soon as your auger got below 10 feet or so, a slurry of mud would get churned up and out of the boring hole, and the "helper" had to keep the area clean of mud, which entailed shoveling as fast as you could, while running back and forth with sample jars, oiling the tubes, fetching augers, and generally doing all of the physical labor. The driller? He stood on a platform (attached to the rig, and therefore high and dry), and monitored the rig's drill speed, down-pressure, made sure of the depths, and operated the hammer. As I quickly learned, it was much, much better to be a driller than a helper. Cleaner, too.

Since I was somewhat of a whirling dervish as a helper, I was given an ATV (off-road) Drill Rig to operate, with a helper, after I had been with the company for only six months. This led to a lot of fun.

A typical day was arriving at the shop at 6 a.m., clocking in, loading the support truck (a Ford F-350 diesel), making sure of the day's assignments (as an ATV operator, I often was assigned a gigantic tract of land, thousands of acres in size, with 300 or 400 borings; I knew what I would be doing for the next 2 or 3 months) , gather my helper, then head out to whichever site I was working before the sun rose. We'd stop at the first gas station, fill the fuel cans for the Rig, and then light up the first joint of the day. We generally worked at a site about a 90-minute drive from the shop, so it was very peaceful to get stoned, chatter with my helper, and fight the Greater-D.C. traffic. The volume of cars never bothered me; I was on the clock.

Usually, we'd arrive at the job site around 8 a.m., and unload the small, 4-wheel ATV that rode in the back of the truck. We'd load that up with supplies, and drive out to wherever the Rig had been parked the day before.

You now know most of what you need to know about the routine.

We were in pristine woodlands, mostly, miles from anyone. The air was clean, (except from my Rig's exhaust), the woods were silent (except for my Rig's rumbles and hammering), and the land was untouched (except where I ran over trees to get to the next boring flag). We were the developers, I am just now realizing, we were the sulliers of beauty. Fuck it, it was fun to work autonomously, stoned out of my head with a 5-ton ATV Rig with 48" tires that could climb up the side of a 30-degree hill.

Some events, 3 tales to give you a feel of the insanity that my employer must have been suffering to put me in charge of a giant, powerful off-road machine:

One fine morning, shortly after an icy-rain, with an ambient temperature about 25 degrees, we were traversing an off-road path following some power lines (the big, metal towers you see in the countryside sometimes, that are inaccessible to normal traffic; they have paths along them so that the electric company's workers can maintain them). The paths were rather slick from the ice, which became a problem when I crested a frozen muddy hill and my Rig began to no longer move forward, but sideways. Down a 75-foot hill towards the power line Towers. The ice had crusted at the top, and my traction went from directional choice to gravity's choice, which was down; gravity was winning, I had no steerage control. About halfway down the hill, my Rig (which was a frame, engine, Drill motor and tower, with a seat, it was not enclosed) began to tilt up so that I was sliding downhill on my two tires on the right side of the Rig, in the direction I was sliding...This I remember quite clearly, action for action...I felt the Rig rise; I was still sawing my wheel back forth, trying to get a bite, when the left side started to rise off the hill...with one foot on the clutch, I stood, sliding, popped the engine down to first, then cleared my legs out from under the engine, ready to jump clear if the Rig began to roll. I had no interest in being crushed inside of a rolling Drill Rig, but as it began to yaw beyond what (I thought) was the point of no return, I jumped off, to the left, just clearing my swinging, giant tires, rolling away from it, and thinking to myself: I just destroyed a $30,000 Drill Rig. I am so fucking fired. My helper, who had been walking alongside the Rig, was running down the hill towards me, he had been chasing my runaway machine...he yelled, wide-eyed, "Are you okay?" I said sure, I was fine, I knew how to roll. We both turned as the Rig, with no operator keeping the gasoline pumping, settled back onto all four tires and then the engine stalled near the bottom of the hill. "I'll be damned, " I said, "I guess I didn't break it."

On that same job site, after the winter had passed, we were working at the bottom of a valley in early Spring. It was chilly (enough for a couple of layers of shirts), but the real freezing had left. I had a new helper, one that fancied himself a hot-dogger on the 4-wheeler that came with my Rig. I always let my helpers drive the 4-wheeler, even when I did not have my Rig; these kids, 18 or 19 year-old high school dropouts, lived for the weekends when they could take their own 4-wheelers out and about, drinking beer and jumping over obstacles. We were moving from one boring to another, and had to take the 4-wheeler up a steep hill to the next. I eyed the incline, and told my heolper to take the ATV up, I would walk, and meet him at the top of the hill. He demurred, insisting he could carry us safely across a small stream, up the bank, and back to the support truck without waiting for me to catch up. Such is the power of marijuana that I believed him and clambered onto the rear of the ATV. We crossed the stream, and as we began to rise up the hill, the mud beneath us betrayed the ATV's grip, and--it felt like slow motion-- We went backwards, me, then him, then the 4-wheeler. I say that it felt like slow motion because as I went backward, I braced for the fall, tucking my chin in to protect my neck; using one arm to catch him as he descended on top of me, and flinging him aside to safety; and using the other arm to guide the ATV so that the steering bar missed my head. I was in six inches of water with 400 pounds of ATV on top of me, but I was completely unharmed, and began yelling at my helper to get "the damned thing off of me." The word "moron" was probably used, as well.

Postscript to this vignette: That helper only worked at the company for another 3 months, because he fractured his femur doing an ATV jump one weekend. Karma is a bitch.

One job site I got was for a single house, a single-acre with 6 borings marked off. 4 were around the perimeter, and 2 were in the center. I had a single-day deadline, as the 18 wheeler that took me from job to job was coming to get me at 4 p.m., and his time was locked in. 5 of the borings were a non-issue; routine, sparse woods, etc. The Engineers, with apparently a twisted and sick sense of humor, had placed the markers for the final boring inside of a 10-foot high pile of deadfall trees. Trees. Not logs, or branches. This pile looked like a fucking log cabin, and dead in the center of this ridiculous pile, was a little flag. The clock was ticking, our chainsaw was pitiful against the strategically-placed forest, and I decided to attempt to drive over it. Now, these Rigs we drove were able to drive over a lot of things; but, looking back, I have no idea what possessed me to attempt to drive over the Matterhorn for a boring. I began my ascent, with the Rig pitching and yawing as each tire would clear another tree, my elevation rising, my helper shrieking at the imminent disaster, until...I had my front tires hanging into space, about 8 feet in the air. Then I lowered my jacks, and drilled in the small clearing beneath us. We drilled in the air. I only went down 10 feet or so, and double sampled instead of going deeper (a no-no, but I was already drilling in an area that would have given my employer apoplexy), and somehow plowed my Rig out of the pile, over a living tree to burst out into the clearing, onto a side road and onto the ramps of the waiting 18 wheeler. I made my deadline, and I thought my helper would pass out. I had to bribe him not to repeat the tale.

O. Construction and Concrete

In 2001, I was driving an airport shuttle to earn my daily bread. When the Twin Towers were attacked in New York City, the country stopped and watched CNN for 3 days. We all suffered in individual ways. On September 12th, 2001, the company I was working for got a call from a business traveler who had been stranded in Baltimore, and needed to get back to New York.After a brief discussion, I told him I would drive him in my van for $300 plus tolls. My in-laws were still living in Queens, and I wanted to make sure all was well with them. After the drive to Westchester (slightly North of the city proper), I drove into Queens, and spent the night with the family-in-law. The following morning, I left to return to Maryland, and driving down the BQE (Brooklyn-Queens Expressway for those who don't know), I got my first good look at Manhattan in person since the attack. This was Thursday the 13th.The World Trade Center rubble was still burning, and would for months. The news from the television became real.After living from hand-to-mouth for months, I decided that I needed to get a better-paying job. Air travel plummeted after the attacks, and I was fortunate to take home $200 a week. I asked a friend to talk to a friend who owned a Geotechnical Drilling Company, and after a brief interview, I was hired as a Driller's Helper. I was 33 years old, and about to begin my third career.

I had spent 3 years driving for the shuttle company, the majority of those trips going to Baltimore-Washington International (BWI) Airport. I calculated that I had driven to BWI about 2,100 times during my tenure. The first day at my new job, the Driller to whom I was assigned had a project scheduled at BWI Airport. The manager asked me if I knew how to get there, as I would be driving the "support" truck for the Dill Rig. I allowed that I had been to BWI once or twice.

Drilling – that ended up being my favorite job that I've ever had. The work was outdoors, you operated a Rig independently (on a schedule), the people were all blue-collar roughnecks, and the money was sufficient, for a while. I left Drilling after two years to work in construction, and later regretted giving up my path in drilling. Another tale for another time, I promise. I am feeling somewhat specific today.The thoughts that I was having just now, outside (which is how I usually do a column; I go outside for a cigarette, and stare at the stars or cars, and something jumps to clarity in my brain), involve a specific exchange that I had when I was foreman of a concrete crew in West Virginia.It was a Friday, and I was visiting various jobsites to deliver paychecks to the crews (we had 3 or 4 jobs going, in West Virginia, Maryland and Washington, D.C.). I had cashed mine, already, near the office. As I gave the crew chief the paychecks, I was counting my cash. It was a nice bundle, since I had made overtime (every week).The crew chief, Mike, saw what I was doing, and said "Rob, you shouldn't flash that cash in front of these guys. Someone could roll you." Mike was a career construction guy, with a hard tan, premature crow's feet and a smoker's rasp. Payday for him was a brawl at the bar and a hooker in bed. I laughed, still counting. "No one here is going to take my money, Mike," I returned, bemused.He shook his head, as if speaking to a slow learner. "You can't say that, you don't know these guys."I slipped my cash into my pocket, the smile leaving my face. I had been promoted from digger to foreman to project manager at the company in the space of a month. My meteoric rise had not gone un-noticed, and now I was being probed to see how soft I was. My kind of people.

"Mike," I said slowly, staring him in the eyes, my tone allowing that play time was over, "There is no one here who can roll me. No one."
I never had another problem with insubordination at that company.

The Romans invented concrete. I am getting the boring part out of the way, so that you can sit on the edge of your seat, being entertained while learning. I am going to teach you, and you'll like it--if not, I will resort to anecdotes about sailing. Hyperbole, of course -- I don't know how interesting I can make it.Concrete is a composite, man-made material that is comprised of cement (that is correct--cement is a component of concrete, so don't call a sidewalk "cement"--it's concrete. Cement is what masons use in between bricks, and even that has sand added to it), aggregate (rocks) and sand. The cement acts as the glue for the rocks and sand, which give concrete its enormous strength. How much strength does it have? (I am glad you are here to feed me the questions). Concrete mix, when purchased commercially from a plant, is sold by its "Pounds Per Square Inch" designation (PSI). Concrete starts at 3,500 PSI tensile-strength. What that refers to (just to get all engineerical and nerdy on you) is that a field engineer at a pour will take a sample tube of concrete, and let it cure (the term for drying). Upon curing, this small tube of concrete is then subjected to a pneumatic press that pushes against the tube until it breaks, and the measure of how much force it takes to break the tube is the PSI designation. 3,500 PSI. Do some math. That means a square foot of concrete can withstand a force of 504,000 pounds. That shit is stout. You could support my SUV on one square inch of the stuff.
To build a Big Thing: First, plans and permissions (the General Contractor's problem). Then, we dig big holes. We fill

those holes with concrete. We level some dirt, electricians and plumbers start running pipes, we pour gravel, and pour some more concrete. Then walls are built upon my floor. Then, a bunch of people run around, adding stuff, and a roof is thrown on. That is pretty much it.After I had spent a few years working as a Geotechnical Driller, I wanted to learn more about construction, and I had a friend (my former martial arts sensei) who owned a commercial concrete construction company, and he graciously offered me a job (when I solicited such). The first week of employment, I was tasked with enlarging a hole under a foundation, unreachable by machine, with a pick-axe. The soil was hard packed, limestone-infested, impossible-to-move dirt. I ended up excavating perhaps a foot a day. The newest employees always got the shit duty; that is merely the way of construction (and most fields, thinking about it).A month later I was running the crew. I had the math skills, the chutzpah, and the ability to sound as if I had a clue.Before I started at that company, my experience with concrete was limited to knocking over a wheelbarrow full of it, that my dad was mixing, when I was 12 years old. I learned quickly enough, and six months later, I was building a Safeway, in Fairfax, Virginia. Scary thought, isn't it? I built the fucking thing based on six months' experience.Concrete is a vicious bitch of a mistress. Once the dry ingredients are mixed, it has a shelf-life; no matter how much water you keep adding, it will eventually set anyway. The curing of concrete is a chemical process, not evaporation (concrete can cure underwater). Commercial projects have limits as to how much water is permissible to add, if you have a truck waiting to pour, delayed for any number of reasons (commercial construction sites are one of the worst cluster-fucks you can imagine; every trade, such as electrical, plumbing, HVAC, etc., thinks that they are the most crucial element, and everyone demands to be accorded priority for everything). Inspectors stand by to reject concrete trucks, if the delay is too long.Imagine, you are a concrete contractor. Without you, there is no foundation. Without a foundation, there is no fucking building. What exactly do you plan to build your walls on, there, Mr. Mason? Dirt? Get the hell out of my way and let me work. Do you plan to set your toilets on some 2x4s and hope for the best, Mr. Plumber? Then shut your pie hole. Everybody would impede my progress. I better set the scene, because I believe I am going out of order.The details: Too numerous to mention. There are porta-johns scattered around a large site, because it is not cool to piss on the ground when someone else has to dig in it. You ever wonder what happens to large quantities of feces and urine inside of a plastic box when the outside temperature drops below freezing? It turns into an impossible-to-pump out piss-sicle. Then it fills, because it can't be emptied, and you have an unusable porta-john. Wait til it thaws--you'll wish it was frozen again, due to the smell.When you drive a concrete truck over a dozen carefully-laid electrical conduits, the electrical contractor is liable to throw an enormous shitfit. Jumping up and down, even. I considered it karma, because his procrastinating self-importance delayed almost every one of my pours (supermarket floors are so massive, concrete pours are broken up into manageable sections, perhaps 60 feet x 120 feet at a time, which is still, as you know, 88 cubic yards of concrete, or 9 full trucks). I had to schedule days ahead of time for a pour; I had to arrange for a fleet of trucks, a crew of ten or so to excavate, level and pour a gravel base; ensure that the electrician had his pipes in, as well as the plumber; make sure I had lights rented (generally, because of the required amount of time for a pour, we would start in the early morning, while it was still dark and cool); and any number of details that had to be juggled for every major pour (we did about 8 for the supermarket, I believe).2 out of 3 times I had to re-schedule because some other trade wasn't ready. Fuck his conduits. I was standing right there, waving the truck to back over them--he wasn't supposed to have them in, yet, so that I could move trucks; he delayed me at every turn, yet was "ahead of schedule" when it inconvenienced me. I stared him right in the eyes as he howled. Then he stomped off to the General Contractor (the Ultimate Arbiter of a job site, the Big Boss), who promptly told him to get fucked, because his conduits weren't supposed to be there. A small moral victory.By the end of that job, I was a cold-hearted bastard, because every jackass on the site would push for every advantage for themselves, while screwing over any other trade that they could; I got along pretty well with the Masons, who were helpful to me, but everybody else--I began to revel in the shrieks of agonal whining that I heard when I arbitrarily delayed somebody else, merely because they had previously been Dicks to me. It is amazing that anything ever gets built, to tell you the truth, and I have been there, on the inside.But, nevertheless, there is now a big building, where before there was none, and I did it (with hundreds of other guys, of course, but still). You're welcome.

P. The perfect kiss

Some names changed for privacy's sake.In August of 1988, I met Irene (my wife Clarissa's sister), and we dated briefly. Meeting Irene also brought me into contact with Clarissa for the first time, and I fell in love/lust right away, but she had a boyfriend at the time.Also in August of 1988 (it was a good month), Charles and I became employed at Tannen Printing, where I would work until 1998, and Charles would work at until 2006.

At Tannen, I had many artists as customers, as it was in SoHo, and one of them was a Brooklyn-based artist named Alison, who had work at a gallery in my area. She was about my height, a redhead, with a gorgeous body, a pleasant, open face, and a great demeanor. We got along well, a friendly rapport whenever she would come in for copies. By 1989, I was 20, she was 34 or 35, so there was an age difference.After a while, I got up the nerve to ask her out for a more or less "date" (I was shyer, then), and she agreed. it may have been as "friends", but not entirely...there was the understanding that I liked her, and she me. She merely thought of me as "young", but obviously, I was precocious.We had a fine time, we went to a falafel shop by Washington Square, and then back to The Prince Street Bar for drinks /and.While we were sitting there, I admitted that I indeed was attracted to her, and I was looking forward to the time if/ and when she would take me into her bed. The bar was crowded, New York-style, with patrons inches away from our elbows, but, for the first time in my life, I felt comfortable being aggressive and vocal and open with a woman. I did forget to mention that she had tight jeans on that night, which molded to one of the finest asses of any woman I have gone out with. Her age was NOT an issue to me.She was somewhat shocked when I told her this, but flushed and pleased, quite obviously. I could see that the idea of sleeping with me was not anathema.After drinks, we walked for a while, until we got to her subway stop at 23rd street. I sat on a short wall, and she faced me, and we kissed.

I tell the whole story to arrive at this juncture, this moment. As I discovered as I told this to Jim, that may have been the single most delightful moment of my life. I was 20, I had a good job, no responsibilities other than rent, no debt, no pets, no warrants. I was young and free, and that moment I can relive as if it were ten seconds ago.I can feel my hands gently cupped around her bottom, sliding into her back pockets. I can taste her lips, the delicious heat of her tongue, the good, clean smell of her breath; I can hear my heartbeat as it paced my own mouth. I can hear her soft, gentle but insistent moans as we locked together, uninhibited, unrestrained, happy.There is no fucking question in my mind, whatsoever, that in the moment I was at my best, my most fulfilled. She went home that night, but I did not feel chagrined or disappointed that we didn't have sex that night: I felt that I finally understood what the fuss about kissing really was. I never had much fun with kissing any woman before that night, and never as good since.

We went out again, but my memory is vague of when...I know she invited me to her brownstone in Brooklyn, on a Sunday morning in November, to watch the NYC marathon pass by her place (a yearly tradition for her block, I was told).It was rare that I got up that early on a Sunday, in those days, being somewhat of a pub-crawler, but arrive on time I did, somewhat fatigued but eager to get nearer to this older woman who excited me so. She was an established artist, a field in which I had sincere interest, and the only "barrier" was age (for her). I think we snuck a few kisses in, but she had a full house, and it was casual.

Around this time (Nov. 1989), she had begun working part-time as a waitress at a bar called Bottom of the 9th (pun---just below 9th and Broadway, and baseball reference). At this bar was a bartender (I'll call him Bill--I absolutely don't remember his name) who began to express interest in Alison. She was quite forthright about it, since we had dated a couple of times, (no lovemaking yet), and was conflicted. Bill was her age, and "appropriate" as a life-partner, for babies and marriage, whereas I was (just turned) 21, a kid, good for a fun fling, but not a "serious" relationship.I'll interject here that I have ONLY the fondest memory of Alison, I harbor no ill-will in any sense. I love thinking about her.

She decided that we could no longer date, that she was going to give a try with Bill, for the aforementioned reasons, and she stopped coming to my copy shop (her decision, I guess she thought it would be awkward).Two months later, Charles and Irene had begun dating, and they were invited to a party in Brooklyn. Clarissa, as they told me, was recently broken up with her boyfriend, and wanted to go to the party, but not as a "third wheel", and would I mind going along as an "escort" (not as a serious date, of course). I said yes.We went out for a drink first (Ironically, to the Bottom of the 9th, which had become my hangout months before for obvious reasons; Alison was not working that night, however), and Charles and Irene immediately became poor company, as they sucked face and did "new lover" swooning. Clarissa and I began to chat, and discovered we both loved, loved, loved cinema. We married 4 months later.Postscript:That August, Alison walks into the copy center, aglow and smiling shyly. She had dated Bill for a time, but it didn't work out. She wanted to know, if I was still interested, would I like to try another date?My jaw dropped as I informed her as nicely as I could (and I hated to say it, actually) that I was now married and expecting a child. I wanted to say, "Your timing sucks". I hated the look on her face as all the emotion crashed down on her as she realized in that instant that she had "backed the wrong horse", so to speak.I wonder if I married Clarissa so that she wouldn't get away like Alison did. I wonder what might have been. Either way, I have the memory of the Perfect Kiss.

S. Earliest Memory

hallway. narrow confines, channel forward. backward. side rooms. route to everything. passage and place. uniform and fixed. enter and move. hallway is not to stand in. hallway is to move through. it is not a place. it is an access. we hear the house. we are always we not for voices but for membership of the humanity club. we are the same but i cannot be we so we must be me.

the house makes insinuations about our bedtimes. we feel the radar must sweep over our head. we are unseen at the level with the unders.

there are hasty patches of dark dark and quick flashing patches of light dark. rumbles echo and touch our skin. we had a purpose moments ago. our purpose has changed with new inputs. anxious pinches fight within our belly making noise that has some message that is just out of reach. there is something we are supposed to think.

there is a dark shadow world of fearful mystery under the long thing where they sit. underneath is unknown. there could be things that whisper like the thing that whispers beneath where we sleep. staying away from the whisper keeps us away from the eyes that glow.

we circle the room looking for the truck. we remember that the truck was in here before. we were asleep but that was also before. sometimes trucks just appear and it is wonderful. we must be in the places where the truck appears. the truck is not there. the truck is not there. we glance meaningfully at the dark place, hoping that the truck is not going to appear there.

that feeling returns and our belly hurts but then it passes and there is something in our pants. we know that we are supposed to put that somewhere else. in our pants is not where it should they said. we must hide it before they come from their sleep place and step over their sleep monsters and find us with it in our pants.

we know -- we will hide it where no one goes -- in the dark place beneath the long sitting place. no one will ever find it there. we have to be quick be quick but we don't know how these things come off ...

....

"Bobby, what are you doing? Oh, it looks like you've got a full diaper. Come on over here, let's get you changed up."

P.S. This is a recounting of my earliest or second-earliest memory, of a time I was wandering the living room in the early morning hours, looking for a toy (I called it a "truck", but what the particular toy was has faded from memory), and I filled my diaper. It must have been just as I was being toilet-trained, or it probably wouldn't reside in my recollections. I have begun to realize (with help from a Constant Reader) that I seem to remember almost all formative incidents in my life, so I will say that this incident is when my brain made the connection between bowel contractions and bowel functions, and the "guilt" associated therewith: potty training. Also, I have tried to interpret the strange and terrible world of a small person, with fearful creatures from bad dreams having a real aspect, since, at the time, we did not know the difference between nightmares and reality.

R. Ex-Girlfriend's Polaroid

So, my buddy Jim was dating this Dominican woman, in the early 1990s. One night, as she was off to Manhattan or New Jersey too visit relatives, I came out to his place in Brooklyn to hang out and drink alcohol and share tales.

We had our wee drams, to be sure, we were old salts and constant drinking companions, so few memories exist of the early part of the evening, and then at some point, Jim says to me, all sly-like, and with a shit-eating grin, "So, do you want to see a naked picture of Josie?" (the aforementioned Dominican lady). I was shocked, initially − Jim is a fairly conservative soul, as regards matters of the heart and sex; I didn't think he had it in him. Of course I said "yes, please", for young Josie was a delicious physical specimen, a creamy, café-con-leche morsel for a red-blooded American Caucasian male such as I was and am. She was young and pretty and curvy and soft and lean; while I had not exactly lusted after her (being the steady gal-pal of my long-time friend), I had not failed to drink in her desirable femininity. Fuck yeah, Jim. Make with the nudie pics.

He took me up to the roof of the building in which they resided, on a night with a sentry moon and clear air, allowing every star in the sky to add candle-power to my vision, when he reached into a pocket (after glancing nervously around, to triple-check that we were alone on the roof), and handed me a Polaroid.

It has been almost twenty years, but I remember the image clearly: A young, caramel-skinned woman, laying a bed (covered with white sheets), legs slightly apart (in a relaxed, not overtly lascivious repose), with her arms behind her head. She had a serious expression on her face (at which I glanced for only a second),her lips were pursed, pensively, as she gazed out from the picture, presumably at the photographer. I stared, drinking in the sight of her trimmed, dark curly pubic hair and at her brown, small nipples and firm breasts.

It was voyeuristic and immeasurably exciting; many nude women have I seen, but this was the first time I had seen a woman I knew (but was not sleeping with, myself) proudly naked. I was instantaneously aroused, sexually excited by the picture of Josie (curly dark pussy fur), and as I handed the picture back to Jim, I said something along the lines of "I am so turned on right now I gotta jack off".

He chuckled as he tucked the picture away, but his face quickly grew serious as he saw me fumbling with the zipper on my jeans, as I settled down onto the roof so that I could masturbate in the cool, crisp air. I think from that point on Jim smoked a cigarette and stared out over Brooklyn and pretended to ignore what I was doing, a few feet away, seated on the roof of his home.

Hey, his girlfriend was sexy. I orgasmed fairly quickly, I suppose (I truly don't remember), and then we went downstairs for more drinking.

Every time I saw Josie after that, I think I was more friendly than I had been previously. (She told me, years later, that she thought that I "Never liked her" or that I disapproved of her being Jim's girlfriend. "Not at all," I assured her, "I just didn't know you yet."

Q. Love Hurts

Love hurts, I have heard repeated so often that it nauseates me.

I have argued for and against the proposition, but I think I will have to settle in the "for" camp. Love does hurt -- if not you, or the one you the love, then someone else.

I met the woman who would become my wife in 1988. She was dating another man at the time, and we kept in intermittent contact over the next couple of years. In February of 1990, her sister (Irene) and my best friend (Charles) were dating; the sisters were invited to a party, to which my wife (Clarissa, having recently broken up with a different boyfriend) had no date. I, being an eligible bachelor, was invited along to create a double-date dynamic, and the four of us attended the party.

Also in attendance at the party was Clarissa's most recent ex-boyfriend (a young man named Jim; a different Jim than has been previously mentioned in these unhallowed pages, to be sure). I was introduced to Jim, and, being the boisterous idiot I was (I have gotten better), would shout his name out at the party whenever I spotted him (JIM!!!), and stand next to him, slugging down a beer and making chit-chat.

I have to clarify my behaviors, to make my point. I was socially inept, for much of my life, and was one of those people at parties who would meet a person, and then talk to them for as long as possible before they ran away, since I was terrible at "meeting" people (That is a "type" of party-goer, isn't it? No? Just me? Oh well). Talking to them I had no difficulties with -- I can ramble on with anyone (perhaps you've noticed). So, I knew only Charles and Irene and Clarissa and now, Jim, at this soiree (hosted by Buddhists, a lively bunch, don't be fooled). Clarissa I spent the evening dancing with. Charles and Irene I barely saw, as they were a "new" couple, and totally immersed in themselves. When I took a break from dancing, I would grab a beer, spot Jim, Hail him loudly (JIM!!), and leap over next to him to catch up with him.

Have you ever been the last one in a room to get a joke? A lot of people are laughing, and you look around, confused, and then you realize: you forgot to wear pants (or underwear)(dreams count, for this exercise), and then you blush bright red and go to therapy for years, or watch a lot of Woody Allen movies. In this case, that was me. Jim was Clarissa's ex-boyfriend, standing there and watching us dance (dirty dancing, too; I was all up in that shizz like nobody's bizz: Because of that night, Clarissa became my wife) with big puppy-dog sad eyes holding a torch and everybody in the room (being members of the same Buddhist cult as Clarissa and Irene and Jim) knew about the break-up and how Jim was pining away, tortured, and then this *loudmouth lout* that had "stolen" away his girlfriend keep jumping at him like some sort of bully, rubbing it in his face.

Seriously: I thought I was just being friendly. I had no idea who the guy was, as he was small and plain and I forgot him as soon as he passed from my view. Clarissa told me much later that everybody there thought that I was a jerk for fucking with him like that. Terrible, horrible.

Anyway, a year and change later, Charles and Irene got married, and at the reception, I was once again, drunk to the point of tunnel-vision (yes, you will find that a lot of stupidities in life -- not just mine -- start with imbibation of alcoholic beverages), and Clarissa (having our infant daughter to tote around) introduced me to a couple of people, and then went off to do mothering stuff. One of the people she introduced me to was a guy named Jim (for the sake of removing suspense, yes, it was the same guy). He and I chatted throughout the reception (which was a fabulous drunken orgy of dancing and food that I remember little of, save this), and at some point, Clarissa returned, and went over to Jim and kissed him and said good night (she was taking the baby upstairs I think), and he made some comment ... it was innocuous (I don't even recall what was said), but the manner struck me, through my drunken haze: you know when you hear such a comment, that the two people exchanging it had been intimate at some point. It dawned on me then, that this was her ex-boyfriend, that she had just left him, right before that party of February of 1990, and I had forgotten him again.

"You're THAT Jim!" I blurted out, to which he smiled sheepishly (probably thinking, *what a fucking jack-ass; she married him instead of me?*). I had done it again.

The next part is a bit darker.

Some years passed, and Clarissa and I hit the lowest point of our marriage in the winter of 1999. Without giving out too much information, some infidelities and drug relapses were involved; I admit everything about myself, but I have to leave some of this out. It was bad. Neither of us wanted to be married to the other, or even to remain living; it was fucking dark and deep hurt and pain and loneliness.

Heroin relapse. And then -- *on that night*. The night between us where it all could have ended, very easily, we lay in the dark, on the bed, both of us crying, as we told each other absolutely everything. Everything. Have you done that with someone you love? Think carefully. There is always some shit that you leave out, or gloss over or omit. You have to. She doesn't need to know about the co-coworker you had been flirting with, and then went out for a couple of drinks with, because it went nowhere. He doesn't need to know that your mother had been sending you money -- as a way of maintaining control of an errant daughter. That night, there was nothing secret that remained. At the end of that night, which seemed to last days, we came to the realization -- together -- that if this was as bad as it got, then we could survive it. We reached what drug counselors call "the bottom" -- everything we were was in danger of falling apart. Instead, we stood back up.

During that night, she told me of one of the triggers for her relapse into heroin usage: she had gotten a letter (we were living in Maryland, then) from one of her former Buddhist friends (temple-mates?) -- Jim, her ex-boyfriend, the man who had asked her on many occasions to marry him (which was the reason she left him, ironically), had committed suicide, driven by pain and unrequited love. JIM!!! was dead.

We cannot blame ourselves (I wouldn't let her blame herself, for certain), but I have to wonder what else could have been. What a waste of life, of joy, of kindness. If nothing else, he never called me a jerk when I was being a jerk. Maybe he should have.

I have no punchline, this time. Love hurts -- if not you, if not your love, then someone else.

P.S. We are entering year 18 of sobriety, thank you very much for   asking.

Part Two: Transfer to Babylon

A. Lobster memories

With nary a prospect for illumination or elucidation, I jump into my autonomous abyss. Hello there, my observers, admirers, students and charges, I return to unsheathe my sword for your passive glee. Behold the magic wand as it turns the alphabet into a rabbit. I haven't talked dirty in a while -- I wonder if my libido is cooling down.

I did think about naked fantasy objects last night (I have a stable of imaginary women that I have invented purely for fantasy purposes. My imagination is such, these days, that when I need an arousing image, I do not think of a Scarlett Johansson or a Raquel Welch: I have assembled certain ideals, in my head, into fucktoys of the mind, so it cannot be said that I objectify women, any more that someone who jacks off while thinking of Jessica Rabbit from "Who Framed Roger Rabbit" can be said to objectify bunnies. I have built dreamgirls with the eyes from this woman I know and the hips from that one, and so forth. My fantasies exist only in Rob-o-vision).

I did not achieve orgasm (by myself, that is, discounting the sexy-fun-times with the wife earlier in the evening), being content to merely ponder my dream girl pouring out a pitcher of water over me, while wearing Daisy Duke-cutoff jeans and a white, button-up blouse (tied at the midriff, naturally). It was like re-reading a favorite passage from Hunter Thompson or

Kurt Vonnegut: Amusing and distracting, while allowing me to drift off to sleep. Imagining the young woman was a means to its own end -- I felt like a voyeur in my own head. Soon, I will find my brain charging me quarters like a Times' Square Peep Booth: please deposit 25 cents for an additional 60 seconds of viewing. My brain really should give me an "owner" discount, not to mention my own V.I.P table; I wish I could convince my imagination to work overtime while I am asleep, and strive to produce the quality of material of which I know my brain is capable.

In my dreams and fantasies, I shouldn't have to settle for re-runs or exploitation flicks: I should be getting first-run, 3D fantasies staring a dozen nubile and naked lasses dripping with honey and perspiration. There should be a story, subplots, intrigue and surprise endings: Every now and then, my brain should let me be James Bond, Ron Jeremy and Stephen Hawking combined into one giant, genius, action-adventure porn burrito. Instead of that, I often find myself playing Woody Allen to my fantasies' Annie Hall, except that there is no R.E.M. sleep deep enough to make me cower in the face of a lobster. I am straight-up pimp bad-ass in the face of a lobster (as long as its claws are bound). I will *fucking kill* a crustacean.

I have to undertake digressions to lay the foundation:

Digression Primus: My father grew up in Maine. As soon as he was old enough (and was encouraged by the local magistrate to do so*), he enlisted in the U.S. Navy to get out of small-town U.S.A., and earn a living. His brothers stayed to home, and earned their livings as lobster fisherman. Sometime in the early 1970s (I would have to guess 1972 or 1973, when I was 3 or 4 years old), we visited Maine during the summer.

I have only snatches of memory from the trip (one was getting lost, in the back-woods area where my grandmother lived, and approaching an older woman sitting on a porch and informing her that I was lost; she gave me a Popsicle, and I sat there eating it, contented, until my mother came along and found me {It was a banana Popsicle, for which I have since had an inordinate fondness}), but one memory that haunts me still, is when we went to the beach, where my uncle was unloading his lobster pots, and he released ... well, I can only call it an unholy abomination in the eyes of God; I was just older than a toddler, and this ... behemoth was the *size of a fucking dog*.

Not a terrier, either, but cocker-spaniel sized. This fucker chilled me so thoroughly my testicles waited two additional years to drop when I reached puberty. As I write this now, 38 or so years later, the hairs on my arms are standing on end -- I am not exaggerating (not much), this lobster looked like a creature from a Harryhausen special-effect. When I watched "The Clash of the Titans", and the film came to the scene where Perseus and Co. battle giant scorpions, my mind flashed back to that beach-front leviathan from my childhood. In Stephen King's "The Drawing of the Three," the second book of his superb Dark Tower series, the heroes Roland and Eddie are confronted by creatures which Eddie titles "lobstrosities", and I had a mental image carved out and waiting for me. Although I have since learned that memory is not a recording of events, but the brain's method of storing information, and therefore suspect as to veracity, I will say that this particular grandfather crustacean was at least 3 feet long. I was so terrified (I was standing perhaps 20 feet away from it, when my uncle was unloading the pots, before I started running) that I don't remember screaming. Maybe it was that I don't remember not screaming. I don't think I ever trusted fisherman or uncles again (I certainly forgave beaches, which are my favorite places on Earth).

Digression Secondus: During my early years -- from about 5-7 years old -- I had a recurring set of nightmares involving Creatures Underneath the Bed. This is the part that I meant, when I referred to the fickleness of memory: At the time, I did not know that they were nightmares. In my memory, with time running linearly forward, these are my memories of bedtime. I thought that every time the lights were turned off, the Creatures would awaken. There were two: One was a wolf, spotted only by his glowing yellow eyes beneath my bed (and, thinking back, I am guessing that image came from "Peter and the Wolf", Disney's classic cartoon of 1946, and a childhood favorite of mine), and the other was ... well, it was Tony the Tiger, the pitchman for Kellog's Frosted Flakes. Visually, anyway, but a lot scarier! Dark and always in shadow ... With a *basso profundo*, James Earl Jones timbre to his voice. Both of these bedroom sentinels would tell me the same thing, every night: If I got off of my bad, in the dark, **they would kill me**. Not the childish fears of "chase me" or "eat me", no; my nightmares *flat-out promised to murder me* if I had to pee in the night. Every morning, when I awoke, I would check beneath the bed in the growing sunlight, make sure all was clear, and then rise for the day's ablutions and toilet. It was many, many years later that I realized that those memories were nightmares. I just thought I had a fucking strict bedtime.

Now that my foundation is in place, I can make my point. I was certain, when recalling the Maine expedition many years afterward that my mind had either invented the experience, or certainly added a gross exaggeration to it. By then, I had eaten lobster, many times, and I figured that the grotesque (and, let's face it, cockroach-esque) quality of the lobster had created in my pre-school brain an image of a Hieronymous Boschian-horror unequaled by reality. *It must have just been the first live lobster I had seen*, I told myself as a young adult -- *remember the wolf beneath the bed?* The brain lies to you.

I had seen images of larger, older lobsters (such as the one pictured above): A couple of feet long, and not tasty eating (the younger lobsters are more desirable for sweetness of the meat; the older and larger ones are released, to go and make more baby lobsters for America's table).

Well, as it turns out, it came to be that I was shooting the breeze with my father, a couple of years ago; we were visiting Florida on vacation, and dad is at an age where he reminisces about a lot of things. That trip to Maine came up (I think I brought it up, being now old and mature enough to confront memories, whether or not they are real), and I mentioned my perception, as a 3 year old, that the lobster that his brother Harold had brought up on the beach was 3 feet long.

Dad told me: Oh, it was at least that. Might have been four feet. Biggest damned lobster he had ever seen, before or since.

Watch where you step, when you awaken. Safer still, *don't get out of bed.*

B. Nothing is What You Expect

I have spent my life as a sort of ombudsman, criticizing and attempting to rectify the wrongs in the universe. I don't believe in being an "armchair" anything: If I rail about an inefficiency, I dust off my hands and go do it myself. I'm not a professor as much as an example.

On the other hand, mistakes have been made. One cannot always perfectly execute an omelet.

C. Flowery prose

A writer practices his craft for ages before proficiency is achieved. A writer must read, must live, must experience pain, sorrow, joy, laughter and love before he / she can truly write about it. A writer becomes a storyteller--a master of holding an audience in thrall, of creating a mental image of a scene, building the story component by component.A writer weaves subtlety into the fabric of words.What if a writer doesn't wish to be subtle? How does one travel from saying: "My heart accelerates its journey, pounding faster when I thought your name, rumbling and vibrating within my chest like an impending volcanic upheaval" to stating "I would be overjoyed to make love to you, to spend a night in your arms, a night that lasts for an eternity".Or, even more simply, "Damn, I want to fuck you."Does the ability to craft flowery prose obligate one to make use of it at all times?

What is cybersex?Well, for the un-initiated, it is when two people use words across a computer screen, usually through a chat format, to speak on sexual matters, while each party is masturbating, for the purposes of higher sexual arousal. It sounds simple, doesn't it? In practice, it is, although I have noticed some discrepancies over time. First of all, cybersex is an activity in which I no longer partake. The succinct reason is that it is old hat; back in 1994, on AOL, I was introduced to the practice by a stranger on a Macintosh in Arizona. The pragmatic reason is that it is lopsided--I am somewhat prosaic and descriptive; not to toot my own horn, but when I describe a thing, whether it be a clitoris or a horse, the other party understands my full meaning. Pick an average person in the U.S., however, and they'd misspell "orgasm" (and not merely while in the throws of one, either, which is forgivable). To wit:Me: I can feel the smoothness of your thighs, as I slide your soft cotton panties down, slowly, inhaling the scent of your wet warmth; my vision is blurred, intoxicated by your smell, making me hungry to taste the heat between your legs...Her: Oo yea I'm so wetMe: Your pussy is exposed, now, I can see your soft curls glisten, warm and inviting and asking me to touch you with my tongue...Her: OooMe: I nibble gently on your clit, as you push your hips against my face, soft noises escaping from your throat as you have forgotten who you are, feeling only my tongue sucking your lips, parting your wetness, opening you to me as go slowly, slowly from your thighs into your pussy....Her: God I am so hot rite nowYou get the point. While that may be exciting (and it is, don't get me wrong; millions of masturbating men and women could be wrong, but they're still getting off), it holds no interest for me, anymore. Words excite women, often, which is why I love them. Men are generally more visually stimulated. Nude images, while seemingly crude to the fairer sex, excite and arouse the primal lust within me. I also see the humor in the moment, especially as I was just writing that passage--it is kind of funny what excites we humans. Give me intelligence and humor; give me quirky, incomprehensible and difficult. I love a bizarre woman, God help me, I love a bright flash of wit while naked and rolling around. I love to make a woman laugh, when she is unclothed and vulnerable (and often self-conscious, even the beautiful ones). Sex is almost funny. I try not to take it too seriously, but it has taken a lot of practice.I will continue practicing until I have it right.

D. The shark's-tooth earring

I am going to intersperse, in an order that pleases me, anecdotes that will presumably build a picture of me for you, the reader. There is a methodology, so forgive any stories told out of sequence – it will all make sense in the end (or not, but it should keep my tale lively).

For this, I change names of the participants—for privacy and closure. I should not need to discuss this anymore.I met my best friend, Chris, in 1982. For this anecdote I dubbed him "Charles".Years of escapades, sadnesses and joys followed, but this is a painful and personal tale that may give you insight, or it may amuse. It may curl your toes or it may not register with you at all; sometimes, events that are too far outside of our own experiences seem like fiction.Everything that follows is true, actually happened. This is the story of the shark's-tooth earring and the filleting knife.Anne, my best friend Charles' mother, was my first infatuation, my first crush. I felt a puppy love, I suppose---she was pretty, and open and vulnerable and brunette. As the years went by, Anne divorced Charles' father, and began to date a much younger man named, for this recollection, Spike. Spike was not the brightest of men, but he was kind and generous to Anne, and they got on well, and Spike even tried to relate to us teenage boys. He was only about 10 years older than we were, and infinitely stupider.Spike was a marijuana smoker, when he and Anne began dating—which was great at the time; he was constantly giving us some with which to get high. Unfortunately, he began to dabble in crack cocaine, and less-pleasant times began in that household.It seems a cliché, but he began to become violent, and abusive, and thieving. Anne was somewhat of a pushover, and in between the shouting matches and loud arguments that began to become commonplace, there were tearful reconciliations and apologies. All this time, we, as young boys, were growing into men. My crush for Anne became obvious, and a mild source of discomfort for Charles; Spike was amused, and Anne filed it away as harmless. The violent outbursts became more and more personal, and directed at Anne; Charles and I began to interfere, and Spike (a larger male than we) would beat us back, when in his cocaine-fueled rages.About a month after I turned 18, Spike (who had finally been kicked out of Anne's house, where I had been living, my own parents divorced and gone) had gone on a particularly violent series of rampages. The details of the provoking incidents are a dead spot in my memory, but what I do remember is this: One night, in December of 1986, we decided that enough was enough, and that we needed to kill Spike. We anticipated his return to the house, for Anne, for money, for whatever reason; we knew he would not knock on the door politely and wait to be allowed inside. We placed weapons by every window and door to the outside—knives and baseball bats and such, and sat down for a murderous vigil with another friend of ours, Rod. After a wait of several hours that night, we began to get restless and hungry. We had coupons for a local sandwich shop, and it was decided that Charles and Rod (who was the only one with a car) would go to fetch food, and I would wait for Spike at the house, alone.Of course it happened that way—the universe has perverse humor unknown to man: About ten minutes after they left, I spotted lights pulling into the driveway. Lights that did not belong to Rod's car, nor Anne's. By the front door had been placed a filleting knife, an old, rusty, thin-bladed knife that we had found in the garage or somewhere; once I spotted the headlights, and my heart began to triphammer in my chest like an impending cardiac arrest, I tucked the knife into the waistband of my pants and slipped into the coat closet, adjacent to the front door.

I remember feeling and hearing a pounding, pounding. I could only hear the blood rushing through my head, filling my ears with a roaring rush, a sensation I had never before felt, nor have I since.I waited forever, it seemed; in reality, perhaps a minute. Then I heard a crashing from the back entrance, a double glass door that opened onto the patio. I heard Spike bellowing as he entered, and I came down to the decision...... stay in the closet, hidden, because I was alone?... step out and face the ogre, the raging addict, the violent man screaming for Anne...I stepped out of the closet, impossibly, and walked out to the kitchen. Spike had been traversing the house, calling for Anne, and when he emerged from the master bedroom, with his eyes blood red and yet still dilated and pale, spotted me standing sheepishly in the kitchen.Words were yelled, that did not enter my ears, as I reached into my waistband and drew out the knife...... which caused him to trumpet with rage, and my hands, shaking, *dropped the knife*. I dropped the knife as he came towards me.At that moment, I was no avenging angel determined to bring down the giant, I became afraid for my own life. Here was an opportunity for him to arm himself at my expense—I suddenly felt that I was about to die.He lunged forward, to the ground in front of me, reaching for the blade; since I was closer, I scooped it up, terrified, and the motion of drawing it away from his grasp slashed the inside of his arm.He truly howled, then, and charged towards me, furious and possessed. I barely had time to drop the blade downwards, over his bull-like charge, into his upper back.I quickly withdrew the knife, believing I had missed anything vital, when he dropped to the floor as if his hamstring had been cut.As it turns out, and if you have seen the movie "Troy", when Achilles defeats Boagrius, a blade more than six inches long, thrust through the trapezius muscle, can puncture the heart or lung from the top. My knife-thrust went directly into Spike's left lung, and his body knew it right away.

I stood, transfixed, with adrenaline pouring throughout my body, as I watched the mortally-wounded Spike begin to crawl away.His yells had become whimpers; his bravado had faded away to desperation. I held a rusty, eight-inch long blade in my hand that had just severely injured another human being in less than the blink of an eye."You're not dead!", I screamed at him, as he vainly tried to make his way towards the door, "No way I'm gonna let you fucking live through this." I jumped onto him, straddling his chest, trying to cover his mouth and nose with my hands to cut off his oxygen supply and finish the termination process. He was too large for me to hold down, however, and fought to throw me off , twisting his head from side to side."I don't want to go to jail for you," I coldly informed him, "I don't want to leave any more marks and go down for murder." I put the knife down in the kitchen and began to rummage through the drawers."Just let me leave," he cried, "I just need to go.""You're not walking out of here, Spike," I growled, looking for masking tape, duct tape, anything that I could use to cover his mouth and nose."Just let me leave. You can have her!!" he shrieked, and my blood ran cold. "You can take Anne, just let me leave!"My shoulders sagged as I shuffled from the kitchen back into the living room, where he had crawled while I was searching. I was defeated. His harsh and pitiful words had highlighted the truth, albeit in an inadvertent and sarcastic way: Anne would never be mine, there was no future for "us". I had stabbed him with a knife— he stabbed me, just as viciously, with his words. His eyes squinted, as he saw by my body language that his cries had hit their mark."Do you know what happened the last time I saw her?" he crowed, coughing blood and grimacing a smile, "I FUCKED HER! MY DICK WAS INSIDE HER and SHE WAS BEGGING FOR MORE!!!"The front door opened, then, and Charles and Rod entered. They had been standing on the porch—they had seen Spike's car, heard shouting inside, and realized Spike was down. They were hoping I would finish him off, and didn't want to have to testify.Spike lived, to shorten the story a touch. I had to go to the police station as they flew him out in a helicopter, and I wrote out my statement of what had happened, much like this but without the prosaic embellishments, and I noticed an odd sensation. I was shocked, since I did not notice when it happened.I had defecated into my pants, presumably from sheer terror.The following year, after I had moved to New York City, I was window-shopping at the South Street Seaport, and my eyes came across a shark's-tooth earring, with gold plating on the root. I bought it, in memory of the knife that I had used when I needed it.I wore it for years until it become lost in the dredges of memory.Here's to you, Spike. I will never be fooled by an ill-wishing human being again. My children, Charles and Anne thank you, also. The last any of us had heard, Spike was doing time in a prison in Georgia. I hope he gets fucked in the ass daily.

E. I am a savage

There must be a rail to grasp, somewhere. Tie up. No need for anyone to fall overboard.

I break. I have been broken.

With no permanence or external acknowledgment of failure, *I heal*. The scars map their own stories -- if you care for an explanation, I will tell you about almost any one. Being held down by a giant is a helpless feeling. How much struggle should one engage in before capitulation, surrender and death?

If you argue in favor of an issue, is it possible (in any non-theoretical realm) to concede error? How many arguments end with the statement, "Oh, yeah. You're right. Thanks for teaching me that."? Few?

Why do we argue? A definition of "insanity" (from Albert Einstein, no less) reads: "Insanity: doing the same thing over and over again and expecting different results." If very few, if any, arguments achieve any form of knowledge progression, is it not then more logical to simply attack one's debate partner, physically? After all, Hollywood Westerns taught us that any disagreement can be solved by a punch in the mouth. Why do we pretend to civilization?

I know I am savage. I remain calm primarily because it is too addictive a sensation to allow the beast to break the chains -- like positive feedback oscillating out of control, I fear a descent into violent debauchery would be a state from which I would have no path to return. There is a rapture in rending flesh, in manual entropy; I have enjoyed the dissolution of corporeal corporations. Death is a dreaded fun, to be feared by the bull's eye, not the arrow.

I like things that are soft and gentle and cool and gentle and pink. My adoration of women may be merely an admiration of their color scheme and textures. Where I lumber, they glide; where I disseminate, they assemble. **It takes two to build a zygote**, much to the chagrin of sexists on both sides of the imaginary battle-lines.

When I call myself "savage", I suppose that I mean *I am unafraid to descend to the level of danger.* I used to have a saying, which I will reprise: I cannot wait to die, but I have things to do, first.

It is very annoying to interrupt a thought in the middle. Concepts are gifts from you to yourself; never look a gift anterior superior temporal gyrus in the mouth (if it had one; since it is part of your right temporal lobe, in your brain, if it has a mouth, you have an absorbed conjoined twin in your head). Don't fuck with the Maestro -- he is rolling.

Eureka. Attributed to Archimedes when he was taking a bath, it is translated as "I have found it". I submit the same answer that I give, when I hear of any scientific or exploratory discovery: **I didn't know it was lost**. Columbus discovered a vast continent full of peoples to rape; they were unaware that they were missing the teachings of Jesus and the joys of smallpox. The Europeans set them straight, for sure. Eureka, Squanto, *I have discovered your land, and if you don't mind, we will put our living room over here.*

Here, Have some Death.

I lost my little R2-D2 action figure, back in 1977. I found out, years later, one of my "friends" had stolen it. Eureka! It is good discover someone else's wisdom -- maybe give 'em a set of quotation marks or footnotes? We who think for ourselves would appreciate the shout-out.

P.S. -- I have just been informed that I am an unlikely candidate for Alzheimer's disease. I like the little things in life that go well. Never mind the necessities, to paraphrase Dorothy Parker; budget the luxuries first. It may be that I die of some form of cancer (several forms run in my family's genetic make-up), but having my wits about me until the Reaper's scythe descends upon my neck gives me optimism. Even more than I had, and I am fairly upbeat, anyway. I've had dudes try to kill me -- I really can't worry about a water bill compared to that.

F. My legacy

Someday, my brain will no longer be able to receive oxygen, and I will stop processing information, and that event will be preceded or proceeded by the stoppage of my heart. This is known as "death". How good will my death be? Will it be better, or worse, than other people's?What is that, you say? There is no rating system for deaths? Then, what are we, as a species, competing for?If we all die, then we all face the same constraints.If you "can't take it with you", then what we accumulate here on this plane is meaningless.If we can only impact the future by what we teach those that survive us, then our children are our students, and our students are our message to eternity.What we do matters less than what we do 50 years from now. Is the World improved--however minutely--by our time here? Native Americans--at least the Plains Indians--take the long view that we improve the World Seven generations from now. Your children's children's children's children's children better get your message etched into the side of Mount Knowledge. Then, you've done some good.I get annoyed too quickly, and I take some inexplicable pride in self-control. I wish that I allowed myself the freedom to have a good mad, now and then.I fear death not ... I do worry over irrelevancy. My legacy is my love of Love.

G. Defending the First Amendment.

Without doing a Wiki search, I refer to a quote that states: "Insanity is the state of repeating an action, over and over, and expecting different results".I hereby posit that the population of the United States of America has cheerfully plodded into a state of insanity as regards religious beliefs.

I refer you to the First Amendment to the Constitution, the very first article of the Bill of Rights. **When you care enough to send the very best, you put it FIRST.**"Congress shall make no law respecting an establishment of religion, or prohibiting the free exercise thereof; or abridging the freedom of speech, or of the press; or the right of the people peaceably to assemble, and to petition the Government for a redress of grievances."Let us analyze this, shall we? I feel like I've done this before, but apparently, the overwhelming weight of hate and ignorance on the part of the peanut gallery of the US of A likes to pick and choose which Amendments it likes."Congress shall make no law respecting an establishment of religion, or prohibiting the free exercise thereof;"is pretty fucking cut and dry. Don't bring out your assertions that America is a "Christian Nation"; according to the *very first fucking line of the very first fucking Amendment*, it ain't. There is no state religion. Period. If you believe otherwise, feel free to fuck yourself in the rectum with a moldy copy of Ann Coulter's autobiography, *"I suck Republican Cock for a Living, and Swallow the Sperm of Conservatism"*. There is no need to research the individual biographies of the writers of the Constitution, to "interpret" what Jefferson, Adams, Paine, et al "meant", with this phrase; Congress shall recuse itself from the Deity rat-race. It isn't the government's business what religion you are. It is a matter of individual choice, not National Policy. It says so right there. "or abridging the freedom of speech, or of the press;"

... has become the favorite clause of pornographers everywhere; I am unsure how a woman's ability to flash beaver is an art of expression, but, since this line has been interpreted to cover all manner of self-expression, I have no beef. Say what you wish to say--I do. "or the right of the people peaceably to assemble, and to petition the Government for a redress of grievances."

...is the line that defends protesters, columnists, and sundry other pundits and wits that like to call G.W. Bush a flaming moron with a jar of pickled onions in his cranial cavity instead of gray matter. It is political satire, and the Constitution says I can verbally assail any public figure. Sweet. Do you have a desire to call Obama a liberal idiot? Protected, welcome to Fox News. To call Rush Limbaugh a corpulent, smegma-coated, drug-addicted child molester with delusions of sentience? Go right ahead. You wish to recommend that Sarah Palin douche with Drano? Welcome to NPR!

In 1892, a Baptist Minister wrote the Pledge of Allegiance, and did a damned fine job of leaving sectarianism by the wayside:"I pledge allegiance to my flag and the republic for which it stands: one nation indivisible with liberty and justice for all."

Changes were made, over the years, to specify the country to which we're pledging (those damned stupid immigrants--they might not have realized they were pledging to the USA), and other, slight grammatical corrections. In 1954, when approximately 88% of Americans considered themselves "Christian", a chaplain named Louis Bowman suggested adding the words "under God" to the pledge. This promoted the controversy in which our country finds itself mildly embroiled.The Christians' recommendation for non-Christians is merely "don't say that line", and the non-Christians' response is "it shouldn't be in there to begin with". Is there a right or wrong? Is it worth fighting in the Supreme Court? Suits have been brought, with mixed success, but the gist of it is (and I am an avowed non-Christian), we do NOT live in a Theocracy. God has no place in our country's pledge, printed on our money, or posted on courthouse walls in the form of the Ten Commandments.

This is a stupid debate; for an allegory to define the principles casting the argument into sharp relief, as if lit by the flames from William F. Buckley's Holy Sword: If Tom Cruise demanded that our pledge include a nod to "Thetan Levels", a component of Scientology's belief structure, the debate would only be whether to castrate Mr. Cruise with a scalpel or with a melon-baller.I vote melon-baller: It would hurt more.

H. Apply within

From a strange place do I speak, as is always true with cusps and creative cupidity:Let the bell sound, signaling the inception of a day's dawn. I want to avoid repetition. I don't feel funny. I am shelving this column until later when I can think about it. I will cast my gaze upon "perception" as a subject.I have 4 stories running through my head. I am fairly adept at creating characters, plot lines, situations, and dialogue, but actually etching the stone, laboring to assemble the pieces, tires me and pisses me off. I need a corporate sponsor to let me create art full time. Working at simplistic jobs whacks my yogurt cupless. I feel the urge to soar. A lottery win would be nice--I don't need all that much money to support the family as I create things. My tastes run to the classic and simple. I see myself as a writer, a painter, a father, a husband; an observer might see me as a raconteur, an EMS dispatcher, a poor man living in a dingy town.My first girlfriend wanted to play around and experiment sexually with me; I think it was her (perceived) "last hurrah" (she was 42, I was 18, and since I am almost 42 now, I can see why people looked askance at that relationship when I told them our ages, then). She covered me in whipped cream, chopped pineapple, chocolate syrup and maraschino cherries one night, to "lick them up". With so much stuff, it became an endurance trial for her, and not very erotic for me. I was watching her pig out on a giant sundae, in essence. I was the vanilla ice cream. It is all about perceptions: in her mind, that would be a sensual, sexy, erotic, titillating experience. In reality, it was mostly sticky and boring for me.I have been with one woman in my life who was a virgin deflowered by me. It sounds as if it would be a teaching experience, an opening, a shining light upon a dawning sexuality--I was too young to be any good, and it was mostly painful and humiliating for us both. Be careful what you wish for. I am in one of those moods where an anonymous sexual encounter sounds appealing. No virgins. No strings attached -- send a resume if interested.

I. Keep up.

Whither my words, my rules,my meaning, my exigencies, there my law.And so forth carried until none can say any other but the obvious--It is his alone, no further other muddles or means such as like him.Hear Me, **Oh Wise Ones:** I find my own meanings within my phrases, avoiding the preponderance ofobfuscating cleverness is my primary millstone; I cannot merely write "I like eggs".There needs must be an explanation of where lost love is found,within the calcified husk containing the embryonic treasure. Were I simpler,I would be elsewhere.Many are the amazing treasures I have found in this plain, glorious gems and jewelsof righteous and loyal. I feel blessed and unworthy to find any who would share a kettle and a fire with one who cannot decide which direction is the sky, and why itshould be so.I will define the word I have forsaken of late, "**love**". Overused and trite, *I lovethat tv show, I love steak and eggs, I love her boots.* What one feels about those who treat us with gentle honesty and caring, those who would clean us when dirty,feed us when hungry, succor us when ill, carries far more weight than how we feel about Hats.We need a new word, a new Love, a word that takes aeons to earn, and cannot be lost orsquandered. I will be up ahead, on the cobbles, searching. I have the blueberries. Keep up.

J. Women on the brain (times infinity)

Women fascinate me.Colors and sounds evolved from the electromagnetic spectrum to give men a voice to describe their desire for women. The wind at my fore, I sally backward.I have tried to put it to words, as I woo;I have tried to explain, as I do what I do;I have tried to understand the things that I feel,I have tried to command the forging of steel.

Women would occupy my thoughts all of the time, except that they don't. When I do think of them, I think of only the things that I like. Perhaps that explains my overwhelming drive; I have no negative thoughts as regards the female sex.Spend enough time in a bar, and you will hear wailing and gnashing of teeth from the gathered imbibers. Listen to Country Music, and you'll get the same effect. If your woman has done you wrong, you're not doing it right.Women have half of the money and all of the pussy. We needs must get along.I am being simple today. A woman on the brain, as always, I am happy to report. Time to go out to the garden and cut off a couple of roses.

K. Boobs

This is an attempt at a humorous take on breasts. If it is not mildly funny, I apologize in advance.It has become much more than a trend--it is now a pandemic: Women everywhere have decided to smuggle cantaloupes under their sweaters. The original breast implants were "over-the-muscle", terribly fake looking, and often ridiculous in scale. The solution? Keep doing them! Never mind the ruination of millions of women's appearance and self-image, practice makes perfect! Except that it doesn't. Some Truth (capital T):

1. Fake boobs look fake. Breasts are composed chiefly of fatty tissue, and therefore are somewhat perky when fresh and new (age 13-19 or so, sorry ladies, Mother Nature's a cruel bitch), and begin to droop, sag and look lived-in as the calendar rolls by. Having babies chew on them (which is, to be fair, THEIR CHIEF FUNCTION) destroys the illusion that the breasts are 16 years-old.

2. Men love to look at breasts, this is not news. We don't obsess over them, in reality, we just like to look. Big ones are easier to see. We don't want them ALL to be big (I prefer a handful to chew on), but the bigger ones kinda stand out there like a flag-waver at a construction site. Move along fellas, nothing to see here. Except that there is.

3. If you get mauled by a tiger, then, by all means, get reconstructed to make yourself feel better. If you have a big nose naturally, keep it. Big noses mean big clits or big cocks. Wear them proudly. If you have small breasts, you don't have to wear a bra. Nipples poking through a shirt will get a man's attention faster than large, brassiere-covered melons.

L. A list of thoughts.

I am indifferent to my own confusion.

I decline to insist upon clarity of execution.

I extinguish no cigarette before its time.

Simple is often enough; when it is not, I excoriate my brevity and remove indecision.

I have been wrong more often than I have been correct; it is why I learn exponentially.

Knowledge is not a stored library, but the ability to access or recall information. Speed, not quantity, can be the difference between witty and dull.

When I crave things, I crave simple things--crusty bread, pungent cheese, fresh cold fruit. Rarely do I crave complications. Entropy is always increasing, anyway, I am a force for distillation.

Never underestimate the power of a smile.

Beauty, genius, and prowess bring tears to the eyes of mankind.

Eternal Life lies within a snapshot.

M. Aggravations

I will start with Clowns.The subject of this batch o'words is "Things that I find to be inexplicably unpleasant". Clowns are an easy target, being a popular subject for horror movies and weird French art films. I have yet to meet anyone who likes Clowns, or enjoys watching Clowns, or has a pleasant story about Clowns, yet circuses and cartoons insist on promoting Clowns as whimsical actors of comedy, instead of the zombie Incubi that they truly are. I have no particular fear of Clowns, but even I have an unpleasant memory of the make-up-coated pedophiles:

When my son was 4 years old or so, my little nuclear family visited the traveling circus when it visited us in Anonymoustown, USA. It was a Small Bigtop, a pleasant little circus with a female acrobat, approximately 17 years of age, about whom I had illegal thoughts. While we sat, various vendors strode around, hawking assorted wares (circus gotta get paid). As these vendors circled, I would ask the chilluns if they wanted whatever it was that the particular vendor shilled; I am nothing if not a doting daddy. My son, an autistic little bugger, affected a blank, disinterested face for most of these goods; popcorn, cotton candy, the usual toxic fun. A man dressed and painted as a clown walked to a point about ten feet in front of us, holding a handful of large balloons on sticks; my son's face lit up, and he indicated that he would very much desire one of those. I waved to the Clown, pulling cash from my pocket, with the intent of purchasing the rubber bauble for my only begotten son. The Clown failed to notice my gentle hailing, so I stood (we were in the front row), and walked the few feet to him, and asked how much the balloons cost to procure. "Not for sale" he rumbled, "Prizes for the next act." Having walked in front of the crowd, waving at a Clown, I found myself forced to go back to my son and tell him he couldn't have one.My son was not one of the kids chosen to win a balloon.Fuck Clowns.Now that I have digressed thoroughly, and perhaps caused a snicker, I address my subject of intent; we all find certain things unpleasant. Feces and refuse and rapists are almost universally loathed (the auteurs of the internet video sensation "2 girls, one cup" might argue the merits of poo, but I shan't); I aim to speak of those things that are not designed or intended to be despicable or ugly, yet somehow are. Much like the oeuvre of Aaron Spelling.1. First against the wall shall be Reality Television.

An idea borne of a complete meltdown of originality and creativity, reality t.v. has plumbed the depths of slack-jawed passivity among viewers and elevated it to a Fart Form. There is almost nothing to recommend about "entertainment" that has Jerry Springer as its Jesus, and Simon Cowell as its Moses. I will not pillory the individual offerings, as it is the very (lack of) concept that makes me want to eat rotten fish so that I may have sufficient incentive and ammunition to projectile vomit towards my television screen when a COMMERCIAL for reality t.v. airs. The programs themselves I can only shudder in recollection at the twelve or thirteen seconds that I was forced to endure while the brick traveled from my hand towards the screen. Pass.2. Second to suffer ridicule shall be Anime (Japanimation).

I am about a hairs-breadth away from being convinced that the Japanese simply hate the United States of America, and specifically loathe the residents thereof. They have foisted shitty art on us for so many years that our youth is beginning to fold under the constant barrage of fecal force-feeding. Let me state that I enjoy certain aspects of Japanese culture, and their understated style of home decor; their animation sucks, has always sucked, and if current trends are indicators of future trends, will always suck until we send them another nuclear "gift" (of the 10,000 megaton variety). They portray us as vapid obsessed rapists (I am not even going to argue whether or not they're wrong) who have casaba melons for eyes and whose main verbal expression is "Huuyaaai!". Japan portrays every roentgen of their impotent rage in their semen-provoked cartoon panels. Anime has simplistic morals, moronic storytelling, and such a disdainfully low standard of "entertainment" that merely perusing a book of Manga (Anime in a book) makes me scream "Fuck You, Too!" I usually respond in kind when insulted, and Anime is the middle finger extended to the U.S.3. Nude Models Post-1996 (or so).

In the back of girly-mags, as I was growing up, were advertised inflatable fuck dolls. These have become more sophisticated, over the years, to a creepy level of realism; fairly soon, the silicone-injected, botoxed and shaven "humans" who spread their legs will appear *less real* than the dolls. On a woman, the pussy should have hair, the breasts are made primarily of fat tissue, and therefore sag and stretch, and lips (on the face) should not look as if the woman has just fellated a Greyhound bus. Get some human females back in these mags or I will be forced to deport Hugh Hefner back to the planet Pimpzorg. That is all. Oh, and thongs are butt-floss; the hole that excretes shit does not turn all men on. Just FYI.

N. Men and Women

In 1962, NASA launched the Mariner 1 spacecraft, whose intended mission was to perform a fly-by of the planet Venus. However, in a move that put a serious crimp on the mission's probability of success, the spacecraft was aborted (also known as "exploded by remote control") 294.5 seconds after lift-off.

The probable error was a software communications error; urban legend has described the $18,500,000 spacecraft abort as "The Most Expensive Hyphen in History". The spacecraft had begun to pitch and yaw, and was about to become uncontrollable, because the software controlling it was confused. Whether it was a hyphen, decimal point, or an overbar transcription error, the only significant information that we can glean from the boondoggle is that it was a serious error in miscommunication. One that had a dollar value attached to it.More often than not, humans--who begin to learn in our mother's womb how to use our senses to interact with the world--are not as successful as we should be at communicating with each other. To assert any other viewpoint is utopian optimism, I fear.Let us use some examples, as a way of 1) keeping this post moving along, 2) entertaining, to some extent, whoever bothers to read it; and 3) so that I can pretend that copious amounts of research buttress my polemic.I have a Social Networking Site Frequent Correspondent (Facebook friend) whom I shall name, for this chapter alone and no other, "Agamemnon", or "Ag" for short. Ag and I are bright people, I feel comfortable in declaring; the top 2% of Intellectual Bad-Assitude fer sher. Ag has a Doctorate in smarty-pants, and I have a black-belt. We freely dissect the foibles and misconstruances of mankind on a daily basis. In my case, those dissections are often in the form of describing love and labia; Ag, having churned out a Doctoral thesis, has thoughts that are generally clear, concise, thoughtful and dryly funny and publishable.

The two of us often take a thread, a discussion on Facebook, about any random subject you please, and turn it into "What did you mean by that?" If Ag and I have bouts of miscommunication, the human race is ultimately doomed to throwing rocks at each others' heads. The medium may dictate the pacing and precision of the responses, but neither of us are illiterate savages who grunt and point to indicate desires; I am the most lucid man I know (personally), and Ag is definitely the most lucid and precise woman.The human race is fucked.I realize that often miscommunication is the result of an unwillingness to codify a thought, rather than an inability; it is for this reason, in fact, that I have said "we're fucked". We are not a race of super-logical Vulcans, stating only eternal verities and raising eyebrows and blowing loads of hot creamed spinach onto the faces of our women; we are illogical, anti-parsimonious demurring vacillators. (I really wanted to write a sentence with the word "parsimonious", there.) We cannot state what we mean, as a species, it seems.I consider myself fairly blunt and direct and free-thinking; those who know me know that if I take an interest in a thing, I proclaim it; if I like a woman, I tell her; if I do not like a thing, I ... well. Thence lays the path of disinterest in universal alienation. Huh? I mean, even behaving as forthrightly as I take pride in doing, I have no wish to hurt someone's feelings, especially when the only serious error that person made was surviving the journey down their mother's birth canal. I am not mean-spirited, per se; however, if said birth-survivor demonstrates an embrace of the moronic, loudly and passionately, I do not mind playing the role of Devil's advocate and ridiculing every statement they make, beginning with their failure to cease biological function.

At least we're communicating.Men and women famously encounter difficulty in transposing each others' intentions. Many stupid books have been issued espousing the subject, fanning the flames, and offering no insight whatsoever. You want solutions? Sure, it is actually relatively simple:Men and women are biologically different, with different evil hormones squirting into our blood. We mean different things with similar phrases. (Woman: Do these pants make me look fat? Man: Yes. (incorrect) No. (incorrect). Correct answer: Ask your girlfriend--I'm the one who fucks you, I can't win. If you want to know if I love you and find you attractive, ask me that. I still won't answer, but at least you'll have the righteous high ground).

There are no solutions, since we are creatures of emotion. My general rule of thumb, advice-wise (to which you won't adhere, be honest) is: Don't get angry about miscommunication. Fix the problem, not the blame. I did not invent that aphorism, but it is one I embrace.

Ag and I have to go fling poo at some sarcastic monkeys, now--it is important to communicate in the method to which a creature is accustomed.

O. Some quotes to appear savvy

Sometimes we find ourselves muted, or even mute.Our thoughts run at their normal speed, but nothing coalesces into cogency or lucidity or even something trite. For the last few days, I have given my head some couch potato time. I was not even thinking about writing, or why I wasn't writing, or whether I was bored by not writing, or...You get my point. The cylinders are once more explosively compressing with just a smidge of fuel vapor, oxygen and fire. (Internal combustion engine humor).The ponderance of the nonce is of quotations. Often, to describe a thought or mood, we pull a quote out of our ass (or out of Google or Wikipedia, these days; the internet has made cleverness harder to detect) and whip it out to amuse or dazzle our friends. Sometimes we do it because it occurs to us; why say a phrase, when Mark Twain has already said it better? Maybe we feel that borrowing a taste of Oscar Wilde's wit will make us smarter--or at least appear to be so.So, let's do some quotations, shall we? Let's have some fun."A diplomat is a man who always remembers a woman's birthday but never remembers her age. "Robert Frost

This one is pretty straightforward--women are vain and shallow creatures who are nothing without their visual aesthetic, so we must slave ourselves to giving them gifts, without reminding them that they are mortal, old and ugly. Got it."Heaven has no rage like love to hatred turned, nor hell a fury like a woman scorned. "William Congreve I chose the first two quotes fairly randomly, so this is not a misogynistic post-- at least not consciously. Maybe I am pissed at the fairer sex and don't know it. Anyway, the popular rendition of this quote is the end part, only, from "hell" to "scorned", indicating that one should not incite a woman to riot, I suppose. A woman whose love has been cast aside burns with furies of a non-existent fairy tale boogey-land? This is one that just smacks of "protecting" the weaker sex from pain and suffering. If we're equals, ladies, the break-ups and lost loves hurt on both sides. "I am become death, the destroyer of worlds. "J. Robert Oppenheimer This is one of my favorite quotes. It sounds so bad-ass, like a spot of pith from a Stallone or a Schwarzenegger. For those who don't know who

Oppenheimer is, and why the quote is truly, madness-inducing scary, fuck you, I am not going to tell you. Look it up, then study the time-period, and draw your own conclusions. This quote crushes--the Perihelion and Aphelion of human existence.

"I have never killed a man, but I have read many obituaries with great pleasure."Clarence DarrowThis one is rather cynical, almost wimpy in its passivity. Like a closet geek whacking off to the Sears Catalog's underwear models, the speaker denotes that he chuckled at another's death, while denying any involvement in speeding the desired process along. Damn, Clarence, shank a brother if he needs killin'. " At the touch of love everyone becomes a poet. "Plato

I am unsure if Plato is criticizing poetry or love, with this one; or merely observing that we all become lyrical and prosaic when the emotions of attraction and desire catch us within their grasp. I have been guilty of such things myself, when I meet a sweet and tender brain that needs the Noms of Love. Unlike Plato, I never got misty-eyed at the thought of a young boy's thighs, but, de gustibus non disputandum est.

P. Men are pigs

What is commonly referred to as "sand" is quartz silica (silicon dioxide), which is, in essence, crushed rock. On our little planet there are estimated to be between 10 to the 20th power and 10 to the 24th power (or, between One Septillion and One Sextillion) grains of sand; the margin for error (which is very large) allows for the fact that no one has ever come close to counting them. A grain of sand can range from 1/16 - 2mm in diameter in size, depending on if it is "very fine" or "coarse" sand. Subatomic particles such as quarks are an order of magnitude smaller, but one can see a grain of sand. For descriptive purposes, that is better to write about.All of the humans that have ever lived on Earth, added up as a total, don't equal the number of grains of sand on an average coastline. We may be more mobile, and we certainly produce more reality shows and Paris Hiltons, but for quantity we cannot compete with grains of sand. Nor can even the stars in the sky--it is estimated that the number of grains of sand are more numerous than the stars in our galaxy, except that many of those stars presumably have planets, some of which also contain sand, which would then make sand grains the reigning champion of proliferation. We are all here to live in the service of sand.A digression, now, because I choose what to write from moment to moment:My women readers (some of them) will know of a Victorian-era pornography novel known as "The Pearl". It was episodes of erotic fiction that had been published in a monthly magazine format, and assembled into a collection that still sells, to this day. I have read this book. Some of the vignettes, were they written today, would qualify as child pornography. It is enough to moisten a woman's lips and stiffen a man's pego; the British can be excused, since we know they are all perverted and repressed, anyway.

Lewis Carroll (Charles Dodgson) was an Anglican Deacon whom History has rewritten as a pedophile; whether it is an attempt to belittle his achievements in literature (Alice's Adventures in Wonderland, Through the Looking-Glass, etc.), or an entirely human desire to demystify high-achievers is unclear to me. It is also irrelevant. The estate of Michael Jackson would like to point out that he was acquitted of all molestation charges; if the accusations were true, do those accusations reduce the spectacular achievement of "Thriller"? Let us separate the man from the Art, so to say.Whether Dodgson showed young Alice his mushroom-tipped male organ does not detract from the lasting grandeur of his legacy in storytelling, Tim Burton (may he rot in hell with his eyes clipped open as in "A Clockwork Orange" forced to view his own movies on an endless loop until the heat-death of the universe) notwithstanding.

Albert Einstein enjoyed the company of women, and was rumored to have stepped out on his wife on numerous occasions; the same rumors apply to John F. Kennedy, Pablo Picasso, Bob Marley, John Lennon, Martin Luther King, Jr., Lionel Richie, Francois Mitterand, Bill Clinton, Bob Crane, Bill Cosby, Bruce Lee, Rudolph Giuliani, Clint Eastwood, Benjamin Franklin, Thomas Jefferson, Desi Arnaz, Nelson Rockefeller...

I have to stop there; otherwise this would become "The List". This is not an unimaginably rare occurrence; I believe is the gist I am getting at. It is not merely the rich or intelligent or the motivated, either--check out Jerry Springer's abominable television program to see how those lacking in hygiene and charisma can also have extra-marital affairs, with their sister's pet poodles. Men do not seek love outside of the marriage because of any actions on the part of their spouse, I think; it is merely who we are. We mean no harm. We aren't doing it to YOU, ladies; we're getting our ashes hauled, mostly from curiosity or boredom or complacency.Sometimes we enjoy the smell of new flesh, different hair. It is nice to be reminded of what vibrancy we can bring to the table when we try to make an impression--which is why, Menfolk, you need to remember to always bring flowers and chocolates to the woman with whom you are currently sharing a bed. You still love them, even if Scarlett Johansson or Kat Dennings walk by, and your eyes follow the soft curves of heir breasts swaying as they stroll.

Which brings me back to sand, and thus, the candy sprinkles on the Forever-Cake; no matter how many of a thing there are, we can never count or experience them all. The universe is inherently unknowable. We have finite brains and memory storage systems, the universe is infinite--do the math. We cannot know it all.It is fun to watch clouds drift across the face of the mirror in the sky, on occasion.Also, to appreciate beauty, whether it is a sparkling sand dune or the fresh skin and curves of a woman.

Q. Men and Women are optional

Part One -- Women Are Optional

Ladies, you are purely optional. Test tubes and gene sampling can replace your reproductive systems. A stereo that is cranked up to full volume playing "Vanilla Ice's Greatest Hits" can replace your annoying proclivities. A Hoover vacuum cleaner can suck a dick better, for a longer duration, and with more attention to detail that any woman ever could -- and swallowing is a foregone conclusion (remember to change your filters frequently, guys). Without a woman in the house, men would devote zero brain cells to which position the toilet seat is in, and ditto the direction that the toilet paper hangs (if there is any available, with no woman in the house; paper towels are rough enough to remind men of their sins, as if the burning diarrhea from the 4th burrito didn't illustrate the shame well enough).

A man can eat take-out seven days a week, so a woman's "cooking skills" (a creature of the pro-woman hype machine) are unnecessary.

Women need to learn to fuck. Because of the over-rated quality of their vaginas, women have a tendency to believe they are unequivocal experts at sex if they have mastered laying prone. They use what little ability they possess to induce men to years of indentured servitude; it is no wonder that old men are grumpy and bitter. After years of indulging the woman of the house for a monthly sniff at the forbidden pussy, men reach an age where even that reward is denied to them, due to the woman's fur-purse drying up like sandpaper and their own peckers shriveling up like used pencil erasers.

Women treat sex like a Government job; they apply themselves at the interview, and afterward, believe that any performance they put in is adequate, no matter how perfunctory. Getting a man to climax is no challenge; a woman's vagina is very slightly better than a room temperature bowl of egg salad for inserting a penis into. After children are born, the problem is attenuated, as her vagina becomes spacious enough to double as a spare bedroom, which is why men beg for anal sex, so that they may remember what little joy there was, back when his penis touched the edges of *something* when he thrust into his listless mate.

And all of that depends on if she is in the mood.

Sex, the primal drive of a man's desire for a union in the first place, becomes a tool for the woman to manipulate the relationship. The man, if he has any lust whatsoever, has two choices; get with her program, and become a slave to her whims on the off chance that he might slip into her while she is asleep, or, fuck his secretary (and hope he doesn't get her pregnant, or the cycle repeats itself with wife #2).

Soon, with virtual-reality and accompanying devices now rapidly being developed by the Japanese (the undisputed champions of repressed perversity), a man will be able to sit in a chair while a gorgeous virtual woman will service his every kinky desire, and it will feel real. Want an underage cheerleader to piss on you while you get blown by Martha Stewart? Program it in. Want 4 super-hot chicks with DD tits to take turns spraying you with their lactation while Ann Coulter rams a garden rake inside her twat? That's number 533, I request THAT one on a Saturday night. Anything your sick-puppy head deems sexually stimulating, these machines will be able to produce in living color, with real tastes, sounds and sensations.

In which case, the human race is doomed, anyway. Men will never leave the virtual couch as long as Megan Fox is masturbating Pamela Anderson in front of them.

Part Two -- Men Are Optional

Women probably already know this part, but fair is fair. Men have such an inflated sense of themselves that as a man, I find it hard to do this part, even though I know my shortcomings are so numerous as to deserve their own column.

If women need a lump on the couch that emits odors and occasionally whines to be fed, she can get herself a retarded sheepdog. If a woman needs an orgasm, vibrators rarely smell like cheap beer and tacos, and if they do, she can wash the vibrator in some lovely scented oil. Men think a sexual encounter is finished when they squirt a drop of mayonnaise into a woman's mouth and then fall asleep. Women can hug, kiss and rub each other with pleasure and gentle knowing after men and their Vienna Sausages (promoted as Kielbasas) are gone.

Men have a name for the enormous slab of lard that they develop when they think they've "reeled in a fish", aka, convinced a woman to marry him: A beer belly. As if they take pride in demonstrating that the only thing in life that they can do well is to serve as a repository for overdoses of tasteless American beer. It is the Badge of Honor of Mediocrity, a bulging bag of blubber with a cutesy nickname -- typical of a gender that refuses to mature. An evolved man is one waits until he is alone in a bathroom to play with his wee-wee or his feces.

Men feel that they are essential to protect the home -- which is true, except that the protection is *from other men*. With no men around, women would leave their doors unlocked, since no woman would want to own another woman's china pattern.

Men feel that they are needed because of their repair and maintenance skills; if any man actually performed such feats, they might be missed. The average man couldn't fix a crooked picture hanging without the feel of the lash on their shoulders.

Men are like unchanged baby diapers; they gain weight exponentially after marriage, at the same rate that they lose hair on their heads, and consider themselves Romance Novel-worthy studs no matter what the evidence to the contrary. Without men, women could save all of the money that they are no longer spending on make-up, and use it to buy designer original dresses for every occasion.

With men gone, women would have clean bathrooms and the toilet seat would always be urine-free, and settled in the down position, as nature and Kohler intended. There would be no laundry scattered randomly on the floor, as if dirty, skid-marked briefs added thermal insulation to the home.

The comedian known as "Gallagher" would cease to exist, which is a worthy accomplishment in and of itself. Without men, there would be no more "chick flicks", just movies. For chicks.

Without men, there would be no more football or boxing, and teeth would once again be held in esteem.

There would be no more war.

Now I am trying to think of how to wrap this piece up, because the "no war" bit got to me. I am almost in favor of women running the joint, while we men go colonize Titan. Without war, our children could grow to maturity in peace and calm, without the worry that some small-dicked Chinaman feels the need to hose his barely-motile sperm over the world in the form of nuclear cumshots.

Without men, would the world be better?

No, I rather think not -- for now. Without men, there would be no *Einstein, Shakespeare, Orwell, Stephenson, Picasso, Washington, Jefferson, Confucius, Gandhi, King, King or Me.*

I will ponder it for another day, and tip my cap to the women -- you have won this round.

We have practiced temper-tantrums, as a gender, to the point where we are apparently less useful than Rosie O'Donnell -- that is an impressive failure as a representation of a sex.

Well, at least Snoopy was a male ... wasn't he?

R. Things I like

I LIKE

Baseball, science-fiction movies, science-fiction books, Stephen King novels, cooking, eating, women in skirts, Harlan Ellison's essays, James Cameron's movies, cats, dogs, humor, Dave Barry, learning anything new, writing, drawing, playing in a band, painting, meeting new people, wry smiles, sidelong glances, witty jibes, Pho, Naan, Vindaloo, sushi, bujutsu, Bruce Lee movies, the original Star Wars trilogy, David Fincher's films, Stanley Kubrick's films, classical music, jazz, waking up in the pre-dawn hours, watching the sky, swimming, sailing, rock-strewn riverbeds, wine, opera, an unabashed laugh, slow dancing, popcorn, conversations that take five years, nipples, clever quotations, margaritas, Captain Morgan spiced rum and cherry coke (*but not with Oreos*), steak with grilled mushrooms, making love for hours, fucking behind a barn, oral sex, a glimpse of pubic hair, bikinis, natural breasts, tight sweaters on a woman, loose cotton shirts on me, lifting heavy weights, strong coffee, gin and politics, sunset over a beach, sunrise over a beach, black clothing, books, Art, working computer software, getting letters, getting messages on Facebook, positive attitudes, whimsical recollections, stories around a campfire, a cold beer on a summer evening after a hard day's labor, building things, repairing things, having an answer to a question, having questions, thoughts, reminiscing, anticipating, remembering, acting in a play, sinking a mid-range golf shot, sitting with friends and saying nothing important, getting butterflies when you first meet someone special, significant glances, sarcastic exchanges, dirty looks, puns, **the smell of moist and green marijuana**, a lit match, driving long distances, driving without shoes, having an extra roll of paper towels tucked away so I don't have to go to the store just for paper towels, fresh bread, apples, pears, figs, fig newtons, rice noodles, not shaving, shaving, sunglasses, funny hats, pierced navels on a young woman, noses of all shapes and sizes, pretty eyes, soft pecks on the lips, vaginas and vulvas, having orgasms, giving orgasms, knees, writing a good poem, fine pens, the smell of fresh paint, the smell of freshly mown grass, autumn in New York City, watching young women stroll to lunch in a city park in New York City on a windy day, grilled hamburgers and hotdogs, shish-kebobs, fire, photography, shy women, bold women, Hunter S. Thompson's worldview, Tom Wolfe, William F. Buckley, Bill Clinton, no condoms, taxicabs, pick-up trucks, an unexpected tune on the radio that makes you smile with a fond memory, cheerleaders and **Cathedrals**.

S. 2B or Not 2b?

Coil-Shuffling 101:

Letterman's Top Twenty Reasons Why You Should Suck an Exhaust Pipe and

Do Everyone a Favor by Dropping Dead (hopefully soon).

20. Solitude. No matter our families or friends, we are, in essence, alone on our journey from birth to death. We can be but one person, and no one can truly feel our personal sorrows or pains.

19. Pointlessness. When summed up, humans are born, they eat, they procreate, and then they die. Few people, if any, have any impact on the world around us--we are insignificant on a cosmic scale.

18. Frustration. Life is replete with impossibilities; lovers we cannot have, places we cannot go, things we will not possess. Life is a series of frustrations until our hearts stop.

17. Hatred. All around us are the envious, the spiteful and the hurtful. We cannot walk through the world without hating fear and violence, and being hated by those who perpetuate it.

16. Equanimity. Life is a zero-sum game; no one comes through it any richer. You are born with nothing, and your body crumbles to dust, with nothing. We advance no purpose, so why worry? We are just hanging out and biding our time until the Grim Reaper arrives.

15. Indifference. Nobody cares, truly, about anyone else. People step over the beaten and mugged on a city street, people brush by the destitute panhandlers without even a glance. People crowd around an accident scene not out of empathy, but out of curiosity as to what the inside of a human skull looks like.

14. Pain. Nature, in its wisdom, has given us nerves to conduct physical pain, as well as the mental capacity to feel emotional pain. The one guiding force in our universe is pain--everything hurts, and the pain never ends until the brain dies, and is incapable of feeling pain any longer.

13. Poverty. The vast majority of humans are like beggars, staring through a window at a King's banquet. The very few have what the most of us don't--and won't--ever have. Starvation is a fact of life for most of the human race.

12. Repetition. Nothing ever changes, in our lives, unless it is for the worse. Every day is a drudgery of labor, pain, grief, hatred, frustration and indifference. Why would anyone volunteer to repeat the same actions, over and over, and not go mad?

11. Incompleteness. Our lives are so brief, as it is, that nothing we could ever do would truly make a difference in the universe. Even the spacecraft Voyager, launched in 1978, has only recently reached the edge of our own Solar System. The cosmos is too big, we are too small. Why start what can never, ever be finished?

10. Irrelevance. Even the CEO of a major American Corporation will leave only the tiniest footnote in history, and that only of recent history. The Library of Alexandria was burned, and all of the wisdom of the ancients disappeared in a cloud of smoke--and they were the *greatest minds of their time.* What hope does a a housewife from Milwaukee have?

9. Eternity. Our recorded history as humans extends backward through time for perhaps 6,000 years. The Earth is almost 6 billion years old. We are an aardvark fart in a hurricane; not only will the Earth forget us, and erase all traces of our existence someday, it doesn't even know we exist *now.* Our time-line is .001% of the Earths. And the universe itself is 3 times older than that.

8. Transience. We are in a single snapshot of forever. The dinosaurs are so much more relevant to history than we are that it is ludicrous to call us a species. We're argumentative algae with God complexes.

7. Incomprehensibility. We have not completely mapped our own world. We don't understand how our own bodies work. The world gets more complicated the more we try to learn about it. We have no clue how we began, and many talking apes believe a bearded ape in the sky spat on dirt to make us.

6. Boredom. There is never, ever, anything to do for more than a few moments that does not require pain.

5. Sour grapes (impossible wishes). If we do foment a desire, it is never a thing we can actually have. We're better off not knowing what we are missing.

4. Impediments. There is no mutual-aid society in the world; self-centeredness is the rule of the day, and no one wishes to help you (unless you help them in some way). The world conspires to make your life harder than it needs to be.

3. Dreams. Why wish for what is unachievable? Heartbreak is inevitable--keep your feet on the ground and realize there is nothing to be gained by dreaming.

2. Goals. We are all encouraged to have goals, which are, in reality, place-markers to remind us that the strong dominate, the greedy thrive, and the humble are sacrificed without hesitation.

1. Love. Love is a contrived human emotion to categorize the pain of attachment, which then rips out our hearts and souls when the objects thereof die.

The Other Side of the Coin:Live, live, at all costs, Live!

1. Love. An emotion that is unique to humanity, it is the ability to subvert everything to benefit someone other than ourselves.

2. Goals. A sense of purpose can drive us to do things that our brains would not foresee as possible. It is in the attempt that we achieve.

3. Dreams. Humans are the animals with imagination--we can conceive of what we desire, and strive to make those desires become real.

4. Impediments. A task, a challenge, is what gets the heart racing, as the crisp, clean air of a fight inspires us to accomplish what naysayers forbid--out of spite, if nothing else.

5. Sour grapes (impossible wishes). If we did not reach beyond our grasp, we would not have invented airplanes. Or ladders, for that matter.

6. Boredom. Sometimes the mind yearns, and cannot communicate to the conscious mind its desires. Thus, we shuffle about, feeling anxious and bored. Then we remember that the neighbor invited us to the baseball game--and we're talking about *one sexy neighbor*.

7. Incomprehensibility. To try to solve a puzzle keeps the mind flexible enough to tackle other tasks, and to find answers where we can.

8. Transience. The opposite of boredom--a new sunrise, a new place to live, a life after our parents have died and moved on; every new experience adds to our stockpile of wisdom.

9. Eternity. Our marks can be made, not in the sand, but in us, ourselves; our children's children will teach their grandchildren's grandchildren the things they learned from us. Our species' memory will include our hopes and fears and love of Pop Tarts.

10. Irrelevance. We are not gifted with our place in the universe, we have to carve out our own meaning. Some of us may pump gas for the others of us that discover how to end hunger.

11. Incompleteness. What we begin, others may finish, though it may take eons. We are cogs, a group mind, a force of will stronger than wind and water--because we can choose to do what we do.

12. Repetition. By doing a thing, over and over, we become skilled, then expert, then qualified to teach, then gurus. Only by becoming a thing can we understand a thing.

13. Poverty. If everyone "had", how would we understand fear of failure? The randomness of the world drives us to stave off our fears.

14. Pain. A simple lesson I have learned, whose wisdom it has taken me years to understand: Pain lets us know we are alive.

15. Indifference. Overcoming the indifference and confusion of others is a great way to be invited to a lot of parties. Make 'em laugh, and they will disrobe.

16. Equanimity. We cannot be too joyous at the high points, or too sad at the lows. We must balance ourselves to prepare for the inevitability of either.

17. Hatred. The marker we may use to identify areas of improvement. Without "up" there would be no "down".

18. Frustration. The ability to deal with failure strengthens us like fire does steel. Adversity builds our awareness, effort builds muscle.

19. Pointlessness. The relevance of a thing is not in the thing itself--it is in the relationship we have with that thing. Understand what you are, and you will see what you are to others, and other things.

20. Solitude. There is no greater joy than having a pleasant conversation with yourself, running down a list of points you wish to make for an article, and enjoying your own reaction and making yourself laugh and weep. Love begins, after all is said, *with the love of one's own self.*

T. I hate school.

I was never very accomplished in school.I have been wandering around my head, as if it were a dusty attic, searching for the elusive tell. I have had alarm bells ringing, intermittent yet constant, miniature chastisements from myself; my consciously unconscious subconscious warns me of fatigue, headaches, hunger, restlessness, solitude, chaos, debt, travel, pain, angst, worry, hell, heaven, death, life, the future, the past, hair, fingernails, toenails and school.I hated school, detested almost every class I was ever in.Have you ever had a half-wit attempt to explain something to you? Not an idiot, per se, but worse: someone who is of average intelligence, at best, but feels, due to their peer group, that they are smarter than the average bear?A gas station attendant pontificating on the workings of a cash register, as if the works of Tesla were but a precursor to the subtle operations of a change drawer?A Wal Mart employee smugly explaining that curtain rods are not in the same section as curtains?A librarian from whom you are trying to exact a library card, and drones with repetitive indifference that a driver's license is required to obtain such a desirable commodity, and who rejects a United States passport, because it has no printed address therein? And who then suggests helpfully that a passport would be accepted if the bearer were to write in the address? In pencil? AND THEN when the fallacy was pointed out to her, that the bearer of said passport could *then write any address he so chose* and so, what would be the proof of the document? Or perhaps you have had to listen to a fast-food restaurant manager, of a chain, whose name rhymes with "Durger Sting"; while said overachiever explains that on the rolling burner, two racks that slowly moved over a gas flame, the top rack was for buns, the bottom rack was for hamburger patties. And, as this Professor of Fast Food physically demonstrated the placement of the materials, the spoken mantra with which he taught this simple and obvious information was the endlessly repeated, "Meat. Bread. Meat. Bread. Meat. Bread. Meat. Bread." (I do not exaggerate, in this instance).Perhaps you have had to listen to a television editorial, wherein the pundits are egregiously less-informed that you are yourself, and the only reaction you can summon after a few minutes of the aural swill is "Oh come on! For Christ's sake!"This is my reaction to schooling. I am steadfastly polite, in my interactions with the outside world; a habit that is learned, not innate. Aggravated and incensed have I been so often that I learned to relax and stare at the walls and go Tharn when a customer in front of me at a supermarket realizes--after the groceries have been scanned, packed, and put into the shopping cart--that she should probably pull out her checkbook, because darn it, those grocery stores want money in exchange for their food. This seems to come as a shock to people, when one judges by their complete lack of preparedness for the inevitable currency exchange most stores expect for goods and / or services rendered. I have a blankish look I employ, in the face of such overweening retardation; However, my wife informs me, she can tell from several rows away what my mood is, and who is annoying me. She has been married to me for 20 years, so there is that. I had always been told that colleges are not like High Schools, and that the quality of teachers improve, and there is not so much emphasis placed upon remedial learning; the classes are faster-paced, studying is a must, and for those who love to learn, it is a revelation after the drudgery that is our Educational System.But I have come to realize that I don't "love to learn", necessarily; I am gifted at it, true, because it has always been effortless. I need only be shown a task or sequence once, usually, and I grasp it. The intricacies of whatever specific nature I absorb soon after, and in short order, will try to improve the process. It is the way my mind works.I do not enjoy Historical programming, documentaries, or the Discovery Channel. I hate NPR, PBS, and Charlie Rose. I learn by observing, I don't enjoy being taught.So I am anxious. That is what is wracking me with symptomatic physical errors. As much as I believe that the class I will attend will be within my intellectual grasp (a humble understatement), I fear that I will ruin my own chances, somehow. I will fume and stamp and chomp at the bit due to a foolish remark, a misspelled word, a mistake in pronunciation. I do not wish to give myself excuses to avoid finishing the course. I am arguing with myself, as my head feels progressively worse, my mood becomes increasingly anti-social, my psyche more fragile.Meat. Bread. Meat. Bread. Meat. Bread. That fucker's voice still echoes within me like the taunts of the mediocre. I stand exposed to the judgment of those not my peers. My eyes are blurring from the pressure. I am angry at having written this. I am too stubborn to delete it, however, I put too much time into it.

U. Endurance

1969. 69. The 8th-grader inside of me says, Beavis and Butthead-style, "Heh heh hehe heh heh". The rest of me says, jolly good year. My first memory. My friend Chris was born. Bobby Kennedy and King were not assassinated again (my birth year of 1968 is notorious for those, not to mention the election of Tricky Dicky Nixon to his first Presidential term).Richard Nixon was a corrupt, vile, paranoid sociopath who forgot to be born in the U.S.S.R. His policies of paranoia, distrust and partisan hate have soiled American politics for all time, and he was elected within a few days of my birth. You're welcome. Any adult, who cares, knows to what the sexual label "69" refers, so I am ... just going to skip it. I can't think of any literary device that would allow me to tackle the subject unless I were writing cyberporn or erotica or sex stories ...which, in general, I don't. Evidence to the contrary notwithstanding. You take his and you stick it in hers. Repeat. It's just not epic literature, or even original weblogging material. I don't often write about pooping, either (I don't think).The flush of a cheek, when regaling another with said tales, that is more my mien. I like to cause a reaction, of any sort. I prefer positive reactions. Why do I write without a tale to tell? Sometimes you whisper to me, and it takes a moment to hear ... if I went back and deleted all of this, it would be crisper, tastier and more nutritious, but then I would not be exposing my soulful examinations to you, I would be stamping out a "product". I have nothing to sell, I will amuse myself for free; if you ride along, you may borrow a seatbelt.Endurance is on my mind. I begin a class, later tonight (it is 12:19 a.m. Central Time as I write this), and I will be committed to 2 four-hour classes a week, in addition to my full-time job. It sounds easy enough, except that I am already exhausted, much of the time, because I work nights and I am not of a vampiric bent. I am historically a morning person; I love sunrises and dew. More Yawning ahead.All I have to do is switch to a vegan diet, quit smoking, and exercise more. Then, if I survive my own suicide attempts, I will feel healthier and more invigorated and much, much paler. The rays of the sun are the work of the devil. Except to a tree. It is hard to sleep inside of such a menagerie as I live; between the pets, and the other pets, I am asleep by 8 am and awake by 1 or 2 pm. A few days in a row and I lose my preternatural calm and settle for acerbic wit and caustic commentary. Entertaining, I hope--otherwise, what is the reason? Why oh Lord oh why?This is an exercise to see if you can spot the hidden message I have so cleverly forgotten to put in this thread. If you can, let me know, so I will feel crafty.I have been offered an inspiration for a post, but I will save it for tomorrow, unless the Yankees lose again, in which case I will be working on my eulogy for the 2010 baseball season.So, this is 69. After 68, before 70, no wiser than I was tomorrow, no dumber than I will be yesterday.Some organ acronyms: New Olfactory Sensory Example (NOSE).Extremis Auditory Receptor (EAR).Penetrative Extrusion Not Illicit Sensor (PENIS).Variable Attenuated Glorious Intake Narrow Area (VAGINA).

V. I am a terrible teacher

My head is screaming at my fingers. Type, it says, type about THINGS.

It won't tell me what things. I have to guess what it is I want--I may have to sneak up on myself and give myself a Roofie so that I babble. Or is that Sodium Pentothal? I am not current on rape drugs--having never seen one, except on CSI. I find that complimenting a woman's shoes and pulling out her chair before she sits down provides the spread-legged experience without the risk of being imprisoned, but what do I know? Women trust me enough to get me hot and bothered, knowing that I will respect the "No means No" credo.I am perpetually fatigued, mentally, physically, and, if I believed in Spirituality (hint: I don't), I would be questioning the meaning of faith and begging John the Baptist to dunk me in a tub full of Holy Apples (not the kind from Eden, of course) and Bless Me back a the State of Sanctity. I need either more, or less caffeine, and only experimentation will provide scrutable revelation.

Did you know "scrutineer" is a word? Holy High School Cheerleaders, Batman. The blond forgot her bra and is signaling "help me" in Morse Code from the black eyes from boob-strikes. There is an image that'll haunt a Guidance Counselor.I suppose it is entirely contextual whether TA means "Teaching Assistant" or "Tits and Ass". Is an ampersand (&) really that crucial in language? What if your Teaching Assistant is stacked like Jayne Maynesfield? Is she a TA with T&A? Is that the root of "ta-tas"? That's the kind of grad student I want helping me, one that distracts me with promises of fleshly delights that turn my brain--the primary organ I would need for teaching, I presume--to be uselessly imagining the TA bent over the desk, panty-hose slid down to the backs of her knees, legs trembling and eager, her breath coming in gasping, erratic pulses....See what I mean? How the fuck am I going to describe Shakespeare's use of puns under those circumstances? I would be a terrible teacher, except at a school for the blind. Or as a lecturer--I could do lectures.I can imagine getting published (eventually), perhaps scoring some guest speaking assignments, and reading THIS VERY

COLUMN while looking at a room full of college-age women (and men, but someone else can fantasize about the men). What are the odds that I'd pick up about fifteen offers for dates / and / or after such a lecture? I'm offering an over / under of 5.

W. Suture the soul

We, the people,

are open wounds,

awaiting a dose of salt,

that we may be indignant at the new source of pain.

To heal our perpetual injurious natures,

we must allow ourselves to be healed,

to give up the bond that we inexplicably feel

for our damaged state.

You don't need to be broken,

to be loved.

You need only be willing

to help another heal themselves.

We, the people,

feel alone, unique, and put-upon;

No one understands, no one empathizes

(we think) with our list of grievous damages.

The unbreakable nature of a peaceful person

is not due to lack of injury, but rather

due to the self's willingness to suture the soul,

to aid the mind and body in once again becoming whole.

A healed person has scars,

a cartograph of their journey

through the blistering pain that exists

when the front door opens.

Only an infant is blemish-free,

for that we instill upon them,

vicariously and unreasonably,

the hopes and wishes of the End of pain.

We mark ourselves voluntarily, with ink,

with jewels, with furs and wraps

and dresses made from dried-out plants;

Hiding a scar does not remove it.

We, the people,

expect to tell all and another

from a hilltop or soapbox that

We are alone and wish to be no longer.

X. Hypocrisy

Since I am at the end of my waking hours, you will pardon me if I elucidate less floridly than with the elegant prose to which you have become accustomed (see how I turned that around, there, and snapped off some Thesaurus-quality words and righteous grammar and shit? I am making sure you're paying attention) and instead write plainly and straightforwardly.On my way home this morning, I was attempting to distract myself (I will not go into how), and instead distracted myself from my distraction, by musing about *excuses*. The initial thrust of this post (insisting on seeing the ghosts and all, S. King shout-out, don't ask) was written between the empty fields near my place of employment and the empty fields near my home, at around 70 mph.Since fatigue is a factor, I will not ponder any academic differentiations between *reasons* and *excuses*; I merely type what I think (thought. Still think? It's been 20 minutes, I might have changed my mind) about humans and their whining.I have supervised several divisions of personnel, from small to medium, in my career(s) and thus, have been in charge of punctuality as it pertains to employees since I was around 19 years old. I was not naturally a responsible adult-- circumstances compelled me to evolve into one. I had had the habit of punctuality since childhood: my father was a 20-year Navy man, and if he was ever late to anything, it never was made public as I was growing up. I emulated his near-pathological obsession -- my wife found that to be one of my less-endearing personality traits, early on in our relationship. I soon discovered that my deploration of tardiness was not widely shared by minimum-wage employees.Look: when you prostrate yourself for employment, usually at an interview, you learn the approximate time that it takes to travel from your home to your potential employer's place of business. Granted, your interview is not often at the time that your future boss arrives to work; if he (she) comes in at, say, 9:00, he (she) isn't going to want you there, eager and disgustingly chipper when he crawls in, hung-over and smelling of feces. He wants a quick nap and a blow job from his secretary before he has to deal with the likes of you, so your interview will more likely be around 11:00 or later.

Your time from home-to-office will be learned, in approximation, on this trip (assuming you weren't at the same party he was, the night before; it is more prudent to arrive from your home, showered and sober for a first impression--you can travel from a kegger to the office, but I don't recommend it, as that would throw off my time-estimation thesis, here, as well as quash your chances of landing this job). (Unless, at the party, you took pictures on your camera phone that he wouldn't want his secretary to see, let alone his wife). If you wow them enough to be offered the job, and it took you, say, 20 minutes to travel there at that mid-morning hour, you know that to commute at the normal rush-hour time you should add 15 minutes for leeway, and depart your home (once again, you can depart a kegger and travel directly to the office for your first day, it is not recommended), and you arrive at 8:50. So, now you have your travel time. I'm getting there... Where we come to *reasons* versus *excuses*: we've all worked with somebody who is 5 -10 minutes late every day. These are the co-workers who give "reasons" such as, *traffic was bad. The kids took longer than usual.* Sorry, those aren't reasons, they're excuses. You know long it takes, with a margin for error--leave 10 minutes earlier. Problem solved. In reality, you're late because you hate your job and you are delaying every second of your departure so you can get just a little bit further on **World of Warcraft**, not because an Army truck carrying missiles tipped over on the highway and traffic closed in both directions and the National Guard was called in and the Governor pissed his Brooks-Brothers suit and declared the entire 10-mile radius area top secret (this actually happened, on the highway I used to get to work, when I was living in Maryland. Was I late? Fuck no. You gotta work for it, sometimes--nobody said life was a bucket of fried chicken with a side order of handjobs).Soon after I was tasked, at my first managerial job, with assuring employee punctuality, I would wait by the time-clock with a machete in my right hand and my erection in my left. I figured those who were late would get one or the other (Kidding, of course; I've never owned a machete). And I would bark some of the platitudes I have been writing here. I hate tardiness. Hate it.There is a whole other section on *pains*, I will try to get through it, but I am getting sleepy. I'll throw it in as an edit, later. More chuckles to come.

What am I writing about? This week, for Jolly Fun, I am thinking about **hypocrisy**, and I am breaking it down, element by element, until I have exculpated the demons from my memory. Too many images float around in my head, and the act of describing them to you--my faithful silent masses--allow me to exorcise these thoughts, and make new ones. Otherwise my brain gets Blue Balls, and I am wary of sneezing--who knows what would come out.

Let me irk the women by addressing **PMS**, (Pre-Menstrual Syndrome) a subject I know nothing about (directly). I only know of perceived effects. I was raised by a mother and father, and I have 2 sisters; I now live in a house with 3 women who have all achieved menarche, so I am used to cohabiting with bleeding women. Not one of the women with which I am familiar is noticeably grumpy, when the cramps begin, signaling the arrival of the Crimson Wave. Instead, they experience pains, and usually mention it, as in "We do still have Motrin, right?", but none of them uses this monthly annoyance as an excuse to hurl raw hamburger at the men in the house (currently, my teenage son and I, not counting critters, who have their own reproductive issues with which to deal).I am not holding up my experiences as a blanket description for the aches and pains of all society; I am aware that the menses affects different women differently. I am speaking about taking carte blanche to be a raging banshee, and pointing at **PMS** as a root cause, and exclaiming, "You don't understand!" I do. I do understand. While my body has never betrayed me by sloughing off a layer of skin from an internal organ once a month, I have had pains, and cramps, and food poisoning, all of which range from unpleasant experiences to hospitalization. What I loathe is a woman -- or any person, but we're addressing the possessors of XX chromosomes, here -- dodging social responsibility because of a pain. A not unexpected pain, no less.It hurts. We know. Chin up, be pleasant, take the afternoon off to eat a vat of butter-pecan ice cream while watching Oprah. We understand, but it isn't my fault. If there were a corollary, it would be **THS** for men --Thumb Hammer Syndrome. About once a month or so, we men demonstrate our masculine, musky, manly skills by "fixing" something around the house; we're as likely to whack our thumbs as we are the nail. Women are permitted (and encouraged, in some states) to snicker behind their hands as we hurl things at walls and kick the dog and blame our 8 year-old sons for moving (sons, when they emerge from the womb, are supposed to have the ability to hold a nail straight). We don't have permission to be grumpy for that pain, either. This is not a condemnation of feeling pain, it is a condemnation of whining about pain.

"I had no shoes, and was sad, until I met a man with no feet". This would be true, except that in our world, a man with no feet usually has a pretty cool wheeled chair. I wonder why you don't see more pimped-out wheelchairs? If I were in one, I would have a sun umbrella and a beer cozy built-in. My chair would have a GPS and satellite t.v. I'd have a Penthouse pin-up on the back and a horn that played Beethoven's 9th (Ode to Joy) when pressed. Everybody has it better -- and everybody has it worse -- than somebody else. Live with what you have, and remember that nobody wants to hear your complaints -- they want to tell you theirs.

Hypocrisy, the theme, fits in thusly: Realistically, one cannot criticize others for performing an action or statement that one undertakes themselves. That was wordy. Don't say "don't do it" and then do it yourself. There it is. Don't cry about it--life is full of pain. During my martial arts days, I once broke almost half of the bones, in *both of my feet* (the metatarsals, which we know as the "balls of the feet"), and my job at the time involved -- wait for it --standing on my feet for 8 hours a day. I had no health insurance, and my family was barely clinging to the lower edge of poverty, at the time. Not working was just not a viable option. I can only speak on my own experiences, so this is not meant as braggadocio, "look how studly I was, suck it up". Not at all. My wife knew about what I was going through, I was not some masculine ideal, keeping it bottled up; I did go to work *everyday*, for the six months I had that machine-shop job, until I found something else. It took an *additional six months* after I left that job for my feet to heal; that is, until they stopped hurting 24 hours a day. That shit *hurt*, as you may imagine. I forgot -- I also had to walk to work, as I had no vehicle. That was another 2 miles, each way. Man, remembering this, I remember how much it sucked. But I didn't whine about it (although tears were formed, often, as I suffered through the hell of those six months), and I tried to be my normal, amiable self.Now, if you'll excuse me, I am feeling the effects of **THS**, and I need some mint-chocolate chip and Oprah, STAT.

Y. Dreaming while awake

I find myself compelled to a fabulous mood, full of giddy and child-like conversations. I was playing with some silly facial morphing software, another friend got involved, and it was very relaxing, unsophisticated fun. Forgotten were concerns over car payments and window repairs; at ease and at peace and pleased I was indeed. That mood was explicable. I know how I came to be laughing, staring at a computer screen. There was an orderly approach that would be quite map-able were I to choose to do so. Today's headlines, about inexplicable moods, (New York Post's Banner: "Mad Dad Fad: Sad or Glad?") comes to us courtesy of my muse. The question is eternal: Why do we awake, sometimes, in a good mood? Or bad mood, for that matter, or a sense of foreboding, a sense of hope, confused, bedraggled, anxious or erotically charged (for men, that is easy: A man's penis becomes erect in response to sexual arousal and excitement, but it can also become erect as a result of deep relaxation, such as that experienced in deep sleep called REM (rapid eye movement) -- a period of sleep during which you dream.)? Morning wood can make or break a day. So what gives? Any second now, I'll hit a groove (you didn't know I write the article as I am writing it, did you? Oh, you knew that? Well hell, I am trying to be "entertaining" anyway). I rarely awaken with a cloud hanging over my head like the Sword of Damocles threatening to skewer my cranium and put a crimp on my day. I am just a chipper guy. It has been known to happen. Were my dreams invaded by Limbaugh-esque boogie-men? Are there demons in my pillow waiting to shave my eyebrows, cover my lips with glue, and pimple my ass? I love the wonder of the world, the everlasting unknowing--I thrill in the discover of menfolk like J and C and women like C and B and G ... knowing that there must be more and treasuring the thought of learning from them and laughing with them and seeing new and different variations of pubic hair and bowling techniques (not all of my desires and wonders are equal, of course). The Universe and Me ... we're good. I know a misspoken phrase, a failed joke, can sour a person's stomach, seemingly highlight one's weaknesses, and draw forth ire and nausea and the urge to piss on your oppressor (there are even websites for that, see below*), but sometimes a failed joke is just a cigar.

Waking up free and happy and in a dream-like suspension of dread? The Universe whispers in your ear when you are asleep--sometimes (after a joyous coital coupling, maybe, or a nice long conversation with your BFF the night before) your brain is relaxed enough to listen. Happiness is the knowledge of one's ignorance, and the willingness to continue railing against said ignorance. Sisyphus should have been happy with his job security, especially in this economy.Sometimes, you hold a door open for someone else, and are not given the courtesy of a "thank you". To me, this is akin to a stranger punching me in the stomach, Houdini-style. The kindest reaction they get from me is a shouted "You're welcome!" to their ungrateful, child-molesting, Republican-voting. slave-owning racist asses. Such a thing can sour one's view of one's neighbors, nay, even Humanity itself; such a cloud may cause one to kick the dog and refuse your spouse a nookie-sandwich (on whole wheat, with extra mayonnaise). A bad mood is contagious like Ebola or John Boehner's smirk. A cloud upon your visage is a thunderstorm of sullen. You feel like smacking yourself. You pick fights with the mailman. You snarl at the grocer. Misery loves company, wrote Aesop, some 2,600 years ago. If only we had known earlier, the Neanderthals could have stopped fucking and allowed our species to grump itself into the fossil record.We all enjoy a friend in a good mood -- vivacious, airy and fluttery, willing to lend a hand or flash panties (once again, some traits of friendship mean more than others), willing to raise one's spirits, share a meal, share an orgasm.A truer test of friendship is weathering the unbidden shit-storms that we all dump on our friends like an unwanted package-bomb.Afterwards, there is always time -- if you make it -- for a cup of tea and a view of the limitless possibilities that we can create, together.

Z. Coffee

My wife and I enjoy coffee to such an extent that we wear out coffeemakers like socks.

Every six months to a year, we go to the local Wal Mart and buy a new Black and Decker or Mr. Coffee automatic-drip coffeemaker, and we make three pots a day or so and burn it out. We received an expensive unit as a gift from my father a few years back -- a coffeemaker and espresso steamer in one unit, with the steam nozzle for cappuccino; we even managed to blow that up.

When we were first married, we thought that we were buying the wrong brands, perhaps; coffeemakers kept burning out on us. Somewhere in there we realized that we were (and are) abusing the machines far past what Mr. Coffee considers acceptable usage; resigned, we endeavor to purchase the cheapest model available, assuming that it will die an appliance-death within six months, anyway. We are the only people I know who keep a spare coffeemaker on hand -- for when the next model breaks, we have a unit available until we get to the store to buy a new one.

We really like coffee.

Coffee was part of our mating ritual; I do believe her lust for coffee was one of the reasons I proposed marriage to her (off-handedly, in a pool hall) in the first place. Never mind the sex or her beauty or her fascinating conversation or the fact that spoke sign language and melted my heart by showing me the words for "pretty" and "shy" and "butterfly"; we both loved coffee, as a beverage, as a stimulation, as a Sunday afternoon activity.

When I first met the sisters (I met one and dated her, and then switched sisters and married the second one), the method they had of making coffee amused and boggled me. They would boil a pot of water on the stove, and then pour in the grounds; after steeping for a moment, they would pour it into a mug, strained through a cloth filter that resembled a fishing net or a wind-sock: It had a handle attached to a loop, and then a length of some sort of material hung from the loop like a sock. "The sock" is what we called it, mildly appalled at the brown, well-used filter; however, the coffee was delicious and strong, stronger than anything to which I had been exposed at that point of my life, save espresso in New York's Little Italy.

So, I think I married my wife because she smoked cigarettes and drank a lot of coffee, as I did. Also, movies. We loved and love movies -- the first week we were dating, we went out every night and saw all of the nominees for Oscar's Best Picture. This was February of 1990, and the nominated movies were the picks from 1989's crop, of course -- My Left Foot, Driving Miss Daisy, Born on the 4th of July, Dead Poets Society and Field of Dreams. I had seen Born on the 4th of July and Field of Dreams, but I had not seen the rest. *I just realized, my former appreciation for Tom Cruise (Scientology has ruined him for me, alas) may have well contributed to my success with Clarissa, my wife.*

We sat, in a bar on a double-date, with a couple that were only interested in each other. I may be a scintillating conversationalist now (I try), but then all I did was work, watch movies (on my brand new VHS player and television, purchased with my first credit card) and masturbate. I also wrote and drew and drank beer, but I am trying to keep it simple; so, we found ourselves sitting there, she only mildly interested in me (she had just broken up with a long-time boyfriend, which is why her sister, my former lover, insisted she come out with us, and how I got the opportunity in the first place -- I was male), and I had not done much at the time. I had, the week before, gone to a theater to see the aforementioned Oliver Stone biopic of Ron Kovic, and used that as an icebreaker. I knew nothing about her, but she mentioned her desire to see "My Left Foot", starring Daniel Day-Lewis, one of the Best Picture nominees, and I had my opening.

That was February of 1990. We were married in June. We're still married, and we still drink 3 pots of coffee a day. Fuck aging -- listen to Roger Daltrey and Pete Townshend -- I hope I die before I get old.

I want to be European, sometimes. I want to sit at a cafe in an urban sprawl with a cup of coffee and a beret and smoke cigarettes and sneer. Well, except for the fact that I haven't been to Paris or Amsterdam (yet), I do that now. I no longer have a beret, but I can get one if provoked.

Part Three: Present Imperfect

A. Implied Friends.

The great casualness of our society--one man's impressions. Fear not, I will keep it from being dull. Don't you trust me by now? Whenever I write an article, I have several goals in mind, including 1) Being entertaining, 2) Not repeating myself when I turn a clever phrase and 3) Amusing myself. Sometimes there is a 4), but that is mainly when my hormones surge and my adoration of Rose reaches fever pitch and I want to make her wetly squirm in her seat (and I think I've only done that twice).Hello, my name is Rob. Some of you have seen me naked, for which I apologize. Some of you don't know me, except as a wraith in the digidorm. Some of you wish for me to be something or someone else, and see me as merely a lump of clay, a starting point. Some of you read my words faithfully, some dabble, some of you I have on my "to do" list.You are all welcome to call me Mr. Anderson, or even Atticus (I temporarily flirted with the idea of having my children address me as Atticus, when I became a father at the age of 22; sanity prevailed, however, and "Daddy" became the standard) if you feel literary. You may call me Neo, in honor of the film "The Matrix", and which also served as my dojo nickname as I got my ass tossed around a mat by a sadistic sensei. You may call me Rabbit, especially if you are Guyanese. You may most certainly call me Rob, which is my name, and the name I hear in my head when I think of myself. Please do not call me "Bobby", which was my childhood nickname, and which I now associate with NASCAR drivers and the son of Hank Hill (as well as Chris' father's name, although "Mr. Lurch" is probably better for him). (Another digression and long story that I am ... simply not going to go into, because Eric K. being a drunk, Penthouse magazine-stealing idiot wasn't even funny at the time).I permit you. You are hereby granted the privileges of familiarity, because I stand naked (metaphorically, that time) before you every night, revealing shit about myself that used to make me cringe in shame, but that I now embrace to take away the power that memory has to hurt me. I refuse to let my past scar me any further than it already has; the past is gone. I am pleased to meet you, and next time I will tell you about the time I jacked-off on a roof in Brooklyn with a good friend nearby, while we howled at the stars and the moon in the dark. That doesn't mean you know me, it means I am not afraid. Sticks and stones may (will, if used correctly) break your bones, but words can provoke a beautiful woman to undress. There have been studies--the rumors you have heard are true: Women actually do prefer smart men with a sense of humor to "dumb jocks". Thank goodness for me.However, the modern social networking that has become our society's substitute for social intercourse permit a kind of anonymous interaction, on an immediate level, that was not previously possible in our world's history. Much has already been spoken on the anonymous web-poster's propensity for slander and rudeness; the epidemic is worldwide. China is instituting an "on-line I.D.", that will accompany every user, so that the days of "FUCK U DIRTBAG"-type posts (or more accurately, 你他媽的污物袋!!!) will be followed, in China, by the sound of rifle fire as another lulz-seeker takes a dirt nap.I am no fan of anonymity--but I am a fan of privacy. If you are posting, say, on Facebook, and you comment on a friend's post, which is then followed by a post by a person who is not on YOUR friend list, but is of course, a friend of your friend, do you immediately assume a familiarity with this person? Who you only know as a row of letters? A row of letters that presumably has some sort of connection with your friend. I may be complicating the question, so follow me:Lacey Hendricks: So, I went out for coffee, right? And then I got back into my car, right? And then I drove, right? And got to my friend's house? And she had lost her leg in a food processor accident last week!!1!11 Like OMG!!Snarky McWry (You): Wow, I was going criticize the banality of your status update, but it sounds as if your appendage-challenged friend is even dumber, so cheers!Squee Pinkskirt: OMG Lacey! Hey Snarky LOL. Isn't Lacey a riot!Snarky McWry: Hello, Ms. Pinkskirt nice to meet you (sound of gagging on own politeness is fortunately inaudible on Facebook).Lacey Hendricks: I know so then I drove, right? and then I...what did I do next? I think it involved food.Squee Pinkskirt: Oh Snarky hit me up we should be friends.Snarky McWry: Who are you, again?

There is nothing wrong with joining a conversation. There is nothing wrong with greeting a fellow poster, who may be unknown to you; however, is it really so difficult to introduce one's self, rather than assume everyone is buds because you happen to share a common human? In person, you wouldn't walk into a conversation, and slap Snarky on the arm and say Ha Ha Snarky without first introducing yourself, would you? Would you? Use condoms, first, you don't know where Snarky's arm has been.I blame Bill W. For those of you who have managed to avoid any knowledge of alcoholism or 12 Step programs in your lifetime, I say, get out of Iowa and wake up to the real world. Bill W. was the moniker of the co-founder of Alcoholics Anonymous, a program that encourages strangers to stand up and greet each other by name at the drop of a hat (Hi, my name is Bill. Hello, Bill). If not for some junkies who can't stop sucking Sterno or chugging mouthwash (I bet you didn't know that one, did you? Mouthwash has a goodly quantity of alcohol in it, and if you drink it before work, you don't smell drunk, you smell orally groomed), we might still be addressing each other as "Mr. Anderson" or "Mrs. Gottschalk" or "Mr. Tibbs". You can call me Rob. But be careful when you talk to strangers--that ain't candy, it's a penis.

B. Men's relationship advice?

Not being a man who uses "Google" to successfully engage women in conversation, I was unaware until five minutes ago of a pick-up technique described as "Cocky and Funny". Apparently, there is a trick (that can be learned) to being Cocky and Funny and thus encouraging women everywhere to shed their panties.The obvious flaws in this approach are many, but I will address a few:1. Women are aliens, and we, as men, have to Figure Out What Makes Them Tick. While it is true that women have differing cultural presumptions than do men, they are members of the human race. They are people with vaginas and breasts; they usually have less body hair and generally smell better. Don't let these differences convince you that they have a "code" that must be "cracked". What works as an icebreaker for the Prom Queen (being attractive, wealthy, or the Quarterback) may not work for the Shy Bookworm (being smart, being very smart, being pleasant and smart). Which is good, because often it is the Shy Bookworm who will fuck you senseless and populate your dreams for the rest of your life. Trust me on that one.2. One Personality Fits All. I have a fairly likable nature, I have been called handsome by more than one woman, and I am fairly clever. I have been rejected far more often than I have been accepted. That's just the way it goes; even Brad Pitt, in his salad days, probably ended up at home alone and jerking off after crashing and burning with the ladies. One size does not fit all, gentlemen; like us, different women are looking for different things. I know a couple of women who think that Roy Scheider was a sexy beast, and other women who experienced labial moistening over Albert Einstein. Some women like a sense of humor, others are attracted to powerful men, and others may revel in sturdy but stupid. There's someone for everyone, but not one way to be for all women.3. Funny. This is one that is difficult to explain. 18 year old women / girls seem to be attracted to powerful and attractive men, but ask any 30+ year-old woman and invariably you will hear the response that she wants "a man with a sense of humor". Perhaps not Woody Allen's self-flagellating sense of humor, precisely, which promotes the reaction in women that I know of "I don't want his sperm in the same zip code as me, let alone inside any of my body cavities", but the easygoing, slightly self-deprecating, aw-shucks humor that says "I know I am a Greek god made flesh, but I still chuckle at the groin impacts on America's Funniest Home Videos". If you can make her laugh, even a little, it shows that you are relaxed, confident and interested in pleasing her. This can't be taught, but it can be learned. Desperation is unattractive.

4. Cocky. This one is slippery, because a lot of women will deny the attraction, but I have found that self-confidence --

even self-confidence elevated to Burt Reynolds-levels of hubris -- drives women wild even as they roll their eyes. I can only speak from what I have observed, but this one holds some water. I will listen to feedback. It is indeed difficult to be funny on cue, especially if you are speaking to a crazy-hot or (in my case), crazy-smart woman whom you wish to bed; my friend Chris is the only man I have known who can be funny on cue. I am sometimes cocky, and sometimes funny. I am neither all of the time; often I am expressionless and blank as my mind is in the Other World.

C. Learn something!

So, what can I use to amuse on this fine evening? I have no ideas yet -- but I have never let that stop me before.

The world was informed of the passing of Leslie Nielsen, yesterday. I don't have a joke for that -- he was not a giant of the acting world, but his work made people laugh, and his name was never associated with rape or murder, so he gets an acknowledgment.

The only subject on my mind is one that I am not going to write about, so I am trying to find an idea...

In the news today was the revelation of leaked diplomatic cables. I am trying to figure out why these would be exciting. Politicians, and those who work in power, in Washington D.C., and around the D.C. Beltway, are so convinced that the rest of the world hangs breathlessly on their every word.

Hello, D.C. isn't the center of the world, geniuses, Exxon and Microsoft are. Nobody cares what Congress feels about pay freezes or leaked cables about reducing Guantanamo's population (which was supposed to be closed by now, Mr. Obama, you promised). We just don't care.

Our oil baron overlords don't give us time to care, what with the daily plans to reduce our health benefits to minimal and our retirement benefits to zero. Washington can certainly diddle themselves into believing that they run things -- the occasional news of a Congressman impregnating a 17 year-old intern breaks up the monotony.

Also, who else is surprised that they still use diplomatic cables? Do they still de-code them with an Enigma, also? Holy shit, you can get your e-mails to your perverted, porn-sharing buddy scrambled with multi-key encryption; shouldn't diplomats have some James-Bondian, Q-Produced cable protecting? Are they strapping notes to birds again? I bet they were using AIM. Or Yahoo Chat.

The old and crusty sect (to which generation I belong, thank you very much) often fails to recognize that things that were specialized or secret when we were younger -- fields such as photography, printing, news reporting, even film-making, have become accessible to the average person with a laptop. No longer does it take a $10,000 camera and a well-lit, dedicated studio, plus a darkroom, to generate stunning visual images; such things can be done with a $150 Nikon Coolpix and a quick trigger finger. In the late 1980s, when I worked in printing, producing business cards was a process that took about a week, and customers were compelled to choose from a set of pre-designed formats; now it can be done with a few minutes' worth of hacking in a cheap program and output on a Laser Printer. I say these are good things; nothing that makes anybody's life easier can be anything but lauded.

However, the ability to cobble together a passable business card with minimal effort does not accord one with Expert Status; there are many elements of layout, design and color and paper matching that take an honest immersion into the field to master. Some things are done passably well by the quick and dirty method; does anybody, anywhere, honestly miss dropping off film at the Fotomat and waiting a day or even an hour for your pictures? I don't think so. Digital photography has not only killed the camera-film industry, it has slain its children and burned down its village, as well.

Some things still require an apprenticeship, and effort, to truly understand. Film-making, for one. "America's Funniest Home Videos" may have made amateur film-makers out of a lot of us, but be assured: Christopher Nolan and Martin Scorsese are in no way threatened by the ascendancy of "VidStud69" and his 37 creations on YouTube. Telling a story with Cinema takes a commitment of skill, artistry and administrative discipline that cannot be learned by splicing footage together on a Mac; I daresay Hollywood and their ilk will not hand a budget of $150 million to anyone who has not proved themselves via the apprenticeship process. Talent is a building block, it is not the skyscraper itself.

I have wandered so far afield I forget if I was making any points. I have already covered the "We know you're talented, but you don't get to be a superstar until you put some time and effort in" mantra; also, VHS, cassettes, CDs, telephones with cords, linotype, film and humility -- these are a few of things that have died since I have been an adult. Not the old "Back in my day we had 8-tracks" rant; 8-tracks were dying when I was a kid, ditto LPs. After I have reached adulthood, technology, which hadn't been moving at a snail's pace previously, sucked down a few cases of Red Bull and got busy trying to emulate the Ouroboros (a snake eating its own tale), transforming so rapidly that it is eating itself while still alive.

D. Road Rage, mildly.

Express Your Frustration!When you are driving, and some yodel moving at half the speed of Turd slows down the closer you get to him, and then speeds up as you pass to keep his Halogens in your rear-view, Express Your Frustration! Pound on the steering wheel, bite your lip, invent a disease, spit yogurt on your spouse!

In Texas, because of the long, empty stretches of road between *here* and *there*, often single-lane highways with 70 mph speed limits, there exists a driving habit that I've not noticed in any other state. Many're are the farm trucks and tractors and such that are traveling along, driving at 45 mph, or in fact any number of mph below the speed limit. When a vehicle is traveling at normal highway speeds (speed limt, or speed limit + 10 or whatever), and comes up behind the lollygagging traffic, the front car will move to the shoulder, out of the way of faster-moving vehicles, and then pull back onto the highway after traffic has passed. The passing vehicle then hits the hazard lights for a 3-blink "thank you", and everyone goes on their way.As I was returning from the fire station, sixty miles from home, I approached an erratic vehicle from behind. He was moving more slowly than I, but not egregiously so, as there was a difference of maybe 2-3 mph between our vehicles. As I approached, the car began to ease onto the right shoulder, but only for a few seconds (to indicate submissive bitch-hood, allowing trailing vehicles to pass one, Miss Manners recommends a shoulder ride of at least 20 seconds). He (she? it?) then swerved back into the lane, discouraging any acceleration on my part lest our cars become One. He/she/it then repeated the action a moment later, prompting a puzzled expression on my face and the (silent) declaration, to myself, "Are you drunk? Or just being courteous?" I then backed off, because I can sniff traffic accidents a mile away, before they happen (anecdote some other time), and I had no interesting in practicing being an EMT on myself. It only took a few extra minutes to get home, as well as giving myself a topic on which to write, a win in my book.

Life is Frustration, broken up into Simon Cowell-sized fragments. I have noticed that clichés help people swallow life like a food. Without the ability to process input, people quote someone who sounds like they know what they're talking about, whether it be Buddha, Jesus or Bill O'Reilly. Why think, when someone else can do it for you?People are afraid of not only making a mistake, but sounding foolish. I think the fear of the herd is biology laughing its ass off at us. Peer pressure -- and yes, adults receive peer pressure, even more so than teenagers -- is responsible for more predictable, drone-like behavior, than any other singular influence. Don't worry about what your neighbors think -- it has been said so often, and ignored so often, that the beginning of my sentence is just white noise to most of you who read it.Don't worry about what your neighbors think -- it has been said so often, and ignored so often, that the beginning of my sentence is just white noise to most of you who read it. So, I said it twice.Respect the group, do not burn down your village with an act of stupidity, but your neighbor's opinions aren't going to pay your mortgage. Try having a thought that does not require the approval of everyone around you.Spend a day lying naked in a kiddie-pool full of jell-o in your backyard for no good reason.

Turn off your electricity and read a book aloud to your children by candlelight.Paint your lawn, in winter and the grass has died, bright colors like purple and red and yellow because it looks nice.Do one thing that no one would expect you to do, every day. Wear a hat.Ultimatums are the unimaginative person's method of dealing with the constant decision making and crises that arise by virtue of living in a world full of pressures. With teenagers, we dismiss their melodramatic ravings, but we give credence to the same idiocy from adults; we do not smack down the stupid with nearly the frequency that we -- as the majority -- probably should. What on Earth do I mean? Well, suicide is the penultimate ultimatum. Screaming "I want to be happy or I'm going to kill myself" seems to be a self-solving problem. An emotional display that culminates in any ultimatum, such as "We need to communicate better, or I want a divorce," is a sticky slope. Often, we don't know how to un-say something, so we feel the need to carry through on our ultimatums, when often, *these things pass* is the best solution. If the ultimatum had not been stated, it would have just been an argument.Many cusps reach us, in our lives, and while every juncture seems crucial, the ability to take action does not necessarily mean we *must* take action. Sometimes, doing nothing is the action. As you gather age, wisdom, and arthritis, you realize that it is important to not only say what you mean, but to mean what you say -- otherwise, you'll gather a reputation as a blow-hard or worse: A Republican. If you are in a bad mood, don't yell out, "I am leaving you!" Unless, you have enough inner-strength (or total lack of dignity) to admit when you are wrong and reverse yourself.I'd rather be right than wrong, even if it means I have been wrong for many years about many things. I am always willing to admit my wrongness, so that I can get on with the righteous feeling of being correct.There's Five Cents worth of analysis for you. I can't wait to see a naked vulva again, soon.

E. Religion

I believe that there is no deity or creator. I think that we are a cosmic accident. We are so arrogant as a species that we have founded an entire faith that states that everything in the universe--*all 93 billion light years of observable universe*--was created for us, homo sapiens. That is hubris on an unimaginable scale. I find the very concept of a God to be impossible. We can measure quarks, leptons, hadrons, protons, electrons, neutrons, baryons, mesons, light, air, earth, water and fire, yet we can find no measurable evidence, nary a trace of a God, except for oral fables handed down for a thousand years before being written down by sexually-frustrated monks. Religion is a members-only club that uses the threat of the invisible to simulate order from chaos. Science is a process of documentation that uses empirical data to promise order from chaos. The methodologies are different at the fundamental level: religion spurns advancement and embraces the "traditional"; science redefines itself as quickly as a new thought can occur.The list of insults to mankind done in the name of a deity are too numerous to list, or even reference; it is fair to say that any belief structure that condones the murder of a fellow human should be closely scrutinized. To kill a fellow human -- to take away all that they have, and all that they are, because someone disagrees with them, is hateful paranoia for which we as a society incarcerate people in padded rooms. Historically, churches do not weather dissenting opinions well. I cannot bring myself to hate a group of people, merely because they hate me; however, I will not invite them over to my house for tea, either. It is acceptable to shoot rabid dogs, and varmint control is in fact a good reason to own a firearm.The knowledgeable and the enlightened have an attitude of "live and let live", it seems to me; the ignorant and spiteful lean towards a mindset of "agree with me or die".I can't recall the last incident I have heard reported in the news of an atheist suicide bomber. Predictably, misguided martyrs believe in a Righteous and Vengeful Deity.Sidebar--if you ruled an entire universe, that you had created from scratch, would it really matter to you--as the big cheese, the head honcho, the creator of heaven and Earth-- that the tiny ant-like peoples of a single rock (among the trillions of planets you had created) did not call your name when those aforementioned ants hit their own thumbs with a hammer? I don't worry whether the fire-ants in my backyard use my name in vain; I cannot even conceive of an omnipotent being becoming agitated at not receiving enough attention.Everything I have ever learned about any religion is equal to anything I have learned about all of them. I give no more credibility to Yahweh than I do to Odin. Hecate and Thoth and Zeus and Saraswati are all eggs from the same Hen of superstition. Jesus is equivalent to Winnie the Pooh, except that Pooh has Tigger and Piglet and Eeyore as friends--Jesus had only his disciples.Advantage Pooh.

F. To buy and sell

Today I am able to express myself with more coherency--I have the feeling that this will lead to writing that is superior to the placemat-gibberish I have been laying before my admirers of late. I have a progression of ideas, and all the time in the world to share them. Are you tapping your toes yet? Perhaps you need a glass of wine before you continue. Very well.

I wanted to address the penchant our culture has for salesmanship. We buy, in America, and we sell. We have been reduced to little else; where once we innovated, we now diet; where once we manufactured, we now market and entertain. We all wish to be wealthy celebrities with gold teeth and a Mercedes SUV that we can exit while flashing our nether regions at hordes of paparazzi that we can loathe.

If you are alive, you are fat and hideous and old. You have no say in the matter--look at the 15 year old girls on television; their breasts are store-bought, their lips are collagen-filled, yet somehow lacking in expression because of the pre-emptive Botox injections. They are beauty incarnate; you, with your wrinkles and your cellulite and your freckles are a Cave Troll that has escaped ostracization in a Tower only due to your parent's pity and forbearance. You cannot ever be attractive, so you might as well make your way onto a reality television show to throw feces at other humanoid wanna-bes. The solution, of course, is to purchase what you need from the benevolent Gods. Debt is your only way to find love--if you spend enough of the money that you don't have, you might achieve bulimic superstar status, and you'll be sneering at the mundane in no time.While you are buying, you should also be selling. Everyone around you is confused and uncertain as to the extent of their ugliness and social awkwardness--they need a sage and wise hand to guide them to all of the many things they should be attempting to procure. Make sure you invade their precious moments and their peaceful serenity; there is no moment during the day when a person doesn't wish to be informed of their choices in consumer electronics. An expletive-filled negative reaction is merely incentive for You to perform better as a salesperson. Only losers can't Close.

Buy and sell. You have no other reason or methodology for existence.Make sure your ugly ass upgrades to Windows 7. Bill Gates knows better.

G. Ranting about things.

Welcome to the Jungle. When I was younger (Zooey Deschanel shout-out, video to be inserted like a diaphragm) I read John Lennon's "A Spaniard in the Works". It is stream-of-consciousness pseudo-writing, but It hit me as if it had meaning at the age of 19, and for a few months, my journal reflected that non-edited, write what you think babble. I found it liberating. I don't know if I can undo my thousands of hours and thousands of pages written, in which I strive to speak with a laser-like focus, but, as an exercise, I will attempt it. I strive to point out, for the readers that happen to be mentioned herein, that this stuff is the subconscious boiling to a froth, it has about as much meaning as a peanut butter and jelly sandwich, nothing is different than five minutes ago, and we already knew I was insane. Forgive me or skip it. (Deep Breath).I state once more: I have no wish to instill feelings in anything or anyone with this piece. It is a primal scream, a self-rape, it is not anything more than that. My mind flies like a pinwheel; you are forewarned.i see emily the goddamned flake when i see that woman whom i liked miked unstuffed like a coddled fish or cuttlefish spinning in the dark angling for a protractor unzipped with pink floyd fucking her and then i am not Stop... reboot that thought there is nothing but anger why anger? why not i take everything inside i think and then i think and then i think and then i speak and sometimes people laugh and if i can get a woman to take off her skirt i like to see the pussy which is most of the fun not even the fucking just seeing a pussy penthouse is as good as a live dead fish so there is that.backtrack and halftrack sherman or is it bradley georgia burn the shit down elton mr john you have a stomach full of cum should have spit some more the carpet is white no need to swallow sparrow undone birds orioles bad baseball insitgate that little quirk no i didnt my fingers did yeah right oover to you barry bad hair day any more typos? yeah i think i'll just let it fly no corrections even WHEN I SHOUT i cannot let it ou but i like a sheer blouse who doesnt nipples are for kissing but babies get first crack breaking your mommas back i first heard that in madrid spain in 1974 that is esoteric shit i remember a sailor told me that and my mom was walking with us right there and i looked at her horrified and skipped the cracks but they were cobblestones oh shit...so the reason is i must say the wherewithal to breathe in the air of the free and the fucked is that i say things and they nod and then i rhyme things and sagely they nod and i paint things and they nod and then i say i love your body and may i take you to bed and they say oh my god or yes or say nothing and i am like well i am just trying to speak because you dont and i can list 1,285 reasons for anything or 5,987 reasons to do nothing it is easier to do nothing it is better to do and i dont mind mistakes in fact i love them and i wish to make more mistakes by the lake and i told her that and we circle so i write to her but also to YOU so dont

feel left out i want to fuck a lot of women---it happens.i have never done a circle jerk. i wonder where is the fun is shooting on your buddys shoes. yet i love cumming on and in women my favorite part it is like my fluid my dna has my code and the right reader you can read my mind or at least tell if i drank enough water or if i had eggs for breakfast. that one woman told me she knows when her husband had eggs because his sperm tasted different and how do i respond to that? good to

know? yeah and the last time i fucked my wife i imagined cumming inside someone else and that would be a confession but everybody knows me and everybody nods like i am so different i think i just admit my screw ups and my fears and

envies and lusts and likes and loves and lovesmy fingers are happy now i am progressing towards a greater truth and i am flying with this thought bought stopgap hold tap reback new finger style of not p and not r and not whatever doesnt flwo wioth the mood so i am now thinking about the bed i have to assemble tomorrow and the shit i have to build and fixing cars and i have no stress about new jobs because i am always the best at whatever i do if i have to try again an again i will be better and if you are better then i get better except bowling i

cant bowl for shit.yep dep johnny oh my fonny he doesnt have the money honey cant you count my sheep in your sleep i wont make a peep ill be under the sheets sewing new barbie doll clothes for my little sister after they cracked open her head and milk has an aftertaste catch an orange catch an orange.That's it.

H. Take a taxi, instead (Small towns suck)

We have heard it broadcast over the airwaves, from radio dramas to television shows; we have heard it espoused in books and articles about "going back to your roots". We have heard that Small Towns (Capital S, Capital T, for the overwhelming oodles of charm dripping from the town halls of Small Towns) are inherently nicer, safer, and just better places to live.I have lived in New York City (for 11 years), I am originally from a suburb of a medium-sized town, and I now live in a Small Town (population 6,000 or so).I am here to call "Bullshit".I cannot judge every municipality in the country, of course, nor am I going to insult Small Towns per se...I am merely going to attempt to clarify that something smaller is NOT automatically more "intimate" or "friendly". Small towns are where residents are afraid to leave, or, have gone to die. I don't sense nobility in either case.

First of all, let me defend New York City from some perceptions that are engendered by the national media. New Yorkers are not rude, they're just busy. That's it, that's the explanation. I have found--and ask any native New Yorker, if my veracity is in question--that anytime I needed directions in New York, I had no trouble asking the next passerby, "Excuse me, where is the XYZ subway stop or the ABC deli?" And I would get an answer. The answer might be brusque or brief, but New Yorkers Know Things. The average person on the street in NYC A)knows where they are and B) how to get to the next place.Sadly, this is less true in my current living environ. Half of the people here don't know where THEY are, let alone how to find anything else.Stores. In New York, I had almost universally good experiences shopping, with few exceptions, and those exceptions are memorable because they were not the norm. Rude salespeople don't last in a city where a competing business is no more than a few blocks in any direction. Once again, the salesperson might be abrupt, but I don't take that as rudeness, because I am usually ready to move on to the next errand, myself. Let's keep it going. Notable exception: I needed refills for my Zippo lighter, fuel and flints. In NYC at that time (in my normal shopping areas), such items were 99 cents each. One afternoon, the wife and I were strolling along the Upper East Side (for those in the rest of the country, the area of NYC where the Trumps and the Hiltons shop--pricey), and I ducked into a smoke shop to procure said items. When the clerk rang up the items, the total came to $19.98. Confused, I looked at the receipt, noting that each item was charged as $9.99. "My good sir, you've accidentally hit an extra "9", I informed him, "This should be about $2.00". He disagreed, asserting that the items were priced correctly. He was unamused that I preferred not to be anally raped, on that particular day, and he should proceed to restock the ridiculously over-priced merchandise. On the other hand, he wasn't particularly rude, so never mind. I have never encountered so many rude, ignorant people that are responsible for selling merchandise as I have in this shithole of a Town. They don't give a damn--they're making minimum wage, and I hope they don't wonder why. I am not even going to address the intelligence factor; the lower the economic standard of a Town is, the education levels drop commensurately. There is a sentence that would be indecipherable to the vast majority of the 6,000 Derps in this burg.I don't understand rudeness, on any scale; we must remember, as a culture, where handshakes originated.When a medieval warrior greeted another warrior, they each extended their strong (usually the Right) hand, to show that it was weaponless. It was a sign of truce, as it were, meaning "I am showing you that I am not going to kill you". We have disarmed our populace, to the point that courtesy is forgotten. Were we all carrying weapons, I guarantee a lower level of sass. Lop off the heads of a few Wal Mart employees, and service would improve.

There must be a middle ground; the last place in which I made my home, in Western Maryland, was not bad. It had some charm, some good restaurants, yet the traffic was not so horrific as to be a hazard to negotiate. The cost of living was prohibitive when I lost my business, however, which is not even a good tale, so I'll skip it.

Thank you for letting me gripe. Avoid small, poor towns. If a place is cheap to live in, you may be assured that is because no one wants to live there.

I work for an ambulance service in a small town.It is a for-profit business; this town is not large enough, as a municipality, to afford an EMS service. We do it for money. There is a supplement paid by the County Government, to ensure we respond to all 911 medical calls; that supplement amounts to about 50 cents per resident, per month. Barely enough to pay me.We get calls, more often than I'd like, of people in real distress--heart attacks, strokes (more accurately known as cerebrovascular accidents, or CVAs) and people who have been in motor-vehicle accidents (MVAs). These are the people that need a genuine emergency response--lights flashing, sirens blazing, helicopters deployed, fire departments assisting. These are people who have the Grim Reaper knocking at the door, and we are the last barricade available.Unfortunately, this town I live in is a low-income town, which means that it is full of low-income residents, which also means low education levels. I do not often receive distress calls from M.I.T. professors. I received a call tonight-- the one that prompted this post -- from a mother who stated that her daughter was "acting funny", and she was unsure whether the daughter "was dehydrated".The prospect of retaining my job prohibited me from asking if the mother had "given her daughter a glass of water".Other calls that I have received, that have scrambled ambulance crews out of bed:-- "I'm constipated"--"My brother's been drinking all night and now he's passed out and won't wake up"--"I don't feel right"--"I have hemorrhoids"--"I've been sick for three days, and I suddenly feel the need to go to the hospital at 2 am." Please, I beg of you. If you're going to have a baby, arrange for a ride. Paramedics hate birthing children--then they have to fill out the birth certificate. Childbirth is not an "emergency".

I.   Perspective

I watched a show today that addressed the mythology of stress (Penn and Teller's Bullshit!, Showtime, now in season 7, Netflix the DVDs, good stuff), and thought I might throw my hat into the ring.

There is always a reason for things I do. You may not know it, hell, I may not even know it, but somewhere in my brain, some gray matter has a reason for something.I find that some pictures reduce my stress level. All I have to do is imagine someone else's face instead of Ms. Jessica Alba (she's pretty enough, but not my type), and then I find Serenity Now! As George "Fucktard" Costanza raved on that television show that time.I am a firm believer that stress is how we react and interact and perceive our environment. If you are feeling "stressed" at work--get a different job. Or, realize that your expectations may not necessarily align with those of your employer. You are being paid to perform a task; whether or not it allows you to chant happy mantras is secondary to whether or not your performance meets completely arbitrary and shifting expectations of a supervisor. Unless you work for yourself, you may argue; then, stress is caused by deadlines, customers, financial issues. To which I say *you* chose this path--you preferred to be aggravated by a customer instead of a boss. It is never too late to turn back; don't think that rubbing lavender oil on your nipples will slow down your adrenal processes and grant you bodhisattva. You will, however, smell like lavender. Wipe clean before nipple chewing commences.I decided a long time ago that other people's expectations were insufficient motivation for me to get excited. I work in an Emergency Services field; I realize a heart attack is urgent--any consternation that ensues during a call is borne of emotional attachment, which I refuse to allow for myself. I want to save every life, and simultaneously, I realize that that goal is unattainable. Some people die today.Some will die tomorrow. Either way, I keep my pulse regular, which allows me to perform in a calm, orderly manner. An automaton I am not; I don't keep this hurt and rage bottled up. When some dingbat calls me complaining that they need an ambulance at 3 am for an "anxiety attack" (which translate as "running out of crystal meth"), we respond in a rapid and professional manner. Then we howl and scream and yell about it back at the station after it is said and done.Because, too often, we get a case like the 22 year-old mother who lost control of her vehicle, over a bridge and into a river with two toddlers in the back seat. The mother, her head slammed against the windshield in the crash, was dazed and swam to shore. She was incoherent. When paramedics arrived, she began to speak more clearly and they realized that two infants had been in the car at the time of the crash. My co-workers, the men I work every day with--the practical jokes alone would indicate a Frat House, rather than an EMS station--these men and women, my friends, dove into the river and freed the babies and frantically performed CPR on the tiny, lifeless forms. This is not CNN, or a newspaper from a thousand miles away. One of the paramedics told me this story, as you would tell a story about a BBQ you went to last weekend. The children died.Don't worry about stress at work--you probably don't have any. Look at the big picture; if your boss is an asshole, you're not alone. Perspective, babies. Keep it real.

J. I hate Halloween

I have been existing in a void of my own making, a space between reality full of refuse and pet hair and blaring car horns and the unreality of clacking keyboards, the silence of the singular digirealm that is my writing and therefore my brain.I feel as if I cannot think unless I am staring at a computer--life, with its breathing and eating and bathing makes me anxious. So, I hate Halloween. Growing up, I always felt out of place and silly and ridiculous being compelled to dress up as something or someone else to beg for candy. I liked the candy. Once, my parents made me a Batman costume, which I wore for weeks afterward. The tights were a blue pair of panty-hose. Somewhere in the muddled gloaming that is the border between childhood and adulthood rose up in me a loathing for this absurd celebration of superstition. Part of me enjoys dressing up babies and toddlers in silly costumes and parading them around, house to house, to illicit groans of ohmy-howcute; part of me wishes to be left alone, which is why my porch lights are off and the dogs unchained--the first canine to get a certified kill tonight gets an extra Snausage.I am guessing that I will think of more to write later; I am watching the World Series, game 4, and perhaps I will rant about the cheers and standing ovation the Presidents Bush, father and son, just received from the rabid, anti-human rights, anti-poor, anti-Democratic crowd in attendance at the Aryan rally--I mean Arlington Stadium.I shouldn't pick on Texas--the Bushes are transplants from the Northeast, carpetbaggers who leached onto Texas as the Bunker from which to launch their plots of World Domination and illegal wars; Iraq was merely a target of convenience; after all, how many cows can one fuck in a day before some other avenue of release is sought? The answer is 4, according to "W."'s memoirs--after you have mounted 4 cows, your body is so drenched with the manure smell that even Dick Cheney won't sit in the same room as you. So, Texas is merely a geographic destination for the Yankee dictator clan--the Lone Star States' embrace of the Bushes merely reinforces the notion that Texans need something to root for that does not involve a martyrdom at the hands of an invading army (that to which I am referring, of course, is The Alamo).Memories are meaningful to the minds to whom they belong.Your memories are not mine. My memories are sometimes filtered and recounted to make stories, but I cannot recount the tastes and smells, not so that they trigger any meaningful response.Sachets are ever associated in memory with anal-retentive elders.

K. Why I am happy, even though everything dies

Do I detail my impressions of beauty to avoid noticing the filth? Do I reject the negative? I am such an optimist. Everything is hopeful and ultimately uplifting.Well, in a word--no. I see the bad things, and foul things that exist in this world, as well as you do, if not better. I have been in the middle of violence and death and disease and hatred and abuse and addiction and infected souls my whole life. I recognize the dark without a flashlight. I just don't think that bad things deserve the press. While the average American may get a thrill from watching a fire on the evening news, or driving slowly past an accident to rubberneck at the gore, my belief is simpler: sooner or later, death will find you. There is no need for you to recognize its impendency. What lives will die. This is a good thing, as it turns out, or none of us would exist--if the older and weaker did not have the grace to die, there would be no resources for us to consume, and we would have eaten our world long ago. Hell, the universe would have eaten itself--thank God for black holes.I hope. In the manner of Andy Dufresne and Red in "Rita Hayworth and the Shawshank Redemption"; a hope not based on Valley Girl-style blind, spoiled optimism, but because I realize the world is full of drippy bad things that want to consume my gizzards and copulate with my corpse. Instead of huddling in a corner (which is, after all, a completely understandable consequence of rational comprehension), I go on with my life until the sands in my personal hourglass run out. Then, I will be done.

First, I will write my name in the snow with urine, because, well, aiming a penis is fun. I am sure women can do it, too--I have been assured that women can pee standing up. We need to address this universal shyness; when I have asked to see such things, of various female friends, I have received a laugh and a rapid subject change. The same goes for

Vajazzling (a trend, brought to the public consciousness by Jennifer Love Hewiit and her breasts); Vajazzling involves gluing crystals to the pudenda, it sounds as if it would be shiny and cute. Several women I spoke to expressed at least a minor interest in it; I asked to be able to see the finished product--out of curiosity. The women demurred, as if I suggested they carve their own initials onto the bottoms of their feet with razor blades. If no one is going to see it, why do it? Just for your girlfriends? The same goes with the peeing standing up thing. The sight of urine does not inspire raging horniness in me (although, it may for some guys), it is genuine curiosity. Or perverseness--I don't mind such a label. I am indeed perverse.So, to sum up:We're all a couple of ventricular contractions away from greasy worm-food. This is normal.The world is full of shiny and pretty. Snuggle up to the sparkly people while you are above ground.Women who have an interest in Vajazzling should know that I will serve as a willing surveyor of the craftwork.

L. Yarnswallowing and bread.

Breads -- Enjoy rye, pumpernickel, wheat, King's Hawaiian Bread, soda bread and farmer's bread. White Wonder bread was designed, marketed and produced by food-haters. I enjoy shredded animal flesh on my sandwiches, but not everyone eats meat. Herbs go well, as do crisp vegetables. No butter. A firm mantra--butter is for mashed potatoes, corn and anal sex, not a Dagwood. Vegetable semen (known by its trade name of "mayonnaise") is also tasty. Food and sex are interchangeable except for the cooking time. Anything more than a braise is a waste for an orgasm.The past is akin to a pile of sand. Disjointed, disconnected, misunderstood and uncomfortable if caught between your butt-cheeks. The past gets in your shoes and tracks all over your mother's freshly-swept floor. The past erodes statues and ruins picnic food.I have no idea what Yarnswallowing is, but it amused me for a title. I had imagery of a dog swallowing panty-hose (which is a bad thing and often requires surgery to remove). I like dogs, I like imagery, and by Jove and by Gum, don't picture a Blue Trumpet inserted into the rectum of an ogre. Especially if he farts out "When the Saints Go Marching In".Often men like "bigger is better" when applied to their penises and their paychecks; vaginas, however, we wish to be infinitely small and snug. A giant vagina is a waste of tissue unless one intends to climb inside and snowboard back and forth across the G-spot. It is not recommended to use the clitoris as a punching bag, no matter how large it is; what if she (whoever this mythological, giant-clammed woman is) is a Squirter? Too much stimulation and you will be a participant in the re-enactment of "Old Faithful's" eruption.The office in which I currently type is a glass-walled storefront. I feel like I am in a anthropological version of a zoo, except that feeding the animals is encouraged. Funyuns and Coca-Cola preferred.The smell of cabbage stew is wafting from the kitchen in the back; upon my arrival, my boss told me that "Fart Soup" was on the menu, which deflated any urge that I might have had to ingest the source of these aromas. Too bad. I am hungry.Why did we, as a species, turn the most pleasurable activity that our physical bodies enjoy (sex) into a source of guilt, jealousy, shame, anger and embarrassment? You know what--fucking is great fun. I love it. I wish I could do it five times a day, each time with a different woman, sometimes with baby oil, and sometimes on a sailboat. Our ancestors ruined it for us, by adding fig leaves and shame. Fuck you, you sandpile shitheads. I hope your memories blow away into an anonymous drift in the Sahara, and men and women begin to walk around bottomless. More fucking = less time for wars and hatred. All we should be doing is advancing human knowledge by teaching the young and studying our universe, farming, eating, fucking and shitting. Everything else falls under shame at our animal lusts. I am not ashamed of lust--I am happy to share it. Even mediocre sex is good for the heart.Fashion. I understand the preening and posturing to engender sexual appeal in a potential mate. Visible cues arouse us, like the hardcore Peacocks and Peapussies we are. I like to dress well when I feel like my hair is sexy.I have not flown a kite in years. What a useless and relaxing activity, like Presidential Primaries with longer tampon strings.

M. Locked doors

Pretend that you understand, for a moment.You must nod and smile, and shrug as if to say, "What could you do? That would be new?"i'd give myself to honest words. i wouldn't backtrack from my balance beam act, i would smile at the times i fell, and use the dust to show the effort. i would scream at my friends, with the hate of ten thousand years, and i would mean it, the dark fucking bile that i felt; but the real ones would know it is temporary, only one side of the cube, becausewe go by dimensions and you know this, too: a dot, a period, is one, a line two, a cube three, and a cube from inception to destruction, four.move a dot around and it becomes more complex-a trifle(1), a path(2), a place(3), a memory(4). dancing is four dimensional, would you feel love if it was frozen?no--a complicated thing, moving through space and time, is a memory. we build them and move them forward, because we cannot move a memory backward.we can build this memory, by beginning at the end, and freeze it: it can never be unborn, because it has already lived. you can fill the palace with death, and tread gently and in fear, or you can fling open the gates and allow the hordes to inhabit and shunt the contents and release the warm air and nothing is controlled it is like a cyclone has arisen messianically from the trellis.a prison and a castle have locks on different sides of the doors. enter the open grassy fields and they will enter you.

N. Preaching

Since I am taking a break from solely-lustful thoughts and discussions these days, I have been trying to figure out just what does garner my attention, when I reject as mundane the archetypes of "women in skirts" or "nubile women in Catholic School-girl skirts being spanked" (my archetypes are type-specific).

Perhaps not mundane, but rejected as repetitive. I leave a trail of blushing and giggling in my wake, for they (the shy) can point to me as perverse, for saying what many think, but are restrained by convention or moral or shyness or embarrassment from openly stating. I apologize--I did not mean to tout myself as the Last Gunfighter against the Moral

Majority (although, were such a battle to take place, you may be assured that I will be Davy Crockett at *that* Alamo); I suppose I mean to say that I can use words to describe sex and sexuality in such a way as to garner the approval of the PTA (soccer moms behind closed doors are often hyper-sexual adult women with little outlet beside Harlequin Romances).

So, I used to mis-hear the term "Pulitzer Prize", when I was younger, as "Pull-It Surprise". That would be an auditory mistake, not a written one. An error such as that, during the early part of your learning process, can lay unstable bricks on which further knowledge will rest, years later. I spelled "business" as "buisness" for years, until adulthood; I still have to be careful typing the word "banana", to count the Ns. I have made so many mistakes in my life, so many errors, that for years I was sure I was a complete fuck-up who would never, ever get anything right or learn anything. It took quite a while for me to realize that mistakes abound, all around me, yet are unacknowledged or glossed-over. I actually do learn from my mistakes; it is, to me, the easiest way to learn something (what is smoking crack like? Is it addictive? Let's find out!).

Life isn't in books, unfortunately. Other people's experiences are, such as mine (in these less-than-hallowed pages), but you will learn from MY mistakes and wisdom no more than I learned from Hunter S. Thompson's, or Samuel Clemens', or whoever. Which is to say -- not very much. Otherwise, you would all be getting fired from your jobs and flirting with the supermarket checkout girls and getting enraged at everything you hear from the media, at all times.

An example of lesson time at my house? When we, as a family, watch the History Channel or the Discovery Channel, and I howl and throw things at the television, loudly decrying the imbecilic oversimplification of the information about whatever "subject" they are currently airing, while correcting, at the top of my lungs, every other nugget of wisdom they espouse.

I wish I were jesting. I am a randomly activated optimist; I smile at the lies. Inside, at all times, I am angry about disinformation and salesmanship. I am so enraged by everything that I have tipped over the other way. I cannot even begin to gather the energy to be angry at the universe; I am resigned to correcting the sands on the beach, one grain at a time.

I know it is futile--which is why I grin and occasionally ask random strangers to send me pictures of their naked bodies.

I need something else to occupy my mind.

O. Bird of paradise

So, there were two relatively clever people, in a pre-arranged location, at a pre-arranged time, both equipped with the modern accoutrements of cellular communication devices-- ...who managed to miss each other completely.New York. I love this place, Part Pi: Harlem, in the gloaming, and I am pale cracker-man, a white boy from the Burbs made flesh, and while glances were made, I was like a wraith in a cloud.Finally, crossing 5th Avenue, I spotted her across the street.I have to clarify a couple of things, for the benefit of my wife, and Her (Sparrow's) spouse (and those who are watching us and betting at Vegas Odds that we will end up fucking someday), that Sparrow and I talk all of the time, but we are both happily married to other people; while we are not unaware of each other's gender, our friendship is built on sincerity, not lust.Still and all. There are moments in time, during the events leading up to any significant events in our lives, when our minds worry over a subject; turning it over and over as if the concept were a hunk of Amber in our hands, our minds preconceive a happening, imagining the variables of yes or no or maybe or Huh. So it was with our first meeting: Pictures, I have seen, and her voice I have heard, but the flesh had not yet been undigitized.My impression, instantly, like a Marquee, like a Headline, was of a Bird of Paradise--expensive and lovely and rippled as if in motion--because she was *in motion*--like a National Geographic documentary about Anthropomorphic Birds of Paradise. It is not kosher to define a thing with itself-- but, Parrot or Parakeet sounds too -- bird-like, and that is not my meaning. "Angel" or "Mermaid" sounds too droolingly sycophantic or like syrupy compliments. But that is what I mean. An artist can look at anything, say, a rock, and see the motion, the sweeping form, the existence of the rock in a 4-dimensional world, moving through time and space. A piece of art does it for you -- you look at it, and know that it is good.So--first impression: good.

P. Road trip

I love road trips.I love the vibration of asphalt under the wheels of an automobile; I love the changes that the landscape undertakes as you travel from *here* to *there*; I love time-zones shifting, the tunnel-vision of driving a highway late at night, the myriad assortment of restrooms, rest areas, soda aisles and quirky signs that pepper our nation's interstates.I say those things to let you know that my descriptions are borne of love--I have no scolding in me, tonight I am too filled with wonder.I have to tell some of it in order. Some of it I'll never tell. Some of it is dull.9:45 p.m. Tues: As I am driving back from my EMT class, I see a dark shape in the middle of my driving lane only a split-second before my car passes over it. I should clarify: my sister's car, a low-to-the-ground Geo Prizm. Instantly, the unpleasant odor of skunk fills my nostrils, and I realize I have either just run over a skunk, killing it, or run over a corpse that someone else squished. Either way-- the smell of skunk lingers, even as I am miles past it. I sigh, knowing that the car now will smell like skunk for the foreseeable future, and I usually leave a window down, because I am a smoker. 10 p.m. Tues: Arrive at work, gather daughter and such. Ditch schoolbooks. Gird the loins for a journey.11 p.m. Tues: Chatting with daughter, I mention that she should stay awake, to talk, to help me stay awake.11:02 p.m. Tues: Daughter is snoring.2:45 a.m. Weds: Enter Arkansas, leaving the Republic of Texas. Somehow, contrary to many Texans' beliefs, my penis does not shrink.5-6 a.m. Weds: I Sleep.6:30 a.m. Weds: Daughter awakens long enough for us to have breakfast at the Cracker Barrel. 7:30 a.m. Weds: Daughter is snoring.1 p.m. Weds: Daughter awakens, refreshed. Driver is beginning to see double.6 p.m. Weds: Dinner.9 p.m. Weds: Rest area. Too tired to see. Somewhere in Tennessee, near the border to Virginia. As driver attempts to sleep, wide-awake daughter decides to type (clack-clack-clack), and change clothes and wash (SLAM

SLAM car door). I sleep in fitful 10 minute bursts. After 4 hours of lying in a small car, cramped, I gain a total of 1.5 hours sleep.3 a.m. Thurs: After succeeding in her mission to ensure driver's fatigue, daughter goes back to sleep.6 a.m. Thurs: Text message from Chris, asking me to stop by his place of employment, with directions.7:30 a.m. Thurs: Arrive at first destination. Unload daughter's shit. Being less-than-thrilled with daughter's First Mate abilities, say goodbye with a grunt.8 a.m. Thurs: Arrive Chris' workplace, a less-than-inviting secure facility that the government uses for storage. Men with sidearms patrol the parking lot. A security vehicle opens the gate and drives up to my car -- it's Chris. A hug and a conversation. Comments on hair. Comments on being behind schedule. Comments on December, when I return to the Northeast. 30 minutes whizzes by, I must be on my way.8:30-ish a.m. Thurs: It is strange to be in the town of my former home; everything is familiar, yet foreign. Haunting.9:30 a.m. Thurs: Finally find the first service area along my route that has a Starbucks in it. Get on this, America; gas station coffee tastes like fermented ass---and *watered-down* fermented ass, at that.2:00 p.m. Thurs: Arrive in Connecticut, home to one of my favorite people, the Jim. JIIIIIIMMMMMM I would scream, in my younger years, whenever we spoke on the phone. I met Jim at a former job, and we have remained friends for 23 years. Jim. He immediately helps me with what I need--he knows I have a train to catch to meet The Sparrow, so we meet and greet quickly, then I jump into the shower. I yell out, because the hot stream of water massaging my battered body feels so good. I shave and change into spiffy black clothing. I wish to impress The Sparrow with clean lines, like a race car (well, a chubby race car, but still). All in black. Hair down, under control. Jim and I go out for a bite of soup, since I have not eaten since a Subway sandwich the night before. Off to the train, with assurances that we will be there to meet him the next morning, when he would be traveling to the city, as well.4:30 p.m. Thurs: Arrive in New York City, Harlem. I walk onto the platform and look around--no one who looks like a waif-like Sparrow. I descend to the terminal, still no success. I walk outside, and use the cell phone. "I was just gonna call you," she laughs into my ear "I'm almost there." Okay, which way do I go I ask, and I assure her I know East from West. "Head West toward Madison," she tells me, and I do so. The tale of that part is the previous Episode. (By the way, Sparrow, I loved the boots).5:00 p.m. or so Thurs: Breathing hard from years of not walking around in New York, and sweating heavily because I am still wearing my sweatshirt, while hauling my backpack, I am beginning to feel decidedly un-me. I pause and remove the hoodie, catching my breath, and hoping I don't seem like a wimpy dweeb.5:30 p.m. Thurs: Arrival at the Sparrowcave. Meet and greet with the family. Coffee brewed almost immediately thereafter. Somewhere in there, we make The Sparrow laugh, and a more pleasant sound there is none; her laugh should be packaged for big money as a ringtone. Scott (the hubby) and I begin to one-up each other in droll humor (I give him the edge due to his age; I am still the apprentice, but he'll die before me, so it all evens out in the end).10:30 p.m. Thurs: With only 2.5 hours of sleep in the 3 previous days, exhaustion overcomes me and I lie down; I raise my arms over my head to stretch out as I set my head on the pillow.7:30 a.m. Fri: I open my eyes with a start; my arms are still over my head, and I look around, thinking I had just cat-napped. I realize I have just been in a 9-hour or so coma. Coffee again.8:00-10-ish a.m. Fri: Catching up on FB. I see little cryptic posts from the Sparrow. I am in the living room, and there is a second computer, a Mac, by the couch. When her first post appears, I turn around to look--no one there. I think she has become ethereal; she assures me her computer is with her in the bedroom, the living room Mac is what her boy watches videos on. At one point, I catch a glimpse of the Sparrow dashing from one room to another--with glasses on! I tell her I need a picture of that, and into the bathroom she darts, to install contact lenses. Foiled. We then depart to meet the Jim.12 noon Fri: Jim and Scott and The Sparrow and I are ready to engage the city on our terms, with no quarter asked and none given. Food and shopping and conversation--it is impossible to describe. You had to be there, truly. Fun times. I am good company; amusing, helpful, weaving tales and explaining things. And all four of us are like that, so extrapolate as you will. We were four smart, funny people hanging together.9 p.m. Fri: Not wanting to depart, but seeing The Sparrow fall sideways on the couch, and Scott reclining in his recliner to a near-horizontal position, we realize that we best skedaddle while we were still welcome guests, and leave our hosts to their peace and quiet. Jim and I depart for Connecticut.12 midnight Fri: Jim plays some guitar while I enjoy a command performance.2-4 a.m. Sat: Sleep, comfortable sleep in Jim's bed. Coffee. Load car. Depart.4 a.m. - 9 p.m. Sat: An unreal blur. I tried to keep the car between the white Unicorns. Borderline psychosis.As I exit for Wood River, Illinois, a shape appears in the road only a few seconds before I run over it. Once again, I have passed over a skunk. The smell of it draws an odd grin, as I remember how my trip started; it was one of those things that if you wrote them as fiction, they would seem hokey or contrived.9:21 p.m. Sat: After 2,921 miles and 14 states (Texas, Arkansas, Tennessee, Virginia, Maryland, Delaware, New Jersey, New

York, Connecticut, Pennsylvania, Ohio, Indiana, Illinois and Missouri), I arrive at my sister's. After walking the previous two days, and then spending 17 hours in a fixed position, my body no longer works. Everything hurts. I eat, soak in a hot bath, kneading the muscles of my legs, and then fall asleep on the couch.7:30 a.m. Sun: I awaken. I feel good, rested and healthy and alive and ready to go home. Leisurely coffee, dressing and loading of suitcases. We go out to a nice breakfast in St. Louis. I see the Arch, which is definitely an arch. I tell my sister and her beau to dump me off at the airport early, and to go enjoy the rest of their day off---I need no babysitting. I revel in the peace and quiet of the airport, and then fly home.6:00 p.m. Sun: Arrive home, kisses, leaping dogs, brief storytelling, promises of more when time permits.9:00 p.m. Sun: You are reading it. Life, as it is, is a continuation of my stories. All of them. I weave now with then, real with imagined, fanciful with pragmatic. I have not yet returned to Earth, save for a couple of things burned into my brain. I love my family, I love Jim, I love Chris, and now I love The Sparrow. I think they all know this, and if not -- now they do.That is all.Moral:Run over skunks and you will have good vacations.

Q. Road trip #2

I just got back from a trip, one that I shall never endeavor to repeat. To sum it up does it no justice, so let me use prose to explain. The facts of the case are these, although trivial:Depart Texas 2 pm Wednesday

Arrive Maryland 11:30 pm Thursday

Arrive Texas 1:30 am Saturday (Friday night).

Now comes the fun part. To explain the journey would diminish it, so I am going to communicate what my head told me, not what actually happened in a linear fashion. This is what I saw, and what I thought.

1 pm Wednesday, I awake, after having slept for 5 hours. Maddie had already packed her stuff into the car, which pleases me greatly. I drink my first cup of coffee, as my wife and mother milled about with Maddie, discussing her departure. My eldest daughter was leaving home. I dressed, made sure I had some clean clothes in my backpack, got my phone charger and stuff, got her dog and related supplies -- leash, food dish, etc.-- and we left at 2.

This is a trip -- between Texas and Maryland -- that I have driven many times, so the early parts are vague, as there was nothing novel. A long drive is a long drive. Maddie and I had long talks about various things, I sipped my travel mug full of coffee, and the miles rolled past. After 30 minutes of restless excitement, the dog settles down and was quietly sleeping.

When I do this trip, I break it into states, in my head, with a certain amount of hours expected for each one. From my house to the Texas border is 5 hours. Arkansas takes 5 hours to traverse, 9 for Tennessee, and 6 for Virginia to Maryland. 25 hours is the expected total. The first day was uneventful -- my goal, when we departed, was to reach the first rest area in Tennessee, which is about 30 minutes outside of Memphis. This we did, arriving at the rest area at 12:30 am. Maddie has brought bedding, so we walk the dog, use the bathroom, and settle down to sleep. It takes Maddie a while to fall asleep, and me, even longer. I finally nod off to sleep at around 3 am.

I awake at 6:08 am (I have an amazing internal clock; when I fall asleep, I just think of what time I wish to be awake, and my body wakes me up at nearly that time; as I lay down to sleep, I wanted to be awake at around 6, and driving by 6:30), and we take care of the dog and pee, and we are off.

As I started the car, I noticed a smattering of rain drops on the windshield, and I hoped that it would not rain too much.

As we got underway, it became apparent from Highway Traffic Signs (the lighted information signs) that Tennessee was suffering through an icy rain storm. I hoped it would be brief, which it turned out not to be. As I was slogging down the highway, traffic was slowed from its normal, frenetic pace, due to ice patches on the road. I began to count cars that had slid off of the road into ditches as we crawled through the mountains of Tennessee in a slick, icy haze.

Fatigue grips. I was tired when we started the trip, and hours of concentrating in poor weather conditions are beginning to take a toll on my nervous system. My hands begin to hurt, from the fixed position they are in gripping the steering wheel. Hour after endless mile of focusing on the roads, the speed, the traffic, the poor light and the sheer length of the trip are beginning to raise tension in my nervous system.

When we reached Virginia, I thought I had entered Hell, with snow and ice and holiday traffic and big rigs.

I didn't know what Hell was, I must foreshadow here.

Upon entering Virginia, I was tired to the bone. Fatigue seeped from my every pore, and I was beginning to feel dirty and grungy from being in a car for so long. My daughter began to receive a series of phone calls from her future roommates (to whose location we were driving), informing her that "because of the weather, they wouldn't be at (the pre-arranged location), they would be at a relative's house, 25 miles further away". Great, I thought. Because of the weather? The same weather that I have just slogged 1,000+ miles through, they can't be bothered to drive 25 miles? And I have to go out of MY way?The roommates were also concerned because our arrival time -- scheduled to be around 9 pm -- was being pushed back to 11:30 pm or so. Tough shit, I thought, and I was glad I was not on the phone, because my daughter is now grown, and needs to learn to deal with problems on her own.

Somewhere, in the middle of Virginia, my well of windshield washer fluid froze from the cold, and I could no longer rinse the road-salt from my windshield. A crust of white began to cake up, and frantic wipes from the wiper blades did little but smear the salt around. Every time I stopped for gas, I scrubbed the windshields clean, until I got far enough North that the reservoirs of cleaning fluid at the gas stations were completely frozen, as well. The squeegee sat on top vats of blue ice, and we used baby-wipes (which I keep in the car on road trips for hygiene) to clean the windshield. At one point, as I pulled out from a gas station, having spent 5 minutes in the bitter cold scrubbing the salt off of my glass, a car passed me not 15 seconds after I had just cleaned them, spraying salty-slush onto the windshield and blinding me. I reached out, while driving, with a paper towel and cleaned a hole big enough for me to see through.

Arrive we did, and I mean to tell you it was cold in Maryland that night, certainly compared to the 77 degrees it had been upon our departure from Texas the previous day. It felt like it was around 20 degrees, and I remembered that when I lived up North, I had gloves in the winter, as well as a proper jacket. Having spent all of the time in the car together, the farewells between Maddie and I were brief, with assurances that she would call, a hug, and I got back into the relative warmth of the car.

Transition.

i know this route better, i am going back this way and avoiding the hellish back roads on the return. the highways are clear. stay away from the big rigs--they spray so much slush that i can't see. cold. keep it cold, so that the body doesn't get sleepy. focus on the lines on the highway. keep it centered, stay focused. good radio station.

ah a gas station that maintains its cleaning fluid--looks like a quarter inch of salt i am wiping off. i can see! i would almost believe in god.

how far should i go tonight. pushing to the point of fatigue is meaningless-i was fatigued when we were still in tennessee yesterday. what day is it? it is early friday. virginia has a lot of trucks, but at least the roads are plowed. tired of the radio. tired of sitting. first thing i do when i get home is take a long bath, soak the cold and grime out of my bones. i can do this. this is hard, but i can do this. the word exhaustion is over used. people use exhaustion when they mean tired. exhaustion, by definition, is when you can't go on any further because your body shuts down. as long as i am awake i am tired. fatigued. worn out. not exhausted -- my reserves have reserves. my hand hurts. my core is beginning to tire from locking my body in an upright position for so long. cold.

where am i? still in virginia. a rest area. should i stop? not yet-- it is only 3 am. i have so far to go. 22 hours more of driving. if i stop and sleep for 2 hours, i'll arrive at 3 am. i want to get there by midnight or so--the wife might still be awake. push on. roll the window down more -- the bitter cold will slash at my face like a knife, keeping me sharp. why do i use that expression? being cut by a knife doesn't hurt that much--it feels like pressure, mostly. the freak out comes when people see the blood. getting hit by a hammer on the thumb, that hurts. i once did it 3 times in a row. i hit my thumb -- darn it, don't do that. i hit it again, on the next swing. dammit rob, i said don't do that. now it is throbbing. i swing again and hey dammit rob i said DON'T DO THAT that fucking hurts. pause, drive the nail. focusing on the pain means that you are focused on the pain -- take the pain, identify it: YES, that is pain -- then set it aside, as if on a chair next to you, and ignore it. you know the pain exists, but you have other things to do. think about the road, keep between the lines, don't think about that.

it is almost 4 am i can't go anymore. i feel like every nerve in my body is sending me signals to rest. there is a rest area, time to stop.

3:51 am. read for a few minutes. if i close my eyes i don't know if i will want to wake up. i need to wake up around six.

5:51 am.

WHAT THE FUCK -----

my eyes bolt open as the world is shaking and roaring like an earthquake, my body is spasming and convulsing. i am alert so rapidly because i am going into shock, from the cold, my body is shivering on an epic scale. put the jacket on, zip it up, turn the car on, let it heat up. close the window. come on legs, stop jerking, hitting the steering wheel is starting to hurt. i am numb and i am sharp and lucid and i am no longer what i thought i was -- i am not a journeyer, i am a soldier in a war against myself trying to survive. 22 hours until i am home. i am hungry i am tired fatigued worn out i am cold.

i know i traveled through tennesse, because i got home alive, but i do not remember it. at around 8 or 9 am i sent a picture of me driving to sparrow and to jim. sparrow responded, and we exchanged a few messages, me typing with one thumb while negotiating the highways. there was driving and driving and there was i am hungry i am tired fatigued worn out i am cold.

the sun set and i was in arkansas. the cold was overwhelming, but every time i roll up the windows, the enveloping warmth of the heater threatened to grant me sleep and death. i roll it up for a few seconds, and then i return to the noisy blowing cold air, which is beginning to have less and less effect. i begin to plot ways of steering my vehicle into oncoming traffic to end my trip painlessly. at 70 miles an hour, head-on with another vehicle, and then i would be able to lay my head down and rest and i would be warm. i see a pair of pick up trucks with loads of goods covered with tarps alternately speeding past me and slowing down and i pass them and it is a sort of game for hundreds of years.

the stars begin to flutter back and forth darting crazily like bats. if i stare at them they go back to where they are supposed to be so i don't yet chastise them. somewhere early in arkansas my odometer rolled over to 100,000 miles (i have had the car since 2006).

i think it took me a month to travel through arkansas but i might be mistaken about the time. i need to keep my brain exercised and sane so i begin to calculate the sleep that i have not had--from 1 pm wednesday, when i awoke, until arkansas, was 57 hours for me, of which i had slept 4 and a half hours. if i count back to when i awoke the day before that, before working and then getting short sleep, and then to the end, i had slept 9 and a half hours out of 80. and i was working or driving in horrible conditions the whole time. i begin to question my reasoning and sanity. i wish the stars would stop distracting me i am hungry i am tired fatigued worn out i am cold. i need to respond to chris he was right that i should say something and i will tell him everything and then i hope he still wants to be my friend.

this should be texas but there is no sign just traffic damn all this construction the road the road is singing to me right between my headlights there is a purple line-drawing, moving, it looks like a crowd of people with fists raised, pumping their arms in time with the music on the radio like a purple string quartet. i can watch them a little bit because they are on the road where i need to be looking anyway but don't forget other cars i am hungry i am tired fatigued worn out i am cold.

the cars traffic sound noise stars moving look at the road dont sleep rob less than five hours less than a trip to new york from maryland that doesnt help bright lights construction damn narrow bridges with jersey walls and there that does look like a crowd at a concert drawn on an etch a sketch and they are transforming with the springsteen song and i am hungry i am tired fatigued worn out i am cold oh hell i hate big trucks damn things of course on a narrow bridge i can pass him speed up remember to focus and stay away from the wall and speed past him STOP dancing for a minute i am trying to drive and clear thank go where THE FUCK did all of these cars come from whirring past me oh shit rob rob youre losing it you didnt see any of those cars and no warning and the lines on the road are calling to you just stop and sleep and then it will all end forever

dallas dallas which road wrong road the salsa the merengue and no rock and i am tired of the cd player silence listen the road screaming and the stars are behind the buildings now get back rob get back to the right place this cannot beat you you can do this you can and everyone wants you to get back home and more cold dammit there is the right road get the hell out of dallas and south blessed road even your dancing will not cower me i cannot lose to a trip i am hungry i am tired fatigued worn out i am cold and i dont care i can make it less than 2 hours now less it is closer i can taste it dont lose focus the damned stars wont stop swooping and damning me and telling me that it is wrong i am wrong and i can never go back because this is life your life in a car you have never been good at anything as good as you can be at this endurance and pain and this is what you are it is pain and it never ends and it should not end because when it ends there will be quiet and silence and

the sign forwherei need to be and now i am gigglingwhat the fuck i am laughing at myself and the home that is close the home that i never thoughtwas real and my body begins to shut down and my bowels screamandthen i scream not yet dammit 2 more miles and the purple quartet tells me not to leave there are miles left on that highway miles and miles and i was just getting started it is only 1:30 am saturday morning and there are thousands of miles left just get more gas and we could go back to new york or san francisco and dont give up rob you can do this i am hungry i am tired fatigued worn out i am cold i am hungry i am tired fatigued worn out i am cold i read somewhere that half of accidents or something occur within 1 mile of home so wake up rob look around slow down almost there no cold no pain no hunger youre there dont give up you can do this they are waiting and the water is warm and stop

am i alive?coda ....1:30 am saturday it is over and i cannot walk and get the gun and the keys the car can be unloaded tomorrow ah hot water is warm so warm and look at the patterns in the swirls that is a gnome feeding a dragon and that is a woman scowling and then write it down tomorrow.

R. How to get fired from any job

I have been worried, at times in my life, that my main area of expertise is pissing off employers. Since my current endeavors lean towards creative soliloquies (I have a lot of time on my hands, here at night, waiting for the Batphone to ring, signaling peril), I have come to realize, Nay! perhaps to accept, that my experiences with employers may make a suitably silly and / or informative column. I already did my "request" of the day, for Nicki, who only gets two more before I cease my performing-monkey act (I am happy to indulge people's whims, but I already work for free; if you want something, bake me some cookies or something) (not literally, I don't eat cookies) and go in search of new inspiration for material. I have an infinite supply of hubris, electricity for my computer, and urges to disrobe women. Wait -- that last bit didn't fit. Strike that -- make it "sources of inspiration".

With the advent of the internet, muses have become devalued.

So, my Ramble du Nuit is about being fired. Summarily dismissed. Outsourced, laid off, disenfranchised, excised from the payroll, handed a pink slip, shown the door, handed your hat, given the boot, and temporarily transitioned to an alternate state of employment.

We shall approach this in terms of decision trees; having some amount of experience in these matters, I will use sample situations, and the reactions and / or decisions a hypothetical employee might use in a given situation. It is not that complicated -- trust me. Complex algorithms aren't funny, and I am trying to be at least a little funny. Here we go:

The Scene: You work at **BetaMogul Company**, sorting **heklorfs** for shipping. You notice that your supervisor, **Mr. Assdick**, has not implemented any improvements since the Dawn of Man (illustrated in the opening sequences of Kubirck's 2001:A Space Odyssey). You notice that rather than keeping the **heklorfs** in 5 different parts of the warehouse, it might be more efficient to store them nearer to each other, thus expediting shipping, and therefore, profits. What approach do you use?

Approaches:

A. You: **Mr. Assdick**, I think the warehouse sorting is outdated; it seems to me that the **heklorfs**, stacked together, would allow us to ship more units. Please notice my initiative, and pay me more money!

B. You: **Mr. Assdick's boss**, I think that **Mr. Assdick** is off his game. He didn't notice that the **heklorfs** are stored badly in the warehouse, and we need to update our stacking. **Mr. Assdick** is a dinosaur, and I think I could do a better job. Please pay me more money!

C. You: **Mr. Assdick's boss**, I think that every manager in this company is clinging to their jobs like a junkie defending his stash of heroin. None of you has the best interest of **BetaMogul Company** in mind, and I have a 12-part plan to improve everything. Can I get a meeting with the president? Please pay me more money and all of you "managers" start updating your resumes!

D. You: Not my problem. I get paid either way. Hopefully, you pay me more money.

E. You: **Mr. Assdick's personal brown-noser**, I think that someone should tell **Mr. Assdick** that the warehouse could be improved. When you speak of me, speak well. Tell them to pay me more money.

Approach "A", on the surface, seems to be the way to go.

"A. You: **Mr. Assdick**, I think the warehouse sorting is outdated; it seems to me that the **heklorfs**, stacked together, would allow us to ship more units. Please notice my initiative, and pay me more money!"

You are showing initiative, by attempting to correct a perceived problem, you are honoring the chain of command by approaching your direct supervisor, and you are not gossiping or ignoring the situation. Some potential branches from that Approach:

A.1. That is a good idea. I like your thinking! Can you write up two or 3 ideas, so that we can pick the one that works best! You are now noticed!

A.2 That is a good idea. I like your thinking! Can you write up two or 3 ideas, so that I can take it to my boss, take credit for it, and you get ignored?

A.3. Don't you think we would have thought of that already? who are you? Go back to work, and keep your focus on what you're supposed to be doing! I am going to take it to my boss, take credit for it, and you get ignored!

A.4. Don't you think we would have thought of that already? who are you? Go back to work, and keep your focus on what you're supposed to be doing! I am going to do nothing.

A.5. Potato chips are salty! (There is a possibility that **Mr. Assdick** is an escaped mental patient).

These are potential results if you do your job in the correct way. Even here, as you can see by the first branches of the decision tree, it may not work out the way you had hoped. It is the Approach that is best in terms of continued employment, and it is not always rewarded (as you can see, and never mind the chance of potato-chip commentary from a drooling idiot of a boss).

Before we summarize, let us analyze potential branches from the other Approaches:

"B. You: **Mr. Assdick's boss**, I think that **Mr. Assdick** is off his game. He didn't notice that the **heklorfs** are stored badly in the warehouse, and we need to update our stacking. **Mr. Assdick** is a dinosaur, and I think I could do a better job. Please pay me more money!"

B.1. Thank you for bringing that to my attention. I like what I am seeing from you! Keep it up, and here is some more money!

B.2. You should tell your supervisor directly.

B.3. You should tell your supervisor directly. Here is a pink slip for your initiative.

B.4. We have already thought of that. There are reasons beyond your pay grade.

B.5. We have already thought of that. There are reasons beyond your pay grade. Here is a pink slip for your initiative.

As you can see, these are more dangerous waters. 2 of the 5 branches lead to unemployment (not the ideal outcome, in case you were wondering).

Approach C: (the correct analysis, if you are worth your salt)

"C. You: **Mr. Assdick's boss**, I think that every manager in this company is clinging to their jobs like a junkie defending his stash of heroin. None of you has the best interest of **BetaMogul Company** in mind, and I have a 12-part plan to improve everything. Can I get a meeting with the president? Please pay me more money and all of you "managers" start updating your resumes!"

C.1. You're fired! (probable)

C.2. Here're the keys to the company! Show us the way! (improbable; Hollywood's version)

Approach D:

"D. You: Not my problem. I get paid either way. Hopefully, you pay me more money."

D.1. Safe (continued drudgery)

D.2. Why didn't you notice this? You're fired.

On the surface, it appears that there is a 50% chance of failure with this approach, but don't be misled. This is the Approach that 99.99% of workers would take, sadly.

Approach E: The crafty, Machiavellian approach: put the heat on someone else, and hope that you reap any benefits by acting as a sycophant to the sycophant. Also known as riding on someone's coat-tails.

"E. You: **Mr. Assdick's personal brown-noser**, I think that someone should tell **Mr. Assdick** that the warehouse could be improved. When you speak of me, speak well. Tell them to pay me more money."

E.1. They said it was a great idea! I am being promoted to Junior Assistant Sub-Supervisor! Please follow my lead, and here is some more money!

E.2. They said it was a great idea! I am being promoted to Junior Assistant Sub-Supervisor! Please clean the dogshit off of my shoes with your tongue!

E.3. They said it was a bad idea. Nothing gained or lost.

E.4. They said it was a bad idea, so I told **Mr. Assdick** it was yours. He wants to see you in his office.

So, we can see that there are pitfalls when seeking rewards. Are you afraid of losing your job, or are you afraid of complacency and inefficiency (as I am). I would rather lose my job (and I have) because of my righteousness in pointing out glaring errors in the system, rather than let poor decisions stand unchallenged. If you are paying me money, you get all of me. You get my observations, my propensity to streamline a process, and my many years experience as a supervisor and a manager. Also, you get my zero-tolerance for office politics and my disdain for disorganization and inefficiency. Managers get no exemption from me. Bad is bad -- I feel foolish for having to explain it.

For the record, in this hypothetical situation (which is merely a fictionalized variation on my own experiences, amalgamated and nomenclatured), my own choices would be A,B and C. (I tried E once, and felt soiled). Which, as you might expect, led to one good experience out of 3. In one case, I ended up as a Vice-President of the company. In the other 2, I was fired.

Fuck complacency. Fire me if you wish. You still suck. I would rather be right than employed.

S. Martial arts and breaking people

Breaking things can be fun.Objects, certainly, especially if they are not our own possessions: the pang of loss may outweigh any endorphin rush brought on by wanton destruction. People, as it turns out, are also fun to break (physically -- I am not among those who take joy in causing emotional pain). The human body is such a fragile thing, really; it takes a moderate amount of foot-pounds of force to break a human bone (only ten for the collarbone, for example), when the force is applied in the correct manner. It only takes approximately four foot-pounds to break the tarsals of the foot. Ligaments and tendons are fragile bindings -- a twist too far, and the ligament will break or pull away from the bone.Punching a person in the face, the common theme and modus operandi of many a movie hero, is not as effective as a judicious heel-kick to the quadriceps muscle, on average. For one thing, punching someone in the orbital socket sounds macho and invasive, just sheer bad-assery in the flesh, but to practice, go pick the nearest oak tree, lean back and whale that trunk as hard as you want to. Let me know how that works out after the cast comes off of your wrist. The human skull is fairly dense and hard; it serves to protect the brain, your body's favorite organ (possibly tied with the heart). There are many other spots on the human body that are easily damaged while saving you the wear and tear on your knuckles.The art I learned (am learning) is called jiu jitsu; you may have heard of it, but you may not have heard what the literal Japanese translation means: "Gentle Art". As my instructors pointed out, it is gentle on you, the performer of the art, not on the recipient thereof. In Martial Arts such as I learned, we practice *on the mat*, but we take those lessons into the real world. Always be courteous -- when two opponents (in *kumate*, or mock-combat) face-off, they bow to each other, first. It is a Japanese custom that carries over, but not in the Western-World style of a bowing English butler; what the bow before *kumate* states is "I respect you, my opponent, and I hereby apologize in advance for any damage I cause you, since we are not supposed to be fighting to the death" It is an art that does not stress the body of the actioner (known as the "*tori*"), but transmits horrible things at the receiver of the technique (known as the "*uke*" or "victim" depending on whether you are *on the mat* or not).I first began training in 1999, because I had dabbled in the Martial Arts previously, having taken some Tae Kwon Do classes in the 1980s, and felt myself approaching my 30s with a restless sense of incomplete body control. I was working on the second shift at a bulk-mailing facility, and could not attend the regular classes; I began to attend only on Saturdays, which were held just before noon. I was often the only student, with anywhere between 1 and 3 senseis of varying ranks holding class; I was instructed at a somewhat accelerated rate. When it came time for the first belt test, I showed up for testing with a whole group who had never seen me before, nor I they; whispered asides to the instructors asked "Who is this guy, and why are you letting him test? He's never been to a single class!"Being the test to graduate from white belts (which is the belt you receive when you walk in the door for the first time) to whatever color was next (I honestly don't remember; it may have been stripes on the white belt, come to think of it), it was fairly simple. One merely had to demonstrate a few rolls, some basic Japanese, and *dojo* etiquette. The white belts tested first, to get us out of the way, and then the higher ranks tested.Well, then the fun began. Many people think of American Martial Arts *dojos* as like chain-style karate schools that became popular after Bruce Lee began to make movies; the type seen in "The Karate Kid", with lots of KI-YAs and *kata* (which are the execution of a technique on the air, which you clearly see in The Karate Kid, rows of white-bread teenagers punching the air and screaming). Our school wasn't quite like that. The Japanese Martial Arts, the root form of which is *bujutsu* (warrior arts), are meant to be performed ON someone, so therefore, we practiced ON someone ... each other. At the testing, after we had demonstrated sufficient proficiency with the techniques, we had to *kumate* the instructors (in some testers' cases, higher-ranking students, also). This means you got on the mat with a tenth degree black belt (a *judan*) with a sadistic streak, and he beat you until he bored of it, and then he choked you unconscious.Welcome to the world of *bujutsu*!

I am not exaggerating even a little bit. God, I loved training. After my Saturday instructor, Jess (who was a "mere" first-degree black belt, a *shodan*) began to realize that I was sturdy and could take a beating, he selected me to be his regular *uke*, as he was also in training for his second-degree belt (*nidan*). I will not digress into the short anecdote of the time that he reviewed all of his *nidan* techniques, with the two senior instructors, on me, ten times for each technique (plus a few times for each of the two senior men to correct him, also *on me*), just before I drove to New York City on a late-night drive, before returning with severely bruised, purple arms and torso and then dropping LSD and spending Sunday moaning in pain and joyous rapture. Not gonna get sidetracked. I gave some of that feedback to let you know just those few things you would need to know, for me to tell the following tale, which is all true: Our *dojo* was in Maryland, and we had a sister *dojo* in Alabama, of all places. Periodically, my sensei Jess and I drove down to Alabama to give seminars (Jess gave the seminars; I demonstrated by being punched, kicked and thrown, how to uke for the techniques). We usually did it over a weekend trip, and they were kinda fun. The instructor down there, Richard, was an amiable guy, who let us stay at his place each time we went down, and the other members of his satellite *dojo* were always hospitable, and took us to cookouts and to have beers at the local bars after we trained. They were good times. On the one particular trip we made, that I am here to speak of, the testing was a bigger affair than usual. The local *dojo* had borrowed or rented a space for a seminar (generally, Jess gave them in Richard's backyard), and we had the families of all of the *dojo* members in the audience (I think they had around 15 students). It was a crowded show, with buffet tables lined up in the back for a potluck dinner after the testing was completed. Being from the home *dojo*, I was not there to test, but to assist Jess, and to *kumate* if needed (I outranked all but one of their students, and as I previously stated, I am sturdy; I am only 5'9", but at the time, I was 190 pounds of muscle). After the testing had commenced, and it was a good show, everyone was prepared, Jess instructed Richard to basically *kumate* everybody (senior instructors are like that -- every now and then they'll make the other teachers fight everybody). Richard fought ---- hold on, I forgot to give you the basic *kumate* rules of our dojo:The lower rank sets the pace. If the lower-ranked person only wants to grapple, he engages the higher-ranked person only in grapples. If the junior fighter punches, the senior can punch, and so on for kicking. If the lower-ranked person bites, all bets are off, and he can expect an ass-whipping.In *kumate*, we do actually use strikes, and you punch as well as you are able; it is considered bad form to strike the face (again, go back to the junior-versus-senior rules; do you really want a high-ranked black belt, who has been training for years, punching you in the jaw? Stick to the torso).Okay, so Richard, the sister-dojo's instructor, fought his highest-ranking student. Jess -- to my surprise, since I was not part of the testing -- told me to go next, since I was next ranked. I stood, and bowed, and off we went.I always liked to release the senior person's shackles as soon as possible; they hate it when you come in and grasp them and wrestle. I waded in and tagged Richard in the ribs, and then kicked him, so he was free to do whatever he wanted. I outweighed Richard by about 40 pounds, so I was trying to do him a favor, allowing him to use strikes, which were his strength, instead of grappling, which would be mine. I was trying to make him look good. For some reason, however, we ended up tussling and rolling around, and then we got back to our feet, and I figured I'd try a throw on him. Richard attempted to use a reversal on that throw, just to show that he was the higher rank, and that he wasn't going to be thrown by a lower-ranked fighter.He got thrown. As he went into the air, shortly before he shrieked, I heard three distinct "pop, pop, pop" noises, as if someone were puncturing bubble-wrap. Exactly that sound, one after the other. Pop pop pop.Surrounding the knee of the human leg are four ligaments: the Anterior Cruciate Ligament (ACL), the Posterior Cruciate Ligament (PCL), the Medial Collateral Ligament (MCL), and the Lateral Collateral Ligament (LCL). Of those four, only Richard's LCL survived that throw intact. By bracing against my throw, he had forced me to pull him over my leg, therefore all-but ripping his leg in half at the knee.When he tried to stand, about 20 minutes later, we all saw a sight that was slightly nauseating: his leg, when he stood up, bent backward, toward his ass, and it was decided at that juncture that a trip to the hospital was not out of order (Martial Artists are notorious hardcases who eschew medical treatment). I like Richard, and enjoyed our trips down there, and I felt horribly guilty for damaging him, afterward. The whole group consoled me, knowing how badly I must feel, for it was at my hands that this heinous injury occurred.The whole point of my article is this: In the first few seconds after Richard had gone airborne, after I heard his knee shatter, after he thudded to the ground screaming "Broken knee! Broken knee!" my very first reaction was "THAT'S RIGHT! YEAH! BOO YA THAT'S WHAT YOU GET!!!" I loved it. I felt righteous, like a conqueror -- I had taken a high-ranking Martial Artist and not only thrown him, but had destroyed him, savagely.That only lasted for a few seconds, and then I felt really, really bad.The moment of impact was delicious, though. Crushing a competitor feels *good*. It feels *right*.

T. Vegetables and autism

Captain's Dog: Beagle-mutt-mix, black with grey beard.

Captain's Blog, 01/02/2011:

We are searching for the truth behind searching. The eternal nature of man and woman seems to be to search. It is rooted in our need for food and shelter, which is to say, survival. Now that survival, for at least 50% of the world, is not a day-to-day worry (and even for the American poor, such as me, it is not really a pressing issue), we should be content with contentment, yes? We have food, we have homes, we have shiny cars and shiny toasters. Is it burned into our brain-matter to search, to seek, to yearn, to eternally quest for the answers that lie over the next hill?

To our bunkers we can retreat; in our minds, we claim to have a "happy place". We need not desire the newest, fastest, most-hyped designs touted by Madison Avenue, yet we still do. I read somewhere that the innate human desire for things that are "shiny" comes from deep within our subconscious, at the murky level of racial memory, as our brain's means to identify clean water supplies: the freshest and purest water reflects light, sparkling and shiny, informing us that the water is safe to drink. This affinity correlates to diamonds and iPods.

Grocers know this; it is the reason your vegetables and fruits (sidebar: you may notice, when a writer types out the category, that it is usually written as "fruits and vegetables". I made a conscious decision to put vegetables first, so as to unsettle your brains and make you read the sentence, instead of skimming it) are polished with oil: to make them shiny, fresh-looking, premium in appearance. A coating of soybean oil does not improve the flavor of your cucumber, but it does increase its appeal. During Texas' long growing season, I buy my vegetables from the local farms, which deserves its own paragraph.

On a day off, I drive the 11 miles or so up to a widening of the road called "Cedar Springs", off of a side road off of a side road. I turn down a dirt path marked with a sign saying "fresh vegetables", underneath which is listed whatever crops they had harvested that day, i.e. "squash", "okra", and invariably, "tomatoes". After a short jaunt down the rutted, gravel road, you arrive at a farm, with several giant greenhouses, and a little table with an awning set up in the yard. On this table are the day's picks, a cardboard box full of small plastic bags, a hand-written sign listing prices, and adjacent to all of these is a wicker basket with small bills and coins in it for change. A scale hangs from the awning's frame. You pick your vegetables, weigh them, and drop the appropriate amount of money into the basket. Very occasionally, one of the farm's residents will come out to help, but generally, the entirety of commerce is conducted on the honor system. The vegetables are usually the best you've ever had, bar none. Never do they oil anything -- they rely on flavor and competitive pricing to sell their product. It is the one aspect of rural living that I will miss, when I eventually return to the urban north -- delicious fresh vegetables, hassle-free shopping, and the buzzing sound of grasshoppers as I peruse the okra.

I am a city-boy, without a doubt; I love the urgency and the immediacy of an urban sprawl. I love encountering 400 different people, every day, on my way to work or grocery shopping. I love breaking down the walls between strangers: It is amazing, to me, how many smiles you can garner in New York City merely by saying "hello" or "nice boots" to a complete stranger. So insulated and afraid are city residents, that the guarded expressions and and blank visages to me are a challenge. Not everyone is a friend in disguise, but more often than not, a random stranger is a searching soul that likes to be touched.

I proclaimed myself to be a pithy idiot (among other things) yesterday, a status I embrace thoroughly. I oftentimes don't think things through, except over time; often, what you get here, is me undergoing the thought-process in real time. I figure out what I mean by writing it out, as if an etching on a cave wall in Lascaux. If I learn something new about what I believe, by attempting to explain it, then I have done what I set out to do. If you, the reader, learn something as well, then I think that is shiny and fabulous. I wish I could go back in time, get the correct sheepskins from the correct Universities, and act as a lecturer or professor. The thing I am best at in this world is analyzing information, and explaining it in a simpler fashion.

My guess is that the root is from my mild autism; to learn anything, as I sprouted, I had to figure out what was being taught, and then explain it to myself. It has made me somewhat of a pedantic, on the surface, but in reality, I am trying to help. I still have the habit, when walking or driving with other people, of reading aloud signs and billboards, and explaining them to whomever I accompany. Some people find it endearing, others find it to be annoying. For most of my life, I was barely aware that I was doing it. Now that I am aware of it, I do it with a tad more self-consciousness.

As I tell my kids, when they complain about my annoying proclivities, You'll miss me when I'm dead.

As usual (and I think it has become my defining characteristic), I begin by speaking on a topic, I never finish my point, and I end up somewhere else. Perhaps it is best that I am not a lecturer at Harvard. However, if and when I ever do garner my Pulitzer prize, or the Nobel (dream big), and I get an offer to bray at soft young minds about whatever my noodle is fixated on, then I would accept. Columbia or Princeton, too, just for the record.

U. Q& A with the author

Some questions from the floor?

Q: Oh, you're a writer? Are you published?

A: Yes. I post almost daily here on the WWW. Unlike Mark Twain and Charles Dickens, who had to settle for paper copies of their work, my work is out here, visible to anyone with an internet connection. In fact, I am going to call it -- my readership is **7,500,000,000** and growing. Every man, woman and child, from a Chinese 120 year-old Luddite who lives without electricity, to the newborn infant born 4 minutes ago, is part of my demographic. I am more widely read than Stephen King, J.K. Rowling and St. Peter combined. Thank you for your support!

Q: Do you get paid to write?

A: Yes, in shekels. It is in my contract, I accept only shekels. It makes for a bitch to pay my electric bill, but I grin and bear it. I am only kidding -- I get paid in moist, snug, willing vaginas. Women every day just throw themselves at me, it's ridonkulous. I sit here every night and write, which gives my poor penis time to heal from all the pussy-lashing it takes. Paying my mortgage truly takes it out of me.

Q: Have you written anything I've seen?

A: You're reading this, so I am going to extend my powers of imagination to speculate, and say yes. Plus, I have written many common words ... "a", "and", "the", "about", "over" ... as I said, *6 billion people*. I am everywhere, like the wind.

Q: I love your work, but you're so vulgar! Does your family read your writing?

A: You're fucking-A right they do, Bubba.

Q: I love your poetry. Can you do more of that?

A: I love your breasts. May I see them, please?

Q: Uh ... no.

A: There you go. Requests must come with cookies, boobs, vaginas or insight. Pick any two. And I don't eat cookies.

Q: Are you really like this? I bet you're some shy nerd who is henpecked by his wife.

A: Yes, yes I am like this. I am also kind, and I love animals (except, *fuck cows*). But my wife is my biggest fan -- she married me to be along for the ride. Also, fuck you for the veiled insult.

Q: How come you don't write every day? Sometimes there are a couple of days that you miss. I would like to see some consistency, please.

A: I want a cheeseburger and a blow job. I don't see any meat patties or little slices of American cheese, so ... (sound of zipper; screams -- "Oh my God -- it's that snake from that terrible Jennifer Lopez movie! *Anaconda!*)

Q: You have used this method before, last summer, the discussion with yourself. At least you are not plagiarizing other writers' methods.

A: We all plagiarize the air when we breathe, and Shakespeare and the Greeks and probably the Sumerians when we write. I try to be as original as I can -- these are my ideas, love them or hate them (and *6 billion* of you love them so much that you have *the link to my sexiest Episode tattooed on your asses*).

Q: I wonder if you are impotent, the way you seem to overcompensate with sexual writing?

A: Not since I discovered powdered Neal Stephenson hair (available at fine Pharmacies everywhere).

Q: Your good friend was quite in his cups, the last few days, wasn't he?

A: He has been, indeed, almost worrisomely so. I would think he needs to find his ideal woman, but alas, he missed Elizabeth Bathory by almost 400 years. Aileen Wuornos he missed by happenstance. Due to a delayed Amtrak train he was going to take to Florida, he missed his chance to ejaculate mightily into Aileen's love-canal as she shot him in the head with a small-caliber pistol -- the course of true love never runs smoothly.

Q: Do women require the purchase of shoes as a proof of a lover's veracity?

A: The Supreme Court has ruled that a woman allowing a man to make love to her without the pre-payment of Manolo Blahniks is the same as rape.

Q: Is "Uncle Doodle and his Strudel Noodle" the type of thing you might say, out of the blue?

A: Yes it is. Often voluminously.

Q: Do you find yourself amusing? Your ego must be huge. This was worth a chuckle, but not much more than that.

A: It is odd, that when I find something that I write to be funny, I am often alone, or get a mixed reaction, but when I rant about a subject, with all sincerity, I have readers falling onto the floor, peeing their pants. Go figure. Remember -- well, hell, it is actually not 6 billion readers, as you may have guessed; the number is closer to *8 billion*. My blog is like a fax machine to poltergeists: The Dead love me, too. Aileen, if you're reading, I am sorry my friend missed the train. He might have straightened you out with the right pair of Jimmy Choo's.

V. Social Network creeping

This column is about a specific sub-culture of internet activities; some of you may recognize parts of it, some of you may be surprised, but very little of it is completely fabricated out of thin air. It is, however, completely and totally a SATIRE. I do not -- let me repeat that -- NOT advocate stalking, creeping, misogyny or disrespect of women in any way, shape or form.

Hello, all you creepers, or creeper wanna-bes! Dr. Teddy Jack has some good advice for you today, so let's get right to it, shall we? There are oh ... so many luscious little tasty bits out there to stalk.

1. Becoming Friends

Of course, the first part of cyber-stalking is gaining access to the ladies you wish to stalk. Making friends with a hottie is not impossible, if you play your cards right.

A. Play games -- For some reason, hot chicks love the silly Facebook games like "Farmville" and "Cafe World". These are stupid and inane games that hot women like to have in the background of their computers while they are at work, pretending to be productive. Most of these games are run by Zynga, which is a front-company for a Russian prostitution ring -- they know what time it is. Zynga has forums where you can "friend" other players of these games; you'll need 1,000s of friends to access the sweet young things.

B. Make friends through other friends. Facebook very graciously "suggests" friends to you, so the more hotties you friend, FB will gladly suggest more in the same vein; Zuckerberg knows when you are chasing hoochie, and encourages it. Facebook allows you to friend up to 5,000 women (per account); you should be able to access untold amounts of personal photos of women to which you can spank your monkey after dark.

2. Making Contact

Okay, now she has accepted your friend request -- now what? Well, we'll show you how to proceed, with examples. The best start to creeper status is to drool over her pictures; chicks love that, especially if you sneak in a few dozen cliches, poor grammar, bad spelling and sexual innuendos into every comment.

Wrong: "This is a great picture. What a lovely family you have!"

Too nice. Too *middle of the road.* She'll think you're a 50 year old married dude with no hair (which you are), and treat you -- at best -- like a "friend". Screw that!

Better: "hey you look great! you must be an angle!"

An improvement toward creeper status; You included the "Angel" cliché, and misspelled it (double-creeper bonus word score), but, you did not mention sex in any way. Too weak for a creeper.

Right: "so sexy so hott! hey your hot i bet you go al night long baby message me and we can "play" together!"

This is the correct way to say hello; let them know you're a "bad boy" who is only interested in her private parts; pay no attention to her marital status or interests -- after all, you're the man, she's there to get YOU off.

3. Closing Escrow

The ideal for you, as a creeper, is to get have the object of your desire send you naked pictures of herself, while you send her sexy messages, until you make your keyboard sticky. Afterward, you can post her nudie pics to 4chan for the Lulz. If she "blocks" you after you've gotten off to her images, so be it. There are lots of girls to stalk. Try to keep the heat on:

A. Poke Her constantly.

Chicks LOVE the "poke" feature of Facebook; some of you may be trying for creeper status and make the mistake of poking too soon. Wait until she has swooned over one of your "baby your so sexxy tits" comments on her pictures from the family reunion; then you "poke" her, and keep doing so until you are dead or in jail.

B. Send her weird rambling poetry about streams and clouds.

Chicks love words, and it doesn't matter if they make any sense -- that's the great part about poetry! Try to rhyme occasionally, but don't get married to it; good poems don't have to mean anything to anyone except her. A good start: "baby im so forever hot for you my dick is full of your faces picture".

She'll know what that means.

C. Hit on all of her friends, too.

Women love competition -- all chicks are trying to compete with each other for the attentions of the best creepers. Make sure all the bitches be slamming on YOUR jock. Insult her and comment on her friends' tits -- she'll be worried that you don't find her "fuck suck-alicious" anymore.

We hope that this has been a useful primer for those men among you who are wishing to step up their game and get some serious creepin' going on. We have seen too many amateurs ruining it for the pros; it is time that the Stalkers got organized, and danced this bitch into the 21st Century.

Remember -- "No" means "my boyfriend is here right now".

W. Feet

Even though there may not have been a recognizable gap, in these my writings, I must confess that there has been. I have not yet done a column about feet. My feet, specifically, and if you don't think that is a glaring discrepancy, you have not seen the world from the viewpoint of feet.

As much as we will all be served by an orderly presentation of subject matter, I do believe that I will edit this post before I offer it for your approval. If I do it correctly, you will not know that I have dipped my quill more than once, you will merely read a tale that has a beginning, a middle, and an end.

Let us begin with shoes, shall we? Shoes: as an adornment, as protection, as an aid to locomotion, shoes have evolved from strips of animal hides tied to the feet to prevent podiatric freezing into strips of animal hide assembled by brown toddlers to make millionaires of homosexual designers.

Shoes can be practical. They are a shield against broken glass, nails and gravel. Shoes can be fabulous -- there is a reason women's sling-back heels are called "fuck-me" pumps. Shoes can speak of moods or poverty or shame or feistiness. There is a shoe for every mood, and a shoe for every apathy.

Breasts have been beaten and much wailing has been made of the high-end sneaker industry's "targeting" of inner-city youth (read: black children) in reference to the sales of Nikes and Reeboks that retail for $150.00 a pair; the protests are inherently racist when you fail to hear similar complaints about Manolo Blahniks and Jimmy Choo's stringy abortions selling for $800.00 (and more) a pop. I think overpricing a pair of footwear shows a natural, forward-thinking progression; if you can convince anyone, of any creed or color, that your leather-and-nylon contraptions are worth a 1,000% mark-up, then you are treating all peoples equally: as consumers. It doesn't matter if the buyer is wealthy, starved white women, or Lebron James-wannabes -- charge them the coin of the realm, as much as the market will bear. We believe in capitalism, yes? Welcome to freedom.

A disdain for shoes gripped me, most of my life. Recently, I have begun to appreciate variety in my footwear, with boots and my first pair of slippers recently purchased. As a youth, however, my feet served as the barrier between me and the environment. I would travel barefoot, on walks to the beach in a Florida summer; with the asphalt cooking in the 100 degree heat, my feet would sear and fry like bacon on a grill. I would reach the shoreline itself, with its blistering-hot sand, and sharp and cloying seashells, and allow the thousands of stabs to attempt to penetrate my soles. So infrequent was my cobbling, that the bottoms of my feet were calloused to a thickness of perhaps a quarter of an inch; I had an unfeeling dead layer of skin as my body's defense against the abuse I doled out on an everyday basis.

I have severely lacerated the bottoms and sides of my feet so many times that I have become indifferent to foot injuries. In another column I detailed how I worked in a machine shop for six months <u>standing on a dozen broken bones</u>. I played in a grassy field in my childhood, and cut my foot open badly enough to need a slew of stitches in *consecutive years*. By the time I reached teenage-hood, I didn't even bother getting sewn up anymore. Two anecdotes guest-starring Chris, real quick, and then back to the post: My first "job" of the honest sort was the summer during my 14th year, when Chris and I got the opportunity to do some scut-work for his uncle, who owned an asphalt-paving company. The work was done at night, due to Florida's prohibitive heat, and the labor was of the "pull this wheelbarrow over here" and "use this shovel to clean that over there" variety. One night, Chris and I were moving this to there, and I stepped onto an exposed piece of rebar, which easily penetrated the side of my sneaker, and blood proceeded to fill my shoe. Chris' uncle was non-plussed (i suppose I wussed out by bleeding), and he allowed me to leave the site, but wouldn't even drive us back to where we staying. I had to walk a couple of miles, in the middle of the night, with a gaping foot wound. I didn't even realize, until now, what a massive fucking cocksucking dickcheese Chris' uncle was (and probably still is). Talk about a workman's comp claim. Bastard. Anyway, the injury to my foot isn't even what sticks my memory -- it was the long walk back (it must have been 2 in the morning or so).

The second anecdote was a piece of stupidity that bit me; Chris and I were about 16 years old, walking along the sidewalks of 3rd Street, in Jacksonville Beach (we never drove, in Florida, which is why all of these stories include a copious amount of walking), when we approached a beer bottle that had been broken, but not completely. The bottle still retained its round shape, being only partially fractured, and I decided to smash it the rest of the way so as to neutralize it (or just to bust shit up; it is hard to discern the motivations of a teenage boy). I stomped my foot down onto it, yet did not hit it squarely; the bottle pivoted as my foot descended on it, and the sharp edges stabbed into the side of my foot with the full force of my stomp. I was wearing fairly new white Reeboks, at the time; I remember, because as soon as I crushed the bottle, and felt the stab in the side of my foot, the shoe began to turn into a maroon color. My shoe was absolutely filled with blood, you could hear it squish as I stepped. I sopped and slid and squelched the mile or two home on that one, as well. For neither of these lacerations did I seek medical attention. Feet bleed, I reckoned, and they would heal, if you left them alone. I think I put a band-aid on the wound, but I am unsure.

At any rate, the abuse and tortures that I have slavered on my feet might lead you, dear reader, to believe that my feet are cruelly neglected and gnarled stumps that connect me to the ground. Oddly enough, this is not the case. Due to sheer luck and grace, my feet are lovely things, my second-favorite feature of my own (after my nose). They are strong, scarred but lived-in symbols of all of the fuckery that life can dole out, yet we as humans can survive. I have always hated to cover up my feet; they show what a person can take without crumbling into dust. I have stabbed them, crushed them, subjected them to burns; I have stood within the chemical morass that is Portland cement, daring my feet to complain at the searing pain. I love my feet, but it is a tough love. I do pamper them, on occasion; I rub them with oil and praise them with soft coo-ing.

Without them, I wouldn't be able to wear shoes.

I make no judgments about people's choices, ultimately; I may grumble, because it is expected (agreements and sycophancy are dull). I generally adhere to a live-and let-live philosophy -- I know of many people, including my wife, who just can't get enough shoes. Are they symbolic of beauty, or of freedom? Are they a form of expression, like a Heavy Metal t-shirt was to a lad when I was a headbanger during the Reagan era? Are they an accessory, a form of protest, a flaunting of wealth, a sexual invitation? I have answered none of these questions, even for myself. I will say that a pair of shoes is like an evocation of a scent; the appeal is to the self, and while we may appreciate when another person admires our selection, the footwear is used to first please us, the wearers. What we may say by our choices depends on what we might say in conversation; I am a practical man with occasional flair, so therefore, my shoes are often nondescript, with a pair or two that are of high quality and noticeable panache. When I was on the prowl for female flesh, I had a pair of handmade Italian boots that I would wear, not because I favored them, but because I knew women did.

Like a peacock with leather feathers, shoes can say: My eyes are down here. The boobs may sag with age, the belly may bloat with laziness, but a new pair of shoes is just a shopping trip away.

X. Entrapment

We begin at the end, this time, because often I get inspired at only the last sentence or two, cut and paste a title from something I write there, and the stuff leading up to it is related only by placement, not congruency.

Among all creatures, man is the animal that ponders himself, and the brain is the only organ that can analyze itself. Now that my point is made, I can move on.

I was given a selection of 3 songs to choose from to write this episode, 1) **John Murphy - Sunshine (Adagio In D Minor), 2)**

Muse- Blackout, and 3) Charlotte Gainsbourg - IRM. I leave it to you to figure out which I chose as my accompaniment; I must have some playtime.

Sincere hopes for happiness are worth the magic beans that you planted in the ground to grow them. I wished for a wristwatch, when younger, received it, and took it as a sign of God's existence. I wished for peace and forbearance among humans, when older, and have not received it, so I take that as a sign of God's absence. Am I to blame for the death of God? Were I more unswavering, would there be peace and understanding throughout the lands? I apologize for the lack of deity under which we currently labor; you have my permission to begin nailing random people to trees if it helps you cope with the electric bill just a little better.

Why we do shout "Oh God!" when we cum (stereotypically -- I say "Oh Carl Sagan!", but I have always been eccentric, if not fey)? I realize God is supposed to be omniscient, but does he really need to see the exchange of fluids? Is he counting sperm, so as to chart the amount of time in Purgatory? If women do a "dry rub" (over the clothes, thinking about Viggo Mortensen or David Boreanaz or the guy from Burn Notice), does God put a checkmark next to their names in the Book of Life? (Or Several checkmarks, as women have the advantage of multiple sins, without rest). The Lord's name taken in vain is a Sin, so they say: It is the first one on the list of commandments. God really, really hates it when we acknowledge Him during our moment of Stupidface. As I see it, you have two choices: Stop cumming (which bodes ill for the continuation of the human race), or pick a new exclamation to yell during the moment of climax. I propose a new cum-shout. I propose that you (and we all) yell "OH PANDA!" the next time you hit your high note; it might help in two ways. One, it will remove the daily sinning from those who fuck, and secondly it might send psychic urges to the goddamned Panda bears who are too holy to bump uglies. Go practice with a lover, and remind each other to shout "Panda!", and we can only hope that we all make it to heaven and the Panda Bears procreate prolifically and take over the world and then we will be caged and afraid to screw in public, as they are now.Perhaps it is merely that -- who the hell wants to fuck with an audience? Some of us do, especially 18 year old (wink, wink) runaways who are trying to break into "modeling", but for the most part, we like to do it in a dark room with the curtains drawn, preferably with the children doped on NyQuil and the neighbors in Guam. That same God who demands that we cum quietly and sinlessly allowed us to discover that out bodies were sinful in nature back in the Garden of Eden. Speaking of that, doesn't that seem like a massive design flaw, or obvious trap? God: *Do whatever you like, EXCEPT to eat from THIS tree.* Adam and Eve: *Okay (crunch crunch) Hey, delicious apple! Hey -- I'm naked! This is ... bad?*You know what, Yahweh? You don't want them to have the fruit of the Tree of knowledge, LEAVE IT OUT. Free will, my ass. ENTRAPMENT. Case dismissed. Homo sapiens, you are free to go.

Y. Fiending for coke

See it:Waiting at three in the morning, huddled in the dark, with only the faint illumination of streetlights coming through the window. A small studio apartment in Queens, New York. Two men, one of them scruffy but handsome, 26 years old, with swept-back medium-length brown hair and a nervous habit of pursing and unpursing his lips as he fidgets in the sofa; the other, even scruffier, with clothing as disheveled as it can be while still maintaining form and function, like a hobo secured by safety-pins, with hair greasing its way from every visible area save for the eye-sockets.The two men were waiting, anxiously so, which was obvious to God, any random observer and the blind Monks shaving sheep in Uruguay; they spoke no words, but every glance they took, at each other, at the floor, at the intercom on the wall by the front door, bespoke an expectation of desperate and interminable and vitally significant events.The only sounds were from the dust-coated box fan in the window, pointing outward for ventilation, and the occasional automobile passing by on the street four floors below. The metropolis that they inhabited is known as the city that never sleeps, and its name was apt, in part because of junkies like these two figures we are watching.We watch them from within, as it were, as no witnesses were present in real time, but the memories and moments of these anguishing languishments shriek across the years and miles. We can see them, cast over in shadows and mired in despair and weak soap; we can hear them, smacking lips and grinding teeth and tapping toes and restless sighs; we can abhor the moment and watch, fascinated, by savage men pushing civility to the brink of casualty. We fear the weakness that prompts grown men to wring their hands as they await the arrival of a narcotic.This moment, the snapshot that we see, is like a flip-card series of drawings, the type that you would practice as a kid: Draw a stick figure in a textbook, near a bottom corner, then move it a tiny bit on the next page, and add other actions as you wish, and so on. Primitive cartoon making, of course, which often featured stick figures perishing in comical ways. This scene of two men is the same, on any night, pick a random witching hour, and look into the window, and they would have exhausted the supply of cocaine that they had purchased earlier in the evening, and unable to deny themselves the completion of that rush, they would send a hapless, homeless musician (who served as their drug connection) all the way out to Brooklyn, on a late-night subway train, armed with cash and the pleading admonition to hurry back with more cocaine, please more cocaine.

Every night seemed the same. We see this diorama, and we feel that we are glimpsing an event, some process by which we may learn something new. Alas, it is but a lie, since this same situational comedy, this tragic mope-opera, played out for all time, an eternity and glancing and fidgeting. When the pressure built to a certain point, the two men would delve even lower into basal instinctive gathering: They would fall to their hands and knees, as if on an unspoken signal, and begin to taste all of the crumbs and detritus that lay about on the floor. They were hoping for an impossible discovery of a piece, a chunk, a grain of crack cocaine would have fallen, unnoticed, in their particular, systematic methods of handling the fresh, tin-foiled packs of the sweet pale rock. Such a dream was laughable, but the search was inevitable: every night, after perhaps an hour of waiting, they would root like hogs to eat the bits of cat litter that were dusted around on the floor.The culmination, the apotheosis, the pinnacle, the zenith, the top of the tower, Everest's peak, was the sound of the buzzer on the intercom. Every second of every bloc of seconds of every minute of every bloc of minutes of --Everything led to that buzzer's sound, knowing that the drugs were safe, the cocaine had come home, that all would be well again, and once more, dear friends, could the reaching for the stratosphere begin again ....See it:Waiting at three in the morning, huddled in the dark, with only the faint illumination of streetlights coming through the window. A small studio apartment in Queens, New York. Two men, one of them scruffy but handsome, 26 years old, with swept-back medium-length brown hair and a nervous habit of pursing and unpursing his lips as he fidgets in the sofa; the other, even scruffier, with clothing as disheveled as it can be while still maintaining form and function, like a hobo secured by safety-pins, with hair greasing its way from every visible area of skin save for the eye-sockets.See it:

Z. The drug crash

The humiliation of sobriety. I decided to send cocaine on its way (and I would go mine), due to a flaming crash and burn when I tried to woo a woman in a bar, the night before Thanksgiving, 1997. She was what we would now call a "MILF", a woman in her 40s, with great legs, wearing a nice skirt, and enjoying the attention (I could tell) of a 29 year-old man. We talked and we flirted and then I got way too drunk and became violently ill and I completely lost whatever suave aura I had had because I couldn't walk.

I had only ended up in the bar in the first place because I had bought $150 worth of crack cocaine that I decided it would be a good idea to smoke all within the space of 20 minutes. I thought my heart was going to explode – the pounding beat seemed to signal my doom, in my paranoia, so I ducked into the first pub I saw and quickly downed a couple of beers, for the central-nervous-system-suppressing nature of alcohol.

It worked quite well – after perhaps three beers, my pulse was approaching normality, and I felt quite smug about my brush with idiocy, and focused my newly-found good mood on the lady seated next to me at the bar.

I can still remember her combined look of loathing and pity as I stumbled out of the restroom. I was to fucked up to flirt, which for me, counted as the "bottom".

Cocaine and I have had an amicable divorce ever since.

Part Four: Fall, Rise and Fable

A.   The Fall

So, a long chain of events came to fruition not with a bang, but with a ticking clock:

I had been running a construction company (new luxury home construction, a focused niche, but a viable one, in Greater Washington, D.C.), with a few small clients, one big one, and another Marlin on a hook. The primary client of mine (a Chinese family; my main contact was the woman of the house, whose Americanized name was "Lily") had introduced me to another Chinese lady, a restaurant owner with an empty lot of land who also wanted to build her own custom McMansion.

With the cash provided by my mother-in-law, I had started a construction company with some industry contacts, a brain, and the internet. I enlisted my new company on several "construction bid" job sites, gotten a license and insurance, and made a living by virtue of having a minuscule payroll and an amiable and knowledgeable nature. I had no employees save myself, hiring crews for individual jobs on a contract basis (as is the norm in construction, at least at first), and I was gaining a reputation as an honest and straightforward contractor. I never exaggerated completion times, problems or costs: I always spelled out for customers (and contracted laborers) exactly what I could provide, how my costs were calculated, and what I expected from everyone involved. My goal was to provide a refreshing difference from what was (and presumably IS) the industry standard: lying.

My credo was my downfall. In order for honesty to work, both parties have to participate.

The impending recession (based upon the collapse of real-estate values) notwithstanding, I ran into irreparable harm when I discovered (about a month too late, as it turns out) that my client was under-capitalized. My company had shut down physical operations for January of 2007, the weather being too prohibitively cold for carpenters, electricians and plumbers alike; I took the opportunity to travel about and see some friends around the country. Before I left on my little mini-vacations, I ordered the windows for the house, since custom windows require a 3-4 week lead time.

I will assume that most of my readers are ignorant as to construction processes, so I will quickly summarize (quickly, so as to avoid boring itemization): You get hired. You acquire plans, then apply for permits, hire sub-contractors including concrete, excavation, demolition, plumbing, electrical, carpenters, and masons, and then you begin to do the job, with city inspections in between. You demolish and clear what exists on the property, and then an inspector signs off on it. You excavate to the required depths, the plumber drops his tie-in pipes in (it is difficult to add plumbing AFTER you have dumped 100 tons of concrete on the area) and lay out footers, and again get inspected. You pour concrete, add the steel, inspect, and then began to build the frame. It is pretty simple, really.

So, since my customer, Lily, was paying for the house herself, we worked on a "pay-as-you-go" basis; every week or two, she would hand me a pile of hundred dollar bills, and I would order supplies, pay off my subs, and drop a little bit for myself into my company bank account (all of which was audited by a CPA, very above-board and legal). Everything was proceeding well and hunky-dory, except for one small issue which had not been resolved, but which Lily assured me we'd take care of when needed.

Oh, did I forget the problem with excavation? Yes, I did. As I said before, I was honest about problems and costs. I bid the job, allowing $25,000 for excavation and disposal (the house had a ten-foot basement), but as soon as we began to dig, we hit a layer of granite. Solid granite. Rock. Did I mention that this house was in the town of "Rockville, Maryland"? I should have seen THAT coming. Anyway, immediately upon notification from my excavators that the costs were about to increase (removal and disposal of rock, as opposed to soil, is an expensive proposition), I called the customer. "We're going to run into cost over-runs on disposal", I told her. "Dumping rock is about 3 times as expensive as dumping soil". Since we were operating on the aforementioned pay-as-you-go, she recommended continuing, since my weekly "draw" (the amount of cash she was putting in, about $10,000 a week) was adequate -- it merely meant that we would run out of money ahead of schedule, months down the line. She assured me that we could tack on costs at the end, rather than at the beginning. Well and good, I foolishly said, and dispose we did, at an over-run of $75,000 (the whole project was $650,000, it was a sweet project, I thought when I signed on).

Of course, I should have stopped immediately and re-negotiated, in writing. I didn't. Hindsight is 20/20.

So, on to January of 2007. I ordered the windows, to be built while the site was closed for the winter, and I paid for the order on my American Express Gold Card.

$35,000.

When I returned, refreshed and happy, from visiting Chris and Jim, and my sister and mother in Texas, I met with the client, and mentioned the forthcoming expenses -- including the AmEx bill -- and told her we would be ready to roll the following week. It was at this moment that she informed me that she was out of money.

There were months of back and forth, and all kinds of recriminations and arguments that I won't detail -- the details are truly dull -- but it was that moment, early in February of 2007, that my company died, murdered by my own honesty and trust.

Then, of course, I decided to take another vacation, and go see some Spring Training baseball in Tampa, with Chris and Todd. Might was well whistle while the house burns down, especially if you have no fire-hose. We limped along in 2007 on loans from friends, attempting to save the company long enough to get the next contract.

My finances began to decline, an understated way of saying that the carefully constructed financial status I had attained was de-constructed, a bit at a time, as loans came due and mortgages screamed for attention. By the summer of 2008, I had taken a job as head of housekeeping in the local hospital, as the banks and lawyers fought over the scraps of money I had left. The construction industry overall declined, at that exact moment in history -- there were no other projects to be had, and all of the sub-contractors who had been screaming for payments only months before began to call me, pleading for leads on jobs, any jobs. I was happy to disconnect THAT phone number, I can tell you. What a cock-up.

I made my last mortgage payment on my house in July of 2007. After that, the money was gone. Maryland is not an inexpensive place to live, and my expenses were running about $4,000 / month, (not counting business expenses), a nut I could not meet. My credit dropped like a rock, and I no longer thought of attaining the status of "upwardly mobile". I began to focus of feeding and housing the family. There is nothing like crisis to dismiss the trivial from your mind.

The hospital job did not proceed as well as I had hoped; perhaps due to the unending stress of bill collections and lawsuits, I was somewhat humorless in my dealings with my superiors in the housecleaning department. I have little tolerance for political posturing and incompetence under the best of circumstances; as my bills fell further and further behind, I became ... I will say *critical* of the management. Vocally critical. Openly critical -- I would tell my boss of his shortcomings (with of course, recommendations as to how to perform more adequately). In my own defense, I had been managing people, budgets, and projects since I was 19 years old; even though my boss was older than I, my experience as a supervisor exceeded his own. Unsurprisingly (in retrospect), he did not appreciate my superiority. My house was foreclosed upon in November of 2008.

In February of 2009, I was fired from the hospital. And I thought I was broke before that.

Thus capped the rapid decline from middle-class business owner to poor (and yet, surprisingly un-bitter) unemployed artist and writer. The main concern, of course, was my wife and two children, whom I had ultimately failed. As a provider and source of stability, I had taken a shot at independent wealth-production and bungled it. Because I trusted another person, in a business deal, to uphold their side of the bargain.

Because my employer, the Chinese woman who called herself Lily, denied that she had ever agreed to pay for the cost over-runs, and expected me to make it up out of my own pocket.

I still trust people, that is my failing, really. I learned a lesson, I suppose -- don't trust HER. Everybody else still gets the benefit of the doubt. Perhaps I am better off not running a business: I don't want to take advantage of anyone.

In April of 2009, while subsisting on food stamps and loans (gifts) from my sister, I went to Texas to do some improvements on my sister's empty house. She had bought it while residing in Central Texas, but was currently employed in a job that required her to hop from town to town; the house stood empty and in disrepair. I drove down, on her dime, and replaced some tile and windows and various things, and then the opportunity to rebuild presented itself: She offered the house to us, as a place to live, rent-free, until such time as I could re-build my self-confidence and fortune. With the rent in Maryland costing us $1,400/month (on earned income of $0.00), it was a decision that made itself for us. I had no where else to go.

Yeah, the Pride went beforeth the Fall. I was not proud of being on the bottom.

And then -- the light. I should say, "Light", capital L. I reconnected with my mother, with whom I had had intermittent contact for several years, and, thanks to a new friend in New York City, re-discovered my ability to channel pain and misery into Art. Stories. Poems. My ability to say everything and nothing, but to sound good doing it.

I have so many people to thank for this award, it is hard to know where to begin ...

I have always wondered (having an inflated ego and sense of self that I do), how I would perform during an award acceptance speech. Would I throw out an amusing quip, loosening up the crowd with a laugh, and then tell an anecdote that offers gratitude to the appropriate people? Would I pull out a written list, and drone out the names of everyone who had ever helped my pursuit of Art? I am currently of the mindset that I would be humble and charming, and as a way of saying thank you, I would say "you know who you are". Since there are not a billion people waiting impatiently for me to finish, I will list some of them here, in no order: Mom, Dad, Todd, Chris, Iris, Sue, Javi, Little Chris, Marianne, Betsy, Jim, Clarissa, Maddie, Elias, Sharon, Karina, Rachel, Ray, John, Fiona, Rebekah, Sue B., John Wayne T., Zack, Bob, Ron, Emily, Debbie, Kim, and every other person on the face of the Earth. Time constraints prevent me from listing you all, but look in a phone book if you need to see your name in print.

I am just a failed building contractor who smiles at the banal trials of life. Strife hasn't killed me, and never will. Only death has what it takes to silence my keyboard, and death better bring some friends to the party -- I hate being interrupted.I still have a universe to save from itself.

P.S. Oh, and I had to add this. The New York Yankees are a team that draws reactions of love or hate -- they seem to command absolutes on the scale of fandom. I am a certified Yankees fan, unapologetic and committed. The World Series Championship run of 2009, while drawing the ire of most baseball fans, helped my karmic mood immeasurably. So, thanks, guys. I won't forget one of the bright spots of that time period.

B. Eureka

I break. I have been broken.

With no permanence or external acknowledgment of failure, *I heal*. The scars map their own stories -- if you care for an explanation, I will tell you about almost any one. Being held down by a giant is a helpless feeling. How much struggle should one engage in before capitulation, surrender and death?

If you argue in favor of an issue, is it possible (in any non-theoretical realm) to concede error? How many arguments end with the statement, "Oh, yeah. You're right. Thanks for teaching me that." ? Few?

Why do we argue? A definition of "insanity" (from Albert Einstein, no less) reads: "Insanity: doing the same thing over and over again and expecting different results." If very few, if any, arguments achieve any form of knowledge progression, is it not then more logical to simply attack one's debate partner, physically? After all, Hollywood Westerns taught us that any disagreement can be solved by a punch in the mouth. Why do we pretend to civilization?

I know I am savage. I remain calm primarily because it is too addictive a sensation to allow the beast to break the chains -- like positive feedback oscillating out of control, I fear a descent into violent debauchery would be a state from which I would have no path to return. There is a rapture in rending flesh, in manual entropy; I have enjoyed the dissolution of corporeal corporations. Death is a dreaded fun, to be feared by the bull's eye, not the arrow.

I like things that are soft and gentle and cool and gentle and pink. My adoration of women may be merely an admiration of their color scheme and textures. Where I lumber, they glide; where I disseminate, they assemble. **It takes two to build a zygote**, much to the chagrin of sexists on both sides of the imaginary battle-lines.

When I call myself "savage", I suppose that I mean *I am unafraid to descend to the level of danger.* I used to have a saying, which I will reprise: I cannot wait to die, but I have things to do, first.

It is very annoying to interrupt a thought in the middle. Concepts are gifts from you to yourself; never look a gift anterior superior temporal gyrus in the mouth (if it had one; since it is part of your right temporal lobe, in your brain, if it has a mouth, you have an absorbed conjoined twin in your head). Don't fuck with the Maestro -- he is rolling.

Eureka. Attributed to Archimedes when he was taking a bath, it is translated as "I have found it". I submit the same answer that I give, when I hear of any scientific or exploratory discovery: **I didn't know it was lost**. Columbus discovered a vast continent full of peoples to rape; they were unaware that they were missing the teachings of Jesus and the joys of smallpox. The Europeans set them straight, for sure. Eureka,

Squanto, *I have discovered your land, and if you don't mind, we will put our living room over here.*

Here, Have some Death.

I lost my little R2-D2 action figure, back in 1977. I found out, years later, one of my "friends" had stolen it. Eureka! It is good discover someone else's wisdom -- maybe give 'em a set of quotation marks or footnotes? We who think for ourselves would appreciate the shout-out.

P.S. -- I have just been informed that I am an unlikely candidate for Alzheimer's disease. I like the little things in life that go well. Never mind the necessities, to paraphrase Dorothy Parker; budget the luxuries first. It may be that I die of some form of cancer (several forms run in my family's genetic make-up), but having my wits about me until the Reaper's scythe descends upon my neck gives me optimism. Even more than I had, and I am fairly upbeat, anyway. I've had dudes try to kill me -- I really can't worry about a water bill compared to that.

C. Relationships

Maintaining a relationship. Hell, I actually have some expertise at that (although, I will stipulate, at the beginning, that it is likely to be from the forbearance of my spouse, more than anything I have done, that has led to my lengthy marriage).

But, I'll write about it, anyway.

People think I am an Enigma. I am a shameless flirter, very open with it on The Social Network (which movie lost to "The King's Speech", last night, at the Academy Awards, in the category of Best Picture; as I have seen neither film, I will reserve commentary until I can speak with information); on Facebook, it has been observed, I speak frankly about sex and fucking and I approach women constantly and I have many female friends.

I have been asked, ad inifinitum and ad nauseum, "Does your wife know you do these things?" and I answer, of course, "Yes". Once I am known to a person for a while, they find that I am telling the truth. Hey -- my wife reads this blog; if she didn't know about all of my habits, wouldn't I be in danger of revealing something, somewhere? So, yeah. I ask women for pictures. Naked pictures, too.

Why so? Well, since the advent of the World Wide Web (I have been wired since 1994, flirting and meeting and such), pictures of unclothed females are no longer at a premium. I can go to Google, type in whatever preference I have in flesh (for example, due to the current infatuation with hairless bodies, I simply type in "hairy pussy" if I am in a random mood), and literally millions of returns come up. I can stare at digital reproductions of naked flesh until it is redundant and dull, which happened to me about 1998.

The days when a young boy needed to sneak into dad's bedroom, while the parents were at work, and pilfer a copy of Playboy to gain a rare and forbidden glimpse at unclothed flesh are long gone. We have, culturally, so far surpassed "saturation" that an image of a naked woman has little value, in coin of the realm. We have oscillated far out of control, to be sure, but it is not my place to analyze the ramifications of pornographic ennui; rather, I speak on my own peccadilloes.

When I meet a woman on-line, and we find ourselves amusing each other in conversation, I sooner or later get around to asking for (usually pretty directly) a photograph of some sinful bit of flesh.

Well, as far as I can tell, here's why: I hate limits and artificial standards. When I hear "no", I try to break down barriers and debate and convince my conversational partner to say "yes". Pictures of oneself are relatively banal, to me: I'll send anyone who asks a picture of any part of me they want. Why would I care? Google works for women, too. If they want to see tushes and penises, there are few limits to the quantity accessible to anyone with a computer. If I have any shyness, it has nothing to do with sex organs. So, to my mind, a picture of boobs, butts and bush are nothing that even registers as noteworthy. However, I do realize that many women consider them very personal and private. To my way of thinking, breaking down that wall is one way of breaking the ice. If they are finally willing to show me what they look like topless, maybe they'll finally speak on important matters without all of the masks, lies and excuses that people accumulate after years of living in this confrontational world.

So, it is kind of a way to say "This is the real me". I am sure that reads as rationalization, which I care not; as far as I can tell (analyzing myself), it is true. Generally, once I have exchanged some wonky pictures with a female friend, then the relationship can begin, for me.

I have no idea how it is for you -- this is not a "self-help" column. You may prefer sharing tales of childhood trauma. The laws of buoyancy, babe: Whatever floats your boat.

So, back to marriage. Early on, I struggled with convention. I found my wife to be infinitely understanding of me, and high on the compatibility chart, from the very beginning. I don't know if she "understands me", or any sort of psycho-shorthand, but she surely realizes my ultimate destination, which is: artistic expression, freedom, love and empathy. That's really all I am. I am not a sex fiend -- I just find it infinitely amusing that people make such a fuss about a thing so natural that our world would disappear if we didn't do it. Every living thing, everywhere, would die, without reproduction.

Shitting, too. What the hell? Feces, I understand, have a taboo due to the high bacteria content (they should be disposed of cleanly, away from food supplies and drinking water). But, Sex? Everybody should love sex. Your body sure does. Sexually active people live longer and happier lives than those who deny their genitals the freedom to get wet with another set of genitalia. Once again, we have to yell at religions and the religious for corrupting a natural process. Adam and Eve (once again to work from the Christian viewpoint) ate from the Tree of Knowledge, and immediately covered their good parts with leaves (I wish they had been poison ivy leaves, and that shit would have stopped right there) in shame. SHAME.

Every man, woman and child on Earth who has ever lived has had either a penis or vagina (for the sake of complete accuracy I will concede that .0002% of children are born with neither sexual characteristic). Everybody has one or the other. I have a penis. Seeing another man's penis just doesn't rattle my chain. It does not sexually stimulate me -- I wasn't made that way -- but, it doesn't bother me, either. I feel fairly certain that most women feel that way about vaginas. They just "are". Mammary glands are not sexual organs -- they are feed bags for nursing young. Sorry, guys -- your affinity for boobs is more Oedipal than sexual. Teats are a good thing; and before it is argued that (some/many) women derive pleasure from a man playing with nipples and breasts during foreplay, let me point out that the same effects can be derived from kissing a woman's neck, right below the ear, while exhaling slowly (results may vary -- I knew one woman who had erogenous elbows). Are we going to criminalize necks? The madness must cease! Neckfuckers of the world, unite!

I am not extolling the virtues of what I do. I have been called perverse, and I take a perverse pleasure in the title. Nobody wants to be thought of as dull. I am here to confess that it is mostly a shtick: The two women I have adored most, in my life, I did not see naked in any casual setting. The first woman of which I speak I first saw unclothed as I undressed her before our first lovemaking session. The other I have not yet seen nude, which tickles me pink.

Sometimes it is good to wait on the fruit from the Tree of Knowledge. I'd rather pluck it myself.

D. Time-Slip

I do enjoy liquefying my ideologies in a word-processor for you -- a verbal smoothie for a Sunday afternoon, perhaps. I awoke too early, fooled by an erroneous clock-setting on our coffee maker (my house has a dearth of clocks; only the computer and coffee maker have time-keeping capabilities), as the coffee machine claimed it was 4:00 p.m., when it was actually 1:30, granting me a total of 4.5 hours of sleep. It is no wonder I felt hung-over when I awoke (although I drank not a drop of alcohol last night). I now know that I was not ill, merely stupid (put not your faith in Mr. Coffee, my son, the great DiMaggio was just cashing checks --[I will make an exception and explain my Dennis Miller-esque obscure sub-references: In Hemingway's "The Old Man and the Sea", the titular Old Man, Santiago, advises his grandson to 'have faith in the great DiMaggio', and after DiMaggio's baseball career, he became a spokesman for Mr. Coffee. The dual pun was in no way intended to disparage Ernest "Papa" Hemingway, Joseph DiMaggio or Mr. Coffee {TM} nor any of their fine products]).

When I arose, prematurely, I heard the sound of my son wheeling in our grocery cart (we have one of those upright, wire wheeled carts for carrying groceries, a carry-over from our New York days, when we used it to carry groceries home, as we never had a car until we moved to suburbia), carting in the fresh vegetables and such we needed for today's planned meal, shish-kebabs. I stumbled out of bed, without shirt or glasses, in a hazy, hang-over-esque fog, and peered in to glare at the coffee maker's clock. The time read 4:02. I then thought that perhaps I was struck with a touch of a flu bug or some such (I am very rarely ill), since I felt terrible. I began to make coffee. When my son returned to the room, I asked him where his mother was, and he told me that she had gone on after the shopping excursion to the Social Security office (our son has Aspergers syndrome, and his medical costs are covered by S.S.), and he walked back by himself.

I was unsure of the time (unknowingly, then), but I was aware that it is Sunday. My wife, oh I love her, but she has never been good with days of the week, let alone dates -- government offices are of course closed on the weekend. I pondered hopping into the car, to go fetch her from her misguided errand (the S.S. office is on the other side of what is admittedly a small town), but -- considering the time -- I decided to fire up the grill, and have dinner prepared for her return.

We generally eat dinner around 5:30 - 6:00 p.m., you understand. So, we started the food prep. My son and I chopped up the marinated beef, and then yellow onions, jalapeños, cherry tomatoes, green peppers, mushrooms and summer squash, and slid everything onto bamboo skewers. I then went outside and lit the grill (I actually let my son light it, for his first time with the flame), and then we started the rice -- a slice of jalapeño and some paprika, salt and marjoram in the water, 3 cups water, 2 cups rice and a tablespoon of E.V.O.O. We skewered the beef on one set of sticks, and the vegetables on another (to allow for disparate cooking times).

It is important to time all these things properly. Once the rice went into the boiling water, I went outside with my first cup of coffee, and had a cigarette in the pleasant warmth from the sun (it is around 68 degrees and clear today in Central Texas) and listened to the meat sizzle. The grill had such focused heat that it took but a few minutes to char the meat, and then switch them with the veggies. They were done just in time to turn off the burner under the rice.

Then my wife got home, just as everything was plated and steaming. Yeah, when it comes to cooking, I am good like that. I may have missed my calling as a short-order cook, except for my temperament. Hurling a cheeseburger at a petulant patron would not have been out of the realm of possibility; come to think of it, that may be a desirable trait.

Anyway, we enjoyed a fresh and friendly and funny family feast (alliteration cheating, I know, fuck me with a dented donkey dong). After the repast, my wife retired to our room (whence resides the television in our electrically-challenged house; do you want to know the definition of a "shack"? A house which is so old that only 4 outlets in the house have three-prongs, so our television can only be run in our bedroom, the kitchen, or the bathroom. We opted for the bedroom, rather than try to fit everyone in the tub during "House"), and as I sat in front of my computer (which is in the living room, run by an extension cord to a source of power), she called out to me "It's only 3:00!"

It was at this time that I realized that my carefully crafted meal-creation and my perfectly synchronized times were all for naught. As a breakfast, however, it was fabulous, and healthy. Minimal fat and starch content. I have every intention of slimming my fat reserves down to sub-Chris Farley levels. I have oodles of muscles that should be displayed for the education and edification of the *greasy-haired, pants-around-ankles stick-figure Justin Timberlake wanna-be lads* who couldn't budge a carton of milk without a hand-truck. These are the same misguided boys who think that a girl that weighs 75 pounds (30 of those pounds in the form of silicone breast implants) is a feminine ideal, as long as she has waxed every hair from her body (save from her over-sized bobblehead that wobbles precariously on her chicken-neck), wears butt-floss thongs and has a tramp-stamp tattoo on her lower back. Kids forgot how to eat and think, but thank god they have Herculean callused thumbs from texting each other so often that they can only speak aloud in emoticons (WTF? LOL! FML. IDK?).

Anyway, make a note. It's fucking Sunday, and at the beep, it is 5:15 p.m. Central Time.

Beep.

E. I am

I am not a representation of anything.

I am not a work of fiction, or an amalgam of traits, or a figment of anyone's imagination.

I am not an obligation or a curse to be borne or a fool to be suffered.

I am a man, and my name is Robert Jon Anderson.

I am stubborn, self-centered, boorish, obnoxious, moody, cantankerous, prideful, elitist, dismissive, obtuse, reticent, lazy, gluttonous, hedonistic and wrathful.

On the positive side, I am generous and kind.

I stand ready to rejoin a world that will not have me; regardless, my preparations are made for the plunge into the breech. Feel the scents, see the singing, hear the rough surface of the eternal optimism.

We, that is me, hopes all will go well,

we know for a fact that it never will;

we pray for heaven and plan for Hell,

We sin with regret until we are still.

We need a thought! Something funny! Dammit, something must be worthy of a rant, a rave, a railing against! Surely, some politician raped a dog, somewhere?

Surely, Lindsay Lohan is in trouble again, this time with a felony charge? Bad example -- the slut is not worthy of my words, nor sperm. I wouldn't fuck her with Pee Wee Herman's pecker.

I never watched the Pee Wee shit, when he was infamous. Every time I would see him on the tube -- pimping for Mtv, or whoring his movies, I had the single, focused, solitary urge to punch him very hard -- Hard, like with full chi and body-mass and intent to damage -- right into his teeth. I wanted to see his incisors and bicuspids and molars explode from his mouth, like a dental orgasm of porcelain caps, blood and calcium and screaming, shrieking Pee Wee ---

Yeah, was I the only one in America completely unsurprised that he was arrested for yodeling while masturbating into the hair of fellow moviegoers in the porn theater in Florida? (editor's note -- needs fact-checking). I only wish he'd been caught with an underage boy doing the stroking for him -- that would have truly fulfilled my preconceived notions of that anorexic ass-plug.

Nah, Pee Wee is old, old news.

What needs yelling about?

Other than the fact that I am alone?

In a crowded room.

I think -- no, I know, I wish to sin again. I don't care about right and wrong, and I am okay with picking up pieces afterward. I want to fuck some other woman, dear god, I won't name names; It may be that desire burns more fiercely than regret. I am sure it does, and I will make that aphorism # 254 by me.

Desire -- the wanting. That feels like a smoldering rush of blood to the cheeks; a flush of everything in your body coming to life at once. Your flesh is on cruise control, and then -- a smell. A smile. A word, an image, a whisper in the ear, a cacophony of innuendos, of flirting, of regressing and forgetting and the encouragement of remembrance. We distill the annoyances and swords of the oppressors into foe, we call them problems or we shrug and tip the bottle into our mouths even if we quaff not moonshine. Our still huddle in the closet with no lights is akin to a drug, a desperate rape of our own intentions, NO I CANNOT but I must I must I must feel it I must touch it I must take her damn all the world for not serving her to me.

And me to her.

Like a drug that I parcel out as if on a cracker, just a nibble, don't do more than dip your tongue in my madness for it is real, this insanity and I am real.

I am not a figment, nor an obligation, but I am a desire.

F. I got a rock

I think the angle of my approach is shifting, which is good, a stagnant paradigm is merely a splash of graffiti on a wall: I have begun to shape the stories or recollections or anecdotes of these "memoirs of a recluse" to demonstrate that I can exhibit my formative experiences like a boa in a frozen glass cage. Instead of twisting my facts to fit my theories, my past is spreading gesso (titanium white, natch) over this organic cotton fabric we shall see as a canvas.

Whew. That was a long-winded (what else? I get paid by the word, 0 cents each, so it behooves me to prattle to the limits of my vocabulary) introduction to a simple chapter.

I am no real fan of Charles Schultz' long-running comic strip "Peanuts", starring Charlie Brown and Snoopy, but I cannot deny the iconic status of its lead characters. It is a twisted childhood, indeed, that deifies a dog as a Hero, a Mensch; I loved Snoopy, but related to Woodstock. I despised Charlie Brown's spineless nature, but felt a sort of kinship with his *schlemiel* status. I hated Lucy with the passion of 1,000 wet pizza-farts. Linus I found to be an enigma (although I, too, had a baby blanket that I kept hold of until I was 10 or 11 years old), Sally reminded me of my own younger sister, and Peppermint Patty reminded me of the girls on my league soccer team who could run faster than I. Snoopy as the Red Baron, however -- ICON. But, and I hate to break my chain of thought, I digress --

In those dark days before cable, we had 4 television channels, and we watched what the networks (ABC, CBS, NBC and to a lesser extent PBS) told us to watch. Our generation (those born between around 1960 and 1980 or so) watched Marlon Perkins wrestle gators on Sunday Night, before watching whatever Z movie Disney felt like tossing to us like a scrap of raw meat to our ravenous appetites. The adults watched "60 Minutes" while we bathed and got our stuff ready for school, and then we all watched the same thing. In that time-before-time, we could all go into school the next morning and talk about whatever programming was on the previous night, because we all watched the same thing.

My parents were always foursquare against violent programming, so I would miss out on being part of the "in-crowd" when the previous night's movie was something violent. I remember, in the late 1970s, when the networks aired "Rocky", and I was not allowed to watch; the next day, the kids were talking excitedly about Rocky getting his eye cut open by a razor blade, in the climactic final bout, and my mind drew terrible images of eyes and blades and blood by the bucket. Years later, when I saw Stanley Kubrick's interpretation of Stephen King's "The Shining", the hallways full of blood were something close to what I had pictured for Stallone's shiner-reduction. My mind carves images from granite and sea-shells -- this is my gift to you, dear lovely-gracious-wonderful-adored-welcome-Reader. Without you, I am listening to my voice echo inside a Bass Drum (a trick I discovered in my basement studio in Long Island to duplicate the "reverb" effects that Lennon used for "You've got to hide your love away").

ANYWAY ---

The networks played the same movies, every year, like an Orwellian metronome: "The Wizard of Oz", "Mr. Roberts", "The Sound of Music," "West Side Story," and of course, the "Peanuts" cartoons, slotted to fit the season. Every Halloween, the "Charlie Brown Halloween Special" would air, and a part of that sticks with me like a punchline. After trick-or-treating, the Peanuts gang returned home to compare their take; Linus spoke of the bounty he had gathered, Lucy declared the fruits of her labor, and Charlie Brown announced, balefully, with an Oscar-worthy delivery that *still* cracks me up: "**I got a rock**."

I have moments in my life of a soaring ego: I know I am fairly adept at writing down my thoughts, I know I am pretty clever about solving puzzles, and I know I am not ugly. There are, of course, moments where I AM the Charlie Brown, the blockhead, standing in front of hordes of hysterically laughing and mocking peers, like the titular "Carrie" (another Stephen King reference), covered in pig's blood, humiliated, worthless and idiotic. It is then, after I run from the room and hide under a shrub in the back yard, that my mind wails to itself:

"I got a rock."

Life gives you lemons, make lemonade, right? What the fuck do you make if life gives you a rock?

Well, the answer could be thus: One saves the rocks, and makes an impregnable fortress, a Keep to wall out the soft and the yearning, the girls in their skirts whose flesh calls, but whose mouths say "Go away, Greaser!" (Self-loathing memory: As a child, I always preferred to bathe shortly before school, and I still do this for work, in fact; I would always arrive at school with wet, slicked-back hair, and earned myself the nickname of "greaser").

I prefer to be like the little pig, and use the rocks to build a modest home that will withstand the oscillations of fortune, but whose appearance is pleasing and inviting. Mine enemies can tear it down not, but neither can the fickleness of natural disasters. Please wipe your feet on the mat, we prefer to keep the dirt outside.

I got a rock.

G. Coffered in Cedar

Every now and then, I see a picture of someone I know, and I feel a spark of recognition, to go along with the shock that I feel: Oh, that's right, that's what she looks like. Now I remember.

I see this which brings me to that: How come I can't tell my mind how to file information? My thoughts get randomly stacked, and I am fortunate that my processing speed helps to overcome a fragmented hard drive. I have, filed away, an image of the woman trying on a blouse stuck next to a kid I knew in 4th grade, which is next to the scent of freshly-mown grass. Of course it is, Brain, how could I doubt you?

Thank goodness the image of my teacher's panties isn't filed next to the mental picture of my grandmother. I think some things should be left unassociated.

Would I be completely stupid if I had no memories? I mean, do I really need to know what happened in 1066, for example, or who Sacajawea was? Why can I not discard the unused information? I seem to be a trivia sponge.

I hate, hate, hate -- as an employee or as a husband -- I hate when something that I have set down is moved. I can put anything down anywhere, and find it at a later time. Always. I don't need a system or to be organized; where I run into problems (as an employee or as a husband), is when another person moves the item after I have set it down (even as little as a foot or two). My wife and I have finally agreed -- after years of the ONE thing that causes me to bark in annoyance -- that I have a desk and a dresser, which she will not touch, ever. Those two areas are sacrosanct, extremely messy, and I can find anything I need without having to think.

In the rest of the house, I am lost. I ask her. I barely know where we keep milk.

At work, I have had to learn the procedures of others. Not a daunting prospect in, say, a dispatcher's office, where there are few items to locate (mostly we need a computer, a phone, and a radio), but more of a task at a print shop, with 20 or 30 active orders for various departments, and I, of course, would set whatever I was working on wherever I dropped it.

That used to drive the other employees nuts, if I wasn't there to locate the item, soothe the customer's frazzled nerves, and essentially swallow the ejecta from the volcano of commerce.

That is a novel metaphor.

I don't miss retail work at all, although the job itself greatly enriched my life and my set of skills. I learned a series of bad habits working in Manhattan (during the late 1980s and all through the 1990s), habits which are of dubious usefulness in Scared Shitless, Indiana: When I was dealing with a customer who was incorrect (or "wrong"), who was rude, or who I just didn't like, I would tell them, quite literally, to "Fuck off and get out of my store". The ideals of customer service in a crazy-busy big city are different than they are in Podunk, and, more honest, to my way of thinking: In small towns, you receive indifferent service and sullen looks. In my shop, if I served you (and there were very, very few that I kicked out arbitrarily; I wasn't the Xerox Nazi), you received good quality work, as expedited as I could make it, and at a fair price. If you swung a stapler at one of my worker's heads (I miss that crazy old bat), I may actually have some grudging respect for you. On the other hand, if you ignore what I say to you, and then bark at me to hurry up, I am going to throw your shit back at you and invite you to exit the establishment, at a faster rate than that of my foot greeting your ass.

Have a nice fucking day. That was my goodbye to the rude.

I do miss Manhattan, and not just for Katz's deli and John' Pizzeria and the subways and the women in skirts (I don't think Texas allows a woman to wear skirts, unless they are made of denim, and she is about to ride a mechanical bull at a strip joint), but for everything. New York is an amalgam of everything.

You like Art? Fuck yeah, they got Art. Some of the finest museums in the world, galleries out the wazoo, and artists themselves, decamped near subway station entrances, with their wares on display.

You like illegal drugs? Fuck yeah, they got drugs -- and they deliver.

Theater? Broadway, baby. Stores? You must have heard of Fifth Avenue -- not to mention, Greenwich Village for those of us whose toilets are made of porcelain, and not gold. Women, men, food, crafts, street performers, parks, the fucked, the funky, the beauteous and the hideous, all things packed together on an island 2 miles wide by 13 miles long. Manhattan is New York, and New York is my adopted home.

Sorry, got a bit wistful, there.

Peace offered, long stood, settled onto new bog; Trials coffered in cedar wood, broken down to log.

I got "Intraductal papillary mucinous neoplasm" in a word game, which plays to the strength of someone who went to school; my response was the jaunty little verse, above, that plays to my strength -- prose.

Never bring a knife to a gunfight, I guess.

As always, I do what I can, I wish I could learn it all, but I am limited by curiosity. My curiosity mostly runs to -- well.

Never mind. Some things you just don't talk about.

I do wander about satisfaction. Is there ever a point, during life, when I will be content with the status quo? Where there will not be something that I wish to change, or see changed?

Sacajawea traveled with her husband, in addition to Lewis and Clark, did you know that? For once, in the History books, it is the guy who gets fucked. No one remembers him (Toussaint Charbonneau). About time. That's what Charbonneau deserves for gaining a wife by winning her in a game of chance -- irrelevance.

Oh, and the Battle of Hastings, which took place in 1066: It was the decisive battle in which the Normans (known as "Frogs" or "French persons") conquered England. The Normans used "combined arms" battle (archers, cavalry and infantry) which rolled over the English. It was fairly important in mankind's history of learning to successfully kill one another other.

I did enjoy watching the woman try on blouses, though. It was sexier than if she had been naked.

H. Intarded

When it comes down to actually putting words in here, I am the arbiter.

I credit my sources and inspirations where due, but the assembler of verbiage is Your Humble Author (and some of you roll your eyes at "humble", since I have a {partially-deserved} reputation for arrogance; in my own defense, I will say that any hubris I display is protective coloration).

Rejection is my way of life. I have to possess a modicum of cocky self-assuredness in order to speak. If I think that my opinions or solutions are worthless, I would remain silent.

If I believed that I could tell no tales to entertain, I wouldn't. Call that arrogant, if you will, while you hide behind the doorway and allow me to absorb the fire and ire of the disenfranchised.

I am wearing black. I mourn the death -- nay, the aborted birth -- of intelligence. We, as a species, came *so close*. Thank goodness the illiterate, by definition, cannot speak well enough to spew bile in any mass-consumed fashion. For that, the illiterate turn to snake-oil salesman, the hateful and the Intarded (a new word I choose for those who can learn, yet choose --seemingly intentionally -- to maintain their ignorance; I blended intentional and retarded, by which I mean no disrespect to those with Down's Syndrome). Some people should know better, yet choose to vomit their crazy on the rest of us.

We, the thinking, may laugh them off as demagogues or Ann Coulter, but the danger lies in the huddled sheep that cringe beneath the overhang of the cave, fecalating at the rumble of thunder. The stupid listen to the crazy people; they don't know any better, because they are stupid. The clever seem to be less entertaining, so we are ignored in favor of the colorful ravings of lunatics.

We, the intelligent, need our own crazy person to throw bread at the masses, while passing along good and smart messages: Love, Peace, Joy, Compassion, Empathy. We need an entertaining madman to lure the sheep back to the fold, but not with hate and fear: Rather, with optimism and hope.

We need another Hero. A funny one. An inspiring screamer who likes people, who does not preach morality, but lives life as a decent person instead. Someone who can inspire a room to laughter, but believes that no one should ever go hungry.

We go back to hubris, now -- I nominate myself.

I don't think entertainment should be centered around hate, but around the funny little differences between you and I ... I don't believe that a yellow person has more or less value than a brown person, or a white person is better or worse than a green one (we must be careful not to exclude extraterrestrials, if we preach inclusion); (while we're at it, white people are really kinda "peach", not really white).

I think the peach people and the brown people need to realize that *people* is what we are, and together we are worth more than divided (I'm stopping before I get all preachy).

Men and Women are all that we are, or can ever be. Let us embrace our humanity and eat the beasts and the fishes (except the cute ones); (side note: I do believe that Panda Bears are inherently evil, but since they are bears {okay, marsupials}, we can continue to use their names for screaming orgasms and ignore them otherwise).

United, We Stand, Divided we what?

Fall.

Street gangs understand this (on a small scale), and so do countries, because we have created divisions where none exist. Instead of "We, the Human Race", we have decreed that we are "We, the human race, from the Right Side of the Tracks, north of where the Supermarket burned down, back in 1921, but just shy of Danny Meachum's Farm". We cannot wait to ally ourselves with a group of like-minded folks, so that we may look down upon others. Why?

Threats that face all of humanity, whether we like it or not: Hunger (because McDonald's just can't build them fast enough)

Alien Invasion (like Klaatu and E.T., not Mexicans)

Bears (fuck bears)

Snakes (fuck snakes)

Meteors and Comets (unless we keep Bruce Willis on retainer -- a small price to pay)

Spiders (definitely, fuck spiders)

The Earth (hurricanes, tornadoes, tsunamis, earthquakes-- face it, our planet hates our shit)

The Universe (entropy always increases -- no matter what, everything that we are made of will one day fall apart)

Things that Humanity threatens itself for:

Land (land that was here before us, and will be here after we're gone; so, technically, the right to stand upon a patch of dirt, presumably with a flag denoting possession, like football)

Hubris (OUR penises are most definitely bigger than the penises of those with yellow skin)

Resources (since the lessons about sharing from "Sesame Street" apparently are lost in the annals of adulthood, much like the concept of "fairness")

Unfamiliarity (differences in cuisine, religion and culture just piss people off)

I say, let the yellow folks eat live octopus, let 'em worship the fat man's statue, and don't worry about how good or bad their driving is: You ain't perfect, either.

We condemn the weaknesses in others that we forgive in ourselves.

I.   Saturday Night (a break)

I almost always have the approach, as I start one of these blank pages, to do something a little off-kilter, to utilize style in my presentation of substance. Just a soupçon, you understand, a dash of panache; I am frustrated, when I read other writers, and they choose write entire columns or novels in some sort of unique "style" that, in my opinion, detracts from the words.

That is to say, I will write stream-of-consciousness, on occasion, but only for a paragraph or two. More than that, and it feels contrived, to me. John Lennon, as magnificent as he was a linchpin of the Beatles, wrote a couple of books, and each one was page after page after page of convoluted rambling. Dude -- use punctuation, for shits and grins, complete a thought. Style does not replace the key element of what it is that we commentators do -- communicate. If the reader is bedazzled by our approach, but is simultaneously unsure of what the writing was trying to say, then the failure is not in the reader for failing to understand the "Art", but in the writer for failing to understand his purpose.

Yes, we writers try to entertain -- I hate being bored by an article or novel or poem, I would not wish that on those whom I ask to read my meager offerings.

Yes, we writers strive for clarity of unique vision, to establish our voice -- but, it does no good if our own voice is in a language that is not commonly understood. I write for myself, but even more so, I write for you. It is imperative that we speak the same language.

I have babbled, in these Halls. I have styled and profiled and complained. I. Have. Spoken. In. Ways that. Annoy. Even. Me, if it went on too long.

I have rhymed, for the girl, I am supposed to say "woman",

I have mis-timed my churl for what amounts to no reason.

I have used prose, unspeakable words in the right places,

I honor my Rose, the girl with the infinite, beautiful faces.

See? I throw out tidbits of style, then I return to my regular speaking voice. Most of you know, yeah, that's how he talks. Just moving along from thought to thought, dabbling, tantalizing, allowing the sum of life's experience to sample the innermost quests. I don't like to expound, I am a buffet of ideas. If you want depth, you talk to the smart ones, the professors; if you want breadth, well, I am your guy. I live my desires, and try everything, so that I know what I dislike.

I like working, the feeling of being productive. I do not mean (necessarily) working for money, as employment, I mean to say I like focusing on an endeavor until the eyes ache from fatigue, the muscles cramp and your bladder is shrieking from neglect.

Still -- there is a delicious sense of emptiness, of the vacuous state of completion or interruption of "taking a break". Allowing one's self a breather. In the midst of even that which you love, there are times when your body and your brain crave a chance to sit on a park bench and watch squirrels hunt Old Folks. A Saturday Night for the Universe, a time when most everything is being plugged into the charger or set on the shelf. In the United States, most everyone enjoys a common hiatus -- as a metaphor, call it Saturday Night.

When hubbub exhales.

THAT is a hellacious introduction to this chapter, this wheat from which I beat the chaff -- a sexual metaphor ONLY when I say so (and I do not, as of yet).

You're going to have to swallow some chaff, every now and then (nope, still no dirty meanings, wait for it). I hate editing these things, except when I am telling a story; the one purpose I have in here is to speak freely and allow you to have a conversation with me, a conversation in which my ears are plugged with silent kisses.

I always volunteer to stand naked before you, having placed my fears aside to chase my greatest gift; either you all are voyeurs or rubberneckers, or I am an exhibitionist -- perhaps the truth is somewhere between.

I have been known to scream in public, but I have also been known to stand silent and roll my eyes. The mood dictates the reaction. For once, I want one of you to stand naked before me (still not it, hang in there), and let me in.

I am open, it is true, by choice -- by nature, I am very reserved and shy and shuttered; I have decided that extroversion leads to more love and sex and laughing.

I know there is a thrill to being touched, when your nerves transmit happy signals to your brain; allowing another soul to come inside you (*that was it*) creates in us the desire to substitute sex for love and can label a gentle touch on the arm to be an invasion.

So many of us are afraid that an honest admission will destroy us. Make yourself vulnerable for one second -- and your heart will be ripped out, shredded by your weakness, by seeking love we have sought our own destruction.

Yes, that is true. When we love, we are unarmed.

I. Night Stills

The dark part of the dusk rapidly slams the door on daylight, here in autumn on the plains. The day surrenders its gray and misty illumination and trades it for an envelope of lightless amnesia. None remember the dark--they forget the light.I can think of few circumstances requiring more optimism and cheer than a cold evening; to accept the dreary reality of the surroundings would initiate a descent into an abdicating madness of dread. To lay eyes upon death and smile knowingly is either courage unbound, or foolish ignorance made flesh.The end of everything, stacked henges and poetic musings of eternal pain and suffering.Stacked stones, peat supports the bones,the skeletons of men whose death alone and bitterdark lack of sunlight shone--stay buried for another year,marry who you wish my dear,no child of children breathe in the clearof the circle of dust that are the citiesof yesteryear;scratch out your wordsyour message what it may be--"do unto others,live free and love, use your eyes to see, your ears,of course, to hear"--leave talismanic rumblings, even call them ramblings,carve your tattoos into your families,your walk, her smile, dad's shrug and mother's wiles;if there is another start, having a card in the deckprobably would smart.If it is all to end, then let us pretend,there is a reason to do anything at all that does notinvolve seeding the ground with ignorant saplings.

K. Women in Skirts

What is the appeal, to me, the sexual excitement and swell from a view of a woman in a skirt? A glimpse of the forbidden. I think my inchoate sexual responses were based on curiosity, and then, once the information about my sexual desires was garnered (i.e., what women hide under their Poodle Skirts), I think a glimpse, a glance, a sudden, expected vision of these lusted-after fruits of trembling became an obsessive focus. During the summer, a woman might go shopping without wearing a brassiere, if her breasts are not too copious to travel unsupported; when she leans over (in a t-shirt), or turns to the side (in a button-up shirt), a sharp eye can catch a hint of nipple, or even the rosy pink of an aureole; such delicious invasions were the stuff of daily fantasy reconstructions. I am sure that it is an affront to the woman, although I never meant for it to be so; I certainly never bothered the individual (unless she noticed my questing gazes), I just wanted to see what I was not allowed to see, like looking through a peephole at a woman undressing (I never had such a peephole to practice on). I worked in SoHo, in Manhattan, for 11 years. The Spring breezes down Broadway, channeled by tall brick buildings, lifted and swirled skirts, displaying the many fashion choices a young lady might make for her undergarments. Once, in a bodega, I was in a line at the register (which was located near the front door). Ahead of me was a lovely young woman (whom I knew as one of my own customers, at my shop across the street from the bodega). She was wearing a modest, knee length skirt. It was a windy day outside, and as we were waiting to be served, the door opened by an entering patron invited a great gust of wind inside, and the woman's skirt flew nearly over her head, revealing a nice grey pair of cotton underwear. She was mildly embarrassed, of course, trying to smooth the skirt back down, and it hung up on the waistband on the way down, continuing her exposure. The waiting customers, mostly Hispanic men (and myself), gave her an honest round of appreciative applause, which garnered a laugh (of embarrassment or relief, I couldn't say).For her, it may have been mortifying, as unwitting as it was, but for men, it was merely a nice view of a smooth and round young female ass, in minimal clothing. We liked it. Nobody bothered her -- she paid for her goods and departed, with no further comment. When next I saw her, I did not reference the event (although, I did watch more carefully as she left, having a better idea of what she was wielding beneath her gowns), paying attention to hip sway and footfalls.Are men pigs, leering uninvited at any potential opened vagina that falls within their purview? Probably -- I do know that I have witnessed many (other) men shout out catcalls and wolf-whistles to attractive women strolling by. Some women seem to take it in stride, smiling at the attention, some women scowl and refuse to acknowledge such invasions -- I have no answer. I don't Holla at a fine miss whose beauty and form or smile and legs and hips tickle my fancy, but I don't ignore them, either. Are we allowed to see what our eyes can see? Does modesty extend to the viewer? If a woman lost her clothing, due to a misfortune, would we not lend her a coat to cover her nakedness until she was succored? Is not a breeze causing a skirt to billow revealingly a mild misfortune, and averting one's eyes the proper thing to do? I don't know. I do know, that when faced with the reality of it, I gazed upon sculpted buttocks, and enjoyed the view.I also know, that on that same street front, Broadway, on a crowded day, a scruffy-looking junkie came down the street, physically assaulting a woman as he traveled. It was obvious that they knew each other, some sort of sordid, drug-related lover's spat, but, he was a man, and she was a woman, and so within they came within grabbing distance of me (I was on the sidewalk, smoking, with Jim and John), I handed my sport coat to Jim (or John), and shouted at the man to leave her alone, and ended up with one hand on his shirt, holding him, as my other arm was drawn back, cocked, threatening to unload on him if he didn't stop touching her. "Within my sight", I think is how I put it, offering to chase him down the street if he manhandled her again on Broadway. Very Reservoir Dogs, Jim put it, a street confrontation between street toughs. A small gesture, to be sure, but nevertheless, my ass is on record as having been put on the line for chivalry.So I will look at your underwear if I can, but I will also protect you as well as I am able. I have no better solution than that.

L. Hands

I have an attachment to hands that do what they will. My hands are what opens the doors in the physical realm; my thoughts and transgressions against complacency unlock the metaphysical doors.

Two hands, eight fingers, two thumbs -- the usual amount.
I can lift things or build them, or gently take pieces of clay and make horses and barns and make miniature art and then dump them into a pile or bake them and give them to children to be piled and forgotten. I can tack a nail, drive a screw, heft a plank, wax a car, pet an animal. haul a line, tie many knots, twist some pipe-cleaners into a scene of cowboys and indians in a not-very politically-correct diorama of instant amusement for myself and observers. My hands are gentle clubs, soft

scars and applied pressure; I can tickle ivories or strum nickel-coated wires to generate rhythmic sound.

I can type rapidly, manipulate charcoal and slather gesso; I can wield a brush or roller or edger and decorate a room. I can squeeze the bridge of my nose while shutting my eyes to exemplify exasperation. I can stroke my penis, tickle a clitoris, pinch a nipple, clasp a face, entwine my fingers into hair; I can crush cans, thread a needle, slap a face, punch a wall or a sternum, thumb-strike a temple or *shuto* a jugular vein. I can open a jar, lift a handle, raise a refrigerator, scoop water to rinse my face, pick a nose, scratch an itch, rub a bruise, take a pulse, butcher a steak, carve a turkey, twirl a bowl of pasta, toss a green salad and pinch off a garden hose.

The combination of power and precision that my versatile extremities possess has taken all of my life to achieve. I shave deliberately strengthened them and taught them to fold paper airplanes, and I have less-intentionally broken them. I have hurt and I have helped others with my hands.

I can maul or caress, create or destroy. The world interacts with me through my sensory inputs -- eyes, ears, nose, skin, tongue. I interact with the world chiefly with my vocal cords and my hands. I wish to have hands that cause sexual desires and dreams of dark occurrences in the wilds of abandon. I am pleased to have hands that can play music or twirl a microphone stand like Jon Bon Jovi did in his video. I have never noticed my hands as being the everything that they are; I would as lief lose a leg before sacrificing even a single digit from my environmental manipulators.

I do lose patience with my fingernails, however. When I broke one of my ribs (the second time), I began a regimen of drinking Knox gelatin, at the recommendation of one of my Dojo-mates who had suffered cartilage damage in his knee. He swore by drinking gelatin (as do I, now, having tried it -- it is a good supplement for calcium or ligament damage), and I began to drink a packet or two a day as my rib healed. Side effects include your fingernails growing stronger and more lustrous. Just what I needed -- a useless (partially useless, I know that they protect my fingertips) re-enforcement for an extraneous body part.

If only Knox gelatin added girth to "that certain part of the male anatomy" as those late-night commercials claim (I don't understand; almost 50% of the world has a penis, and much of the other 50% has heard of a penis -- how come we can't say "penis", especially at 2 am? My guess is that the vagaries protect the manufacturer from lawsuits brought on by unfulfilled claims: "Hey, we didn't claim you'd get a longer donk, we said a 'certain part of the male anatomy'. If you read the fine print, we meant that it would enlarge your prostate and kill you. Happy Fucking!!!")

But no -- a broken rib led to stronger and faster-growing nails on my fingers and toes. Swell. I am the envy of secretaries everywhere.

I once awoke in the dark to an unknown sensation of danger. I had only been asleep for a couple of hours, but I thought I smelled smoke.

I stumbled downstairs, and out the front door, to sniff at the air. I was hazy and not-quite-awake. When I sensed nothing, I turned to re-enter the house.

Staying with us in the house was my younger sister, who had a boyfriend over that night. When I exited the house, to check the air in the yard, she closed and locked the door behind me (she thought, in her 16 year-old way, she was being funny). We had a nice front door with glass panels in it. When I reached the door, and felt that it was locked, my sister waved at me and laughed from inside the house.

I punched through the window in the door, so that I could reach through and unlock it. When half-asleep, I had minimal impulse control, at that age, I suppose.

I still have a long, jagged scar that runs across the middle knuckle on the back of my right hand.

After punching through the glass, the entire house woke up and stirred into action. I stood dumbly on the front porch, my hand draining copious amounts of blood onto the porch, as my younger sister ran to the bathroom; a piece of the inward-flying glass had cut her face near her left eye. My older sister (also staying in the house, in the basement -- it was a four story house) came and grabbed me and washed my hand under the sink and told me I would need to go to the hospital for stitches. My wife stood in the living room, holding our young baby daughter, shaking her head.

I didn't mean to cause a ruckus -- I didn't want to be locked outside. Sometimes the key is to control the bleeding. I received thirteen stitches over the knuckle, another two in my index finger, and I nearly severed the ligament that controls my middle finger (which I had to point out to the half-asleep resident; he was about to sew me up when -- because the wound gaped, and I could watch the white cord of my ligament move up and down as I flexed and extended my fingers, I am nothing if not fascinated by how the insides of a body works -- I pointed out that the ligament was about 90% cut, held together by the slimmest remaining fraction. A consult and an aluminum popsicle stick later, I had a heavily-gauzed hand (which I re-dressed, the next day, minimizing it to a band-aid, for range of motion; the brace for my ligament I threw away).

Because I ignored the medicine that the Shaman sprinkled on me, my hand hurt (presumably healing, it works hunk-dory now) for five years.

As precious as my hands are to me, as much as I need them to manipulate my world, I just cannot abide somebody locking me out, and I will risk anything to pass through walls.

There are many ways to open doors.

M. Song for the Girl

prepare the clean sheets, to prepare the bed.for there must be a place to rest your head.there must be the smell, that clean scent bright,there must be side table, books and candlelight.there must be sounds, gentle, contrived and sweet;there must be sweet nothings for your lover to eat.there must be the wind, urged to dance and swirl,there must be a dance floor to indulge a sudden whirl.there must be time, allotted and fiercely guarded,there must be adoration to soften the hard-hearted.there must be like feelings, shared and urgent desires,there must be passions that rage like lustful fires.there must be two, for one feels only their own pain,there must be touching and wetness from the rain.there must be creation, a foundation for the start,there must be someone with whom you can be the Art

N. Non-sequiturs

I keep an eye-patch handy, for when I need to Rule the Kingdom of the Blind.

I do believe my Christmas Stocking is racist ... the white chocolate and dark chocolate are separated.

I do believe we have a triumvirate of syncopation.

I am never silent -- there are moments when you can't hear me,because you are listening with the wrong kind of ears.

When no one is talking, no one is listening; when silence reigns, death bides.When suffering advances, succor retreats, when waxes the mooncome forth the tides.

Please pray quietly -- I can only mock what comes to my attention.

"Delaying the inevitable" could be a definition of life.

Laughter is medicine, and I have no HMO.

Shards of expected walls crumble as I stomp on them,pieces of eight deaths pierce my eyes.Dread stock fills my cabinetry, redundantas my den is filled with the corpses of unexpected visitors.

The status is Quo. The albatross has fled. The monkey seeks a wrench.

"Spunk McNuggets: Fast Food and Fast Sex in America", Andy Warhol's last film, was unearthed today. It stars Peter North, John Holmes, and Edie Sedgewick as "French Fry".

Being randy is dandy, but if you lick her, it's quicker.

The Flat-Earth society grades on a curve.

I want to swim in words until I drown.

Thank Goodness I appear thoughtful; it allows me to skate by when I am not.

In Texas, all of the animals scream if you forget to gag them.

Boots are the first barrier between savage and savant.

Barbarians with a malfunctioning GPS are at my gate; what gestures are sign-language for "Rome"?

For the single woman in your life, try the new " iCock ", which comes with its own dock and Bluetooth-compatibility.

James Cameron should re-make "Deep Throat" in 3D. Starring Nicholas Cage as the penis.

If you could "taste the rainbow", would it be Leprechaun-flavored?

"The Onion" planned to release a spoof book on George W. Bush's presidency, but George W. Bush beat them to it. "Decision Points" is on sale now at The Salvation Army everywhere.

The dyslexic went out on New Year's Eve to get "Pucked Uf".

Reduce your carbon footprint: Don't exhale.

O. My First Tree

I want you -- yes you, reading this right now, not her or him or even her -- to remember the mental picture of the first tree that comes to mind. My first tree: When I was 8 years old, my family moved into our first owned property, a small ranch style house in Jacksonville Beach, Florida. On the left side of the yard, facing the road, was a tall cedar tree at the edge of the property, one with regularly spaced branches that an 8 year old boy could (and did) climb. I used to spend afternoons up there, thinking; from about 40 feet in the air, looking over the neighborhood, I spent many a friendless afternoon keeping myself company. Most of my childhood was wishing to be in the tree. That was not the first tree I had encountered, to be sure, but it is the one that I will remember, always.

I was atop the tree when the Blue Angels (defined by Wikipedia: The United States Navy's Navy Flight Demonstration Squadron, popularly known as the **Blue Angels**, first performed in 1946 and is currently the oldest formal flying aerobatic team. The squadron's six demonstration pilots fly the McDonnell Douglas F/A-18 Hornet) performed their aerobatic show in the beach area, and I had a glorious view; it felt as if the Hornets were only 50 feet above my head -- the engines roar and the vibration from their passing made me feel more alive than I did at any other time.

When I was a kid, I wanted to be an astronaut, like so many others; I had genius-level aptitudes for science and math, and I have never and will never be motion-sick in my life; a childhood full of ear infections rendered that dream impossible. I still remember the doctor visit, when I was 8 years old, wherein my doctor told me, in no uncertain terms, that due to the perforations in my eardrums, I would never be able to be a pilot, let alone an astronaut. Do you remember how old you were when your dreams were first crushed?

So, I climbed the tree.

I have been higher, since, on the Empire State Building, and the World Trade Center towers before jet airplanes piloted by terrorists destroyed them, not to mention on many an airplane ride; my cedar tree was me, under my own power, climbing toward the stars.

Now I do it with words.

I dream again.

Does my writing make me better than I was?

Would I be less if I were silent? Does reaching out to others increase my value to mankind?

The skin. The skin. It keeps me in.

I am confused by this thing we know as "writing". It is merely talking -- with the chance to edit. When I speak, I tend to ramble and babble (as I did on one opportunity to rattle off factoids about the human heart to a PhD), and if you take every third word, you might have a conversation of interest. I attempt to duplicate that, here.

I just feel so inspired right now that I grabbed a chapter from the shelf, one in which I had scribbled a few lines, and decided to ransack it -- any attempt to add value. Maybe I will do the best I ever have.

Anything less is failure.

P. The pig in charge

Driving thoughts. In the interest of surprising myself, this is a lecture I give on the nature of man's incapacity to forgive man.

"We are social creatures who don't know how to talk.

We make grunting noises at each other, and our bodies give us away, to be sure; if I am sexually attracted to that beautiful girl in the corner, my cheeks will flush, my breath will quicken, and my body's desire to rut will thrash me sideways with its desire to penetrate her orifices, but nowhere within those behaviors will be any conscious genuflection to what religious folk -- those that I deem to be afraid of the unconventional -- decide should be the proper approach. To smile, to display that my hands are empty of weapon or threat, to compliment or admire her attractiveness, whether of the childbearing nature, such as wide hips and large breasts, or of the skilled-gatherer nature, such as keen eyes and a sharp mind. Social networks such as ours require these behaviors, so that none of us may surprise another.We all want to know what will happen before it happens.

Since this is impossible, we must now consider how a species grew from the basis of such insane and counter-productive beliefs. Why are we here, if we cannot behave in a manner that is natural? From fear of the dark, we have harnessed light; from fear of sickness, we have tamed fire for cooking and mold for antibiotics; from fear of homelessness we have mastered tools to build shelters; from fear of predators we have developed weapons and bars for our cages.

Many of us have distinguishing natures or characteristics; some of us are more intelligent than others. Being smart is like being tall, or being beautiful -- it is in the nature of itself alone. Being smart is not better than other things, it is merely the state of being more intelligent. Aphorisms are the teaching to the stupid from the marginally less-stupid, simple ways of explaining for those who cannot ingest polysyllabic terminology.

Non sequiturs are manna from the divine. It is not through the hierarchy that comes wisdom, it is from the lowerarchy. The lowest common denominator is the only referent of importance for a society, or your beliefs and hopes are elitist. If that is the case, so mote it be -- but don't ask for me to donate to your church. I have my own set of problems, I have no need to adopt yours.

An embrace of that same divine, of a deity, leads to many more quandaries. For every mistake we make, we must invent a new God. A single error, a single action that is contrary to your own arbitrarily self-imposed moral system, belies and disavows that moral system. Hypocrisy is the enemy of the righteous. If you truly believe in "Thou shalt not kill", then there is no room for "just a little killing". Either you believe, and you are righteous, or you allow for backtracking, which means that you don't believe, you just "sort of believe", which is contrary to any moral standing. There is no God that we do not see every day. If we are the inventors of Gods, then we are the Gods.In George Orwell's "Animal Farm", totalitarianism is broken down to a fable, in such a manner as to be nothing short of a work of genius; one of its lines is: "All animals are created equal, but some are more equal than others". I love this, as it sums up the dilemma of any person ruling another person: To be in a superior position over the rights or freedoms or survival of another, it is necessary to be a servant. Doing it the other way around, as every form of government has done, puts the person in charge of making the rules in a position of superiority over the governed; this has not worked, cannot work and will never work, as the old saw says it best: That is putting the mice in charge of the cheese. There is no morality for denying one's self an advantage -- it is contrary to the evolution of a complex, competitive predator such as we humans are. It is not a moral failing for Bill Clinton to fuck every woman within reach; what else would a rutting, sexual carnivore such as he do? Abstain? Why? When one is a pig, it is always best to be the pig in charge.

I want to be the pig in charge."

Q. The brown-eyed girl in the cab

The woman on the other side of the digital interface was special. All women, Rabbit had found, were special in their own way; some were pretty and preening, some were thoughtful and boisterous, but never had Rabbit encountered a duplicate among women on our world. The one he was currently interacting with, however, seemed to have a built-in bullshit detector, as well well as a forgiving nature. That way, she called him out on his mercurial proclivities, but did not hold them over him as if tabulating his faults. Her name, she had told him, was Rose, a simple title or euphemism that Rabbit could remember easily. Differences between conversational partners almost begged for an index card system, or notebook; Rabbit preferred to work unencumbered and inspired, trusting his memory to catalog the myriad voices that whispered from the computer screen. Rabbit lived within his routines, almost measured as if poured from a Pyrex divinity, a certain number of hours for sleep, a certain number of hours to be parceled around to confidants and lovers. A minimum set of time per week he set aside for himself, to laugh, to drink alcohol, to remember or forget, to flirt, to hunt. Rose was open, as open as a half-seen novella could be; she shared details of her existence eagerly, and refused to address some subjects just as readily. Rabbit believed that his personality was such to feed from challenges, be strengthened by rejections; far from fooling himself, he was merely incomplete in his information-gathering. Rose was next on Rabbit's "To Fuck" list, real or imagined. All that remained was to gather Rose's whole-hearted participation. Rose was a Legal Secretary, taking classes to become a paralegal, married to an unknown male competitor of Rabbit's, and exceptionally pretty and gifted at conversation. Rabbit had always used charm like a wrench, a tool to convert, convince and manipulate. He was courteous so that he could proclaim a love of courtesy, and wryly humorous so that he could watch a naked woman laugh. Women intrigued him ferociously, from within and without. He loved their physical differences, in a way that he found difficult to adequately explain--the soft slope of a pudendum could capture his attention for hours as he traced the verses of the Songs of Solomon into a partner's pubic hair. He loved the higher pitch of their voices, the aggravation they underwent to compete with other women; the fussy focus on makeup and appearance and clothing and footwear. Women drove him mad with desire and confusion, in equal measure, yet he stood undaunted at the tidal wave of the mysterious that a new lover represented.He met Rose on-line, and over time had seen her pictures, heard her voice on the phone, and imagined the rest of her as untarnished perfection, as the unknown is often believed to be; he was sure she was snug as a bug, a tireless romper, a voracious kitten with claws that would scratch but never scar.If her photographs were to be believed, Rose was a petite brunette, small breasted, with lean muscles developed from years of jogging. In the jpegs that Rabbit had seen, she always had a diffident smile, as if she gave up on posing halfway through the motion.There had been several times before that her voice or her image had stayed with him in the dark, as he masturbated; her laugh alone caused him to become partially aroused. When a newness defines a relationship, every familiarity carries the value of a diamond to a De Beer. He savored her exotic stature, and was undecided if he preferred real or digital.He began to imagine she knew him, in the real world, under a different name: he couldn't identify what had put that thought into his mind, but she always had the correct answer for everything that they discussed. He was not firm believer in fate or destiny, but he didn't disbelieve in nuance, either. Sometimes, a pair fits together in unpredictable ways. He assumed she was married, and thus somewhat secretive; he was unconcerned, as the chasing was more fun than the catching, to him. His desire for her was rich and real, like a sudden glimpse of a young woman's thigh when a gust of wind afforded a sneak peek. The brain is the organ of arousal, and passes the message on to the appropriate body parts. Sometimes the arousal is foreseeable, often it is not. Rabbit liked surprises in matters of lust.Rabbit wanted Rose to surprise him, and thus she became his pet project. She was vulnerable to his literate methods of wooing, but cynical enough to keep him at arm's length, even while her heart palpitated whenever she saw that he had sent her a message. Rabbit enjoyed someone who enjoyed him, whether through imagined insecurities, or merely a suppressed need for attention. He had no desire to fix his own broken soul, considering that his flaws would draw many women to him with an urge to repair and enlighten his quirky mania.Rabbit gave himself an answer, to an unbidden question, and set to task his female interest with an an-amorphous destination:Rose, the little flower that is a sonnet of sincerity,I don't need to know, call it just a Want,but we have danced, we have rambled, we have played as if coy teens;I render none of these things to be unseemly or amiss,but lecture me boldly only this:May I see you, with real tears clouding my eyes,might my real lips taste a kiss?Sometimes, a diving board is greater fun than wading.On the phone, a woman can sigh and arouse the mind and body of an attentive listener. Even an avowed wordsmith falls mute. In person, the scents that women wear can reduce a charismatic conversationalist to an illiterate lump of clay. These interactions may be pheremonal, but to deny exposing oneself to such joys is to stand up from the table and exist only in the gallery. Rabbit often lost with his cards, but he was always willing to play.Unable to temper his words any longer, Rabbit asked to meet Rose in the real world. Rose agreed to do so--she felt that she would not be able to live with herself, going forward, if she didn't at least meet with this man whom she found to be so exceptional in so many ways. She was wracked with excited trepidation, nervous joy, paralyzing fear, and the expectation that no reality would match her imagination. All of these things she thought or said, and Rabbit would answer with his definitive sincerity.The moment arrived, at a public house of transportation:Rose had spent three days before traveling agonizing over how she would allow herself to appear before their first meeting. She found herself torn between two outfits, and decided to leave the final decision for the morning of her travel. She had her hair done at her favorite shop the day before, choosing to maintain the hairstyle that she had favored for the last couple of years, but having the ends trimmed and, finding herself relaxed by her stylist's droning and familiar voice. She trimmed her nails and painted them in a quiet shade of pink, because Rabbit had mentioned -- in one of their many, delightful all-night talking sessions -- that he really enjoyed a woman who could wear pink without appearing childish. She bought herself a new pair of shoes, the purchase of which decided the outfit she would wear for her. She also found herself blushing like a teenager as she agonized over which color panties to buy at the Victoria's Secret store in her town's shopping mall. She fretted over her makeup before she left her house, and debated how much perfume to apply -- and exactly where to apply it -- before deciding that she was a grown woman, not a twittering virgin, and dabbed herself with the applicator behind her ears, on her wrists, and yes, a dab below the band of her panties. She spent two hours packing for a short trip the morning she was to depart. Preparing for the journey had been the focus of her attention for two weeks.The morning that he was to meet Rose, Rabbit arranged himself to be casual and happily scruffy.He sat in a chair at the depot, at the time she had arranged to arrive, unshaven, unkempt, as unaesthetic as he could easily manage. When the gates opened, he watched the crowds spill forth, and Rose was easy to spot, matching her picture perfectly, as tense and grim as he'd imagined, and he sat on the aisle of the seats in the waiting area, a grin cracking his visage.She walked past him without noticing.Somewhat nonplussed, he sighed, and arose to follow her. She walked several yards before entering a ladies' room, and Rabbit planted himself directly outside of the doors, as if he was waiting on a woman, which he was, which allowed him to realize that he was also a tad nervous. He frowned to acknowledge that he was not as cool as he had supposed.When Rose came out of the bathroom, Rabbit waited for the soundtrack to kick in, something dramatic, without being too sweet...maybe Debussy, tempered by Clapton, with a dash of The Moody Blues. Instead, she smiled, momentarily startled, and Rabbit did not feel the need to kick into his manic persona."Hey," she smiled, and it was alright.Her appearance was stunning to him, as was her intention; he struggled to hide any approval, for nothing is worthwhile that is simple. They exited and caught a cab, since she needed to go to her hotel; her stay was to be brief, and he had every intention of displaying his township--that had been glorified as a city--to her.She tended to her hotel, and towards the heart of the urban magnet they journeyed; many times before they had spoken, but never met. In the cab ride across the bridge, he sat transfixed. He was flabbergasted by her brown eyes, and found himself unable to avoid staring. She, being more practiced as a human, cast sidelong glances at him when he was distracted with his own soliloquies.They both had wondered, and pondered still, if the romance and friendship that had developed in the pseudo-reality would translate into the physical realm. He took her to his favorite museum, and to dinner at his favorite pizza restaurant. When the night fell, the question that had never been asked become a lingering wraith--would they sleep together?They sat upon the bed in her hotel room, and she stated that she had decided that sex would not be on the menu.He grinned, and responded:"I wondered what I would do or say, when you made your decision, and I had decided that if that was to be your answer, I would not argue or try to convince you. But, then I changed my mind and I have decided to try to talk you into it. I could state my case as a poet, and recite some verse, either invented on the spot, and therefore real, and cogent, and applicable only to you, your face, your eyes--my god, your eyes, the liquid brown depths at which I have been staring all night;I could state my case as a friend, as one who has made you laugh, who has listened as you told me of problems with your spouse, your children, your in-laws; one who has regaled with the silly, formative moments of his own existence;I could state my case as a lover, for so close have we been that I feel that I have been inside you, already, felt you wrap around me and taken me in; felt your breath in my mouth as I am speechless in the warmth and fury; I could state my case as an appreciative artist, who has cast you into gold and poured you from obscurity into eternity;I could, and will, do all of those things, if only you are honest with me and tell me if there is a reason for doing so. You are just a woman, and I am just a man. We did not invent the world, or even this moment, for in fifteen years or so I will tell our story as a metaphor for so many things, and distance makes the pain lessen, but never disappear. Whenever disappointment and heartbreak strike, one can either lash out at others, or barricade the damaged part; or, one can use the pain to build a castle that will love the world, all who are in it, and everyone who can understand.Even if you don't love me, I can and will love you."

R. Chemoerection

I feel the need to prolong my indifference to myself.

I like me, very much -- I am the only me I have, and I fill the need for a me, most every day. When I need to talk to myself, I am always there. When I feel the need to chastise myself, I sulk, but I don't hold a grudge. I forgive myself, nearly always.

When I need to criticize myself, I can almost always find constructive deconstructions, and I often take my own advice (but not always -- for which I tend to absolve myself, because no one else but me remembers the snake-berries).

I am collating data, Ash said, before he sprayed milk and Parker whacked him with a fire extinguisher (switch the order of those). Soon, I will publish my books! And I will sell 12 units! Which will put almost $22 in my pocket, and I can retire to a life of luxury. Fuck these small town blues.

I cannot wait to be a pundit. I make myself laugh, by thinking about being interviewed by the famous and semi-famous about *things*. I will take great pleasure in pleasing no one but myself -- the advantage of my middle-aged years, I suppose. I give no fucks about anything except that which I currently give a fuck -- my friends, family, pets and penis. All of the rest is figmental space-filler, anyway. There is no such thing as "reality television": It is a bad piece of pork chop that my intestines have rejected and turned into waking daymares.

I do believe I was born to be infamous. If only I had awesome, Tom Cruise-like teeth. Then I might smile more about being "glib". I just heard, from the television in the other room, a line that should have never existed: "Eric Bana is an ex-C.I.A. agent". Please stop foisting Eric Bana on us. Also, Jake Gyllenhaal. Thank you, Hollywood. Also, stop making pretty girls subsist on one saltine and 2 grapes per week (plus 4 or 5 eight-balls of cocaine). Women need food, otherwise they look like coat hangers with wigs. A re-tread of a statement -- especially since I like women in all varieties (when healthy): Thin, chubby, tall, short. Sick women don't hold any sort of appeal to me (I have a slight aversion to pustules and genital warts).

Chemotherapy, on the other hand, creates a vulnerability that I find oddly sexy. In the film "The Doctor", starring William Hurt, one of the sub-plots involved a young woman that the titular lead befriends, played by Elizabeth Perkins. During the film, the character (a not so proud possessor of a brain tumor) undergoes chemotherapy, and I find myself uncomfortably erect ever time I see her bald head. Perhaps I am in need of shock treatments to re-align my brain with the commonweal.

I am foursquare against a lobotomy, however. I like my odd nature.

S. Backyard Thoughts

in which all who came before are felt in presence if not in nameand all who lay down upon the sand and leaves remember me to my cousins and featured players in the storm in front of the curtainsand then all was speaking including the brew of tea leaves on the fire and the slow steam of tarts within the kitchen and then no more can I smell the room I am in only is the past with the ice-cream maker churning the peaches from our backyard tree and the rock salt is in a box which is needed why? I don't know why but you must pour in the rock salt periodicallyso therefore it is fruit and ice and salt and sweet cream and Florida horseflies and I suppose that is a memory but all I feel is that it is just on the tip of my tongue since my earliest memory is trailing cousins while barely able to walk and then I ate corn.Later then there was a roof in Brooklyn and howling at the moon undressed while looking at a polaroid of a friend's fiancé and she also was naked and I approved and approve of her nice little dark triangle and though it could not be! Cannot be! No such exists but I was pleasuring my own physical body while seeing this plantain tart lightly crisped and the thought was good and that was Brooklyn in the summer so many years ago.and five minutes ago I sat in the stubby eternity that is my jungle though freshly mowed and the heat keeps the bugs dead and whatever else there is the air greets you with a caress like a brickbat and I sit in my chair and remember trying to keep dogs here and not exploring and there are random wood slabs patching the fence and that is this backyard but also there have been cold beers with no sunlight and many smoky fires and this is good because I live here now.

T. How to dispose of an annoying person (Satire)

A recipeYou'll need :an intended victim 1 motorboat1 van or pick-up truck1 chainsawFlunitrazepam4 pieces of rubber tubingmaterials for bonfireseveral buckets of rotted fisha remote beachan accomplice1 rusty filleting knifeAnother way of dispatching the annoying among us:First build a good bonfire on a beach. It is probably best to have an accomplice with a small (15') motorboat. Your accomplice can be trolling about 100 yards from the beach with a bucket of day-old chopped fish bits, 2 or 3 buckets worth, chumming the waters to attract hungry sharks.

While he (or she) is doing that, you capture the offending party and knock them unconscious (**Flunitrazepam will do fine, as it is a** strong hypnotic and powerful sedative, anticonvulsant, anxiolytic, amnestic, and skeletal muscle relaxant drug.) Then, you get some tourniquet material (rubber tubing is fine), and tie off the upper arms, and upper thighs of the proposed victim. Use the chainsaw to remove the arms and legs of your (now probably awake) victim. Toss the limbs onto the bonfire to dispose of evidence. Use a flaming branch from the bonfire to cauterize the wounds. Lug the victim onto the motorboat, and find a nice school of hungry sharks. Lightly stab the victim in the stomach with the rusty filleting knife--not too deep; you want a blood flow, but not enough so that the victim faints from blood loss. Toss the victim into the feeding frenzy. Enjoy the spectacle.This has been hyperbole.

U. Danger Zone

All of my life, I have existed in mortal fear of error. I hate making mistakes, of any sort, at any level. Since life (and the act of living it) is of necessity rife with incorrect actions and behaviors, I have spent many a moment soaked with anxiety and frustration.

In the 1980s, Tony Scott directed a terrible movie called "Top Gun", a Reagan-era mythological fable about homo-erotic jet pilots who are just too bursting with semen to obey any rules whatsoever. Val Kilmer plays a Naval Aviator (and former member of the musical group "The Village People") who was jilted by lover "Maverick" (played in pristine Liberace mode by Tom Cruise, in his star-making role), and they find themselves in the Navy's "Top Gun" school together.

The sexual tension ripples across the screen as they sneer and toss their impeccably-coiffed heads at each other. In the film's original finale, the pair consummated their reconciliation with a ground-breaking (for a major Hollywood motion picture) 15 minute graphic sexual orgy, in which they writhe around in full, K-Y lubricated, shiny glistening glory in a 69 position, culminating in simultaneous, graphic ejaculations (Kilmer spits, but Cruise swallows like a dehydrated Rockette). The MPAA ratings board, in typical, short-sighted fashion, slapped an "*Ohy My God* NC-17" rating on the movie, naturally, and the scene was trimmed to garner the more commercially acceptable "PG" rating, wherein the climactic reconciliation was filmed as merely a "man-hug" on the deck of an aircraft carrier after the pair had started World War 3.

I think I digressed.

Oh yeah, mistakes. When the movie came out, smack in the middle of the time period in which MTV was still hip with young folks (because they played music videos; can you imagine that, a musical video channel that plays music videos?) This was before Youtube, of course, but ask your parents -- at one time, MTV was mostly videos, interspersed with parasympathetic pre-mongoloid "Video Jockeys (V.J.s)".

When a video would launch, in the lower left corner of the screen (a format which has been used ever since) would list the artist, the song title, the album title, and the music's publisher, in a four line scrawl, thusly:

"Danger Zone"

Kenny Loggins

"Some Stupid Compilation Album"

RCA Virgin Mega Records

The song received enormous quantities of radio airplay, and the video was constantly interrupting commercials on MTV. The movie was a smash hit, and for a few months, the song was pervasive. It was one of those songs (like Springsteen's "Dancing in the Dark", Jackson's "Billy Jean", and Madonna's "Like A Virgin") that you merely had to be alive to become familiar with. It was ubiquitous, at the time.

My point, such as it is, is this: The song's title was "Danger Zone", and the lyrics were the essence of simplicity:

Highway to the Danger Zone

Gonna take a ride into the Danger Zone

I won't denigrate the song, itself. It's catchy. For almost 20 years, however (most of that time during a period when lyrics to songs were not immediately available for perusal on the Internet), What I heard the lyrics as was this:

I went to the Danger Zone

Gonna Take it right into the Danger Zone

A slight difference, but a difference, nonetheless. In 2004, as I was driving back from a drilling job, in Washington, D.C.'s rush-hour traffic, the song came on the radio. Not having heard it in many years, I suppose I listened to it with fresh ears, and I realized that the refrain was speaking of a "Highway" to a "Danger Zone". Not that he (presumably, Mr. Loggins) *went to it* -- he was describing a roadway, a path to a "Danger Zone". The song subtly, yet completely, shifted meaning for me. I had been mis-hearing it for nigh on 20 years.

This has been an analogy, an allegory, or a fable.

What if everything that I have ever perceived, at any point in my brief existence, has been mis-heard, mis-read, or mis-interpreted in the manner of this song's lyrics? Everything that I am that is knowledge-based would be wrong.

I love wondering if that is true.

Afterword. Wrap-Up.

Welcome, my friends and despots, to the Twenty 'Leven.
I expect we'll finish some of these things this year. I can never
know what I will do next -- I don't share that information with
myself, since information should be disseminated on a need-
to-know basis, and I don't need to know what tomorrow will
bring to get out of bed.

Instead of relying on prediction or hope, we can wish for
bread. In the yeast is the future. It expands when warm, and
kills itself with its own excrement. What a pseudo-metaphor.
Global warming makes bread bigger.

Lost in much of the debate and breast-beating about Global
Warming is the fact the it (G.W.) would yield a net benefit to
most of the world, due to longer growing seasons and
reduction of heating costs. Bring on the toasty and fuck the
Ice.

One of my favorite quotes of all time, in or out of context, is a
line from Neal Stephenson's "Snow Crash":
"Jack the sound barrier. Bring the noise."

'n context, the quote refers to the shedding of convention by a
'borg guard, called a "rat-thing"; the guard was treated with
dness by the female protagonist of the tale, in a former
tence as a dog, and when the cyborg, known as Fido, was
ed for an injury. When the female character becomes
ngered near the end of the book, Fido dismisses all
mming that restricts his movement and accelerates to
' in his single-minded desire to aid her. It may read a
lonky, but it plays out beautifully in the story. A dog's
Fido nsplanted into a Terminator's body -- never mind that
programmed to stay at subsonic speeds within city

limits: The girl was in trouble! JACK the sound barrier. Bring the noise. Read the book. It is one of the more unique novels I have ever read.

Out of context, the quote to me means: Never mind the restrictions. Do it.

At the ending of the "Star Trek" re-boot, from 2009, the character of Captain Kirk, in typically Captain-like decisiveness, shouts at Engineer Scott "DO IT! DO IT! DO IT!", as an order to jettison the Warp core into a Black Hole (some of these plot devices sound silly when summarized, to be sure). It should have been melodramatic and silly, but it worked within the confines of a science-fiction world where sound travels through the vacuum of space, and *every single character that commands a war-vessel* should be court-martialed for "abandonment of post" (seriously, every one. The captain of the Kelvin, in the opening scene, leaves his ship. Captain Pike shuttles away from the Enterprise. Kirk and Spock abandon the Enterprise, leaving in command a 17 year-old rookie, Chekhov. Chekhov runs off of the bridge -- without appointing a replacement -- to operate a transporter. The coda of Star Trek should have been a war-crimes tribunal wherein Kirk, Spock and Chekhov are executed for dereliction of duty. Pike escapes execution only because he was in a wheelchair, anyway).

I am unsure what the point of that was -- I didn't dig deep enough.

I love Youtube and Twitter and Facebook and MySpace and Bluetooth and iPod and iPhone and iPad and Blackberry ar Android and all of the other things that simply did not exist or 5 years ago. We have changed so far, so fast, that the no referent, except to say "When I was a kid ... " whic' always hated to hear when we we children, ourselves. I love change. I thrive in the novel.

I just saw a picture on my Facebook feed, one of the oodles that fly by at any given time: It was a heart, pseudo-artistic, with the inscription: " If I had known it would hurt this bad, I would never have said I loved you".My thoughts and dissection of this picture are going to unfold live, on this keyboard, as you read them. I will not go back and edit this. (as far as you know).First of all, someone young and / or ignorant (simple gentility prevents me from calling the author stupid, just yet) wrote that inscription. There has been three thousand years worth of poems, and hundreds of years' worth of songs describing the experience of "Love", so I will only re-hash it so much, but honestly, it is akin to a kid crying because he got his hand caught in the cookie jar. He isn't crying over guilty feelings, he is crying because he was caught and punished (presumably). Love is a grand experience, and if you wish to avoid pain in this life, you might consider that you should go ahead and swallow some opiates now, because it is unavoidable. Being born hurts--for you and your mother. Dying is generally considered unpleasant. In between, if you open yourself to joy, you open yourself to having your heart and soul ripped out, due to the nature of the vulnerability you have accepted. Welcome to pain, pal, welcome to life.I try not to Pre-Live my life, I just try to Live it; many things that appear in retrospect to be bad ideas were probably bad ideas looking forward, also. So what? Many great things have happened because some damned fool genius didn't accept the fear and reticence of the monkeys around him / her, and went ahead and jumped off of a cliff anyway. Marie Curie dies of Radium poisoning--didn't the silly woman know that radiation can kill? She sure as hell learned.And we are all richer for it. When my child asked me what would happen if he stuck a nail an electric wall socket, I gave him the same answer my father me: Go ahead.The same can be said for love: Will it hurt? yeah. It can hurt something awful.But there is no greater d available to humankind.

no God that we do not see everyday.

About the Author

Robert Jon Anderson was born on a Navy Base in 1968. After many years of traveling the country, and working in a multitude of fields, he has settled down in the south, in the lush bayous of Southwest Louisiana. He began writing in the mid-1970s, finding his own voice through the written word. He has worked in digital print shops, seafood restaurants, construction sites all over the country, as well as owning two businesses, writing freelance, and, in 2018, running for the House of Representatives in the Louisiana 3rd District.

He has been married since 1990 to his lovely wife, Clari and together they raised two children, both of whom w engineering fields. They have too many cats and a zombie dog who seems to be immortal.